QUALITATIVE ANALYSIS USING NVivo

Software is cut and dried—every button you press has a predictable effect—but qualitative analysis is open ended and unfolds in unpredictable ways. This contradiction is best resolved by separating analytic strategies—*what you plan to do*—from software tactics—*how you plan to do it*. Expert NVivo users have unconsciously learned to do this. The *Five-Level QDA*® method unpacks the process so that you can learn it consciously and efficiently.

The first part of the book explains how the contradiction between analytic strategies and software tactics is reconciled by "translating" between them. The second part provides both an in-depth description of how NVivo works and comprehensive instruction in the five steps of "translation." These steps are illustrated with examples from a variety of research projects. The third part contains real-world qualitative research projects from a variety of disciplines, methodologies, and kinds of qualitative analysis, all illustrated in NVivo using the *Five-Level QDA* method. The book is accompanied by three sets of video demonstrations on the companion website.

The book and accompanying videos illustrate the Windows version of NVivo. As there are some differences in screen and interface design between the Mac and Windows versions please watch the video 'The NVivo Mac Interface' in the Component Orientation series of videos (available on the companion website).

The *Five-Level QDA* method is based on the authors' combined 40 years of experience teaching NVivo and other software packages used as platforms for conducting qualitative analysis. After many years observing their students' challenges, they developed the *Five-Level QDA* method to describe the process that long-time NVivo experts unconsciously adopt. The *Five-Level QDA* method is independent of software program or methodology, and the principles apply to any type of qualitative project.

Nicholas H. Woolf has worked as an independent qualitative research consultant, coach, and trainer since 1998. He has conducted or consulted on numerous research studies, from single-site to multinational studies in various fields in the behavioral sciences using a wide range of methodologies, from highly structured content analyses, to evaluations, grounded theory-style projects, and interpretive phenomenology. As a trainer Nick specializes in teaching qualitative analysis using ATLAS.ti. He has conducted 285 workshops at over 100 universities and other institutions, primarily in the USA and Canada, for more than 3,000 PhD students, professors, and research and evaluation consultants. In 2013 Nick introduced *Five-Level QDA* in his keynote address at the first ATLAS.ti user's conference in Berlin (Woolf, 2014).

Christina Silver has worked at the CAQDAS Networking Project at the University of Surrey, UK, since 1998. She is responsible for capacity-building activities and has designed and led training in all the major qualitative software programs, including ATLAS.ti, Dedoose, MAXQDA, NVivo, Transana, QDA Miner, Qualrus, and Quirkos. Christina also works as an independent researcher, consultant, and trainer, supporting researchers to plan and implement computer-assisted analysis and contributing to doctoral research programs in several UK universities.

Developing Qualitative Inquiry

Series Editor: Janice Morse
University of Utah

Books in the *Developing Qualitative Inquiry* series, written by leaders in qualitative inquiry, address important topics in qualitative methods. Targeted to a broad multi-disciplinary readership, the books are intended for mid-level to advanced researchers and advanced students. The series forwards the field of qualitative inquiry by describing new methods or developing particular aspects of established methods.

Other Volumes in This Series Include

Mixed Methods in Ethnographic Research
Historical Perspectives
Pertti J. Pelto

Engaging in Narrative Inquiries with Children and Youth
Jean Clandinin, Vera Caine, Sean Lessard, Janice Huber

Interpretive Description
Qualitative Research for Applied Practice, 2nd Edition
Sally Thorne

Qualitative Ethics in Practice
Martin Tolich

For a full list of titles in this series, please visit **www.routledge.com**

QUALITATIVE ANALYSIS USING NVivo

The Five-Level QDA® Method

Nicholas H. Woolf and Christina Silver

Routledge
Taylor & Francis Group

NEW YORK AND LONDON

First published 2018
by Routledge
711 Third Avenue, New York, NY 10017

and by Routledge
2 Park Square, Milton Park, Abingdon, Oxon, OX14 4RN

Routledge is an imprint of the Taylor & Francis Group, an informa business

Library of Congress Cataloging-in-Publication Data
A catalog record for this book has been requested

ISBN: 978-1-138-74366-3 (hbk)
ISBN: 978-1-138-74367-0 (pbk)
ISBN: 978-1-315-18166-0 (ebk)

Typeset in Bembo
by Apex CoVantage, LLC

Visit the companion website: www.routledgetextbooks.com/textbooks/5LQDA

Dedicated to Ben Woolf,
who fearlessly overcame
seemingly insurmountable obstacles
with grace and humor.

1980–2015

CONTENTS

EXTENDED CONTENTS

FIGURES

TABLES

BOXES

ACKNOWLEDGMENTS

This long, long labor of love would have never reached fruition without the enthusiastic support of many people. Jan Morse believed in the project when it was still a germinating seed, and it would not have happened without her encouragement. Trena Paulus stands out for critiquing early drafts, asking if she could test the *Five-Level QDA* method at the University of Georgia and inviting us to join her and Elizabeth Pope in their research of the use of the method. Trena has a knack for critiquing our writing with an apparently innocuous question that cuts to the core of an issue, and we thank her for the contributions she made to our thinking. We are also indebted to Sarajane Woolf for her relentless editing; we turned over chapters to Sarajane thinking them in excellent shape, but quickly learned otherwise.

Numerous leaders and teachers in the CAQDAS community have provided the encouragement we needed to keep going. As you will soon be reading, the *Five-Level QDA* method is all about making conscious what CAQDAS experts have unconsciously learned to do. We want to thank all the CAQDAS experts who have told us so enthusiastically in their own different ways that the *Five-Level QDA* approach spells out what they have been thinking but haven't been able to articulate. We particularly want to thank Ann Lewins, Kristi Jackson, Michelle Salmona, Sarah L. Bulloch, Eli Lieber, Judy Davidson, Daniel Turner, Steve Wright, Pat Bazeley, Susanne Friese, and also Chris Astle and Silvana di Gregorio at QSR International for their positive encouragement and support over the years. Finally we would like to thank Hannah Shakespeare at Routledge for her efficient and cheerful shepherding of this project through to completion.

We solicited case contributions for the book and for the numerous mini-cases on the companion website. We were delighted to find experienced researchers who recognized that the *Five-Level QDA* method resonated with their work and were eager to take the time to write up their projects for us. We thank them all for the courteous and collaborative manner in which they contributed their work. We particularly thank Elizabeth Pope and Kristi Jackson for the cases that are printed in Chapters 8 and 9 of this book.

Each of us received invaluable encouragement from so many colleagues, family, and friends through the many years of this project—to all our supporters, a heartfelt thank you. Nick would particularly like to thank Jim Quinn for his never-ending support, expertise, and encouragement, and Sarajane for her standard response to the long hours and late nights on the project: "keep working." Christina would particularly like to thank Ann Lewins for commenting on early drafts with wit and detailed perception, and Sarah L. Bulloch for her accuracy checks and enthusiasm in integrating the *Five-Level QDA* method into her own teaching. In addition Christina thanks her family: Jason, Christopher, Nelleke, Derek, and Deanna, for their ceaseless support and encouragement, and Nathanael and Magdalena for illustrating that there is always light at the end of the tunnel.

CASE CONTRIBUTORS

Chapter 8: An Exploratory Literature Review

Elizabeth M. Pope is a doctoral candidate pursuing a degree in Adult Education and a Certificate in Interdisciplinary Qualitative Studies at the University of Georgia, Department of Lifelong Education, Administration, and Policy. With a background in the field of religion, Elizabeth is merging the two disciplines in her dissertation, "This Is a Head, Hearts, and Hands Enterprise: Interfaith Dialogue and Perspective Transformation." Her research interests are in religious studies, adult learning, qualitative research, and transformational learning in interfaith and cross-cultural contexts.

Chapter 9: A Program Evaluation

Kristi Jackson, PhD, is co-author with Patricia Bazeley of the book *Qualitative Data Analysis with NVivo,* now in its second edition, and in 2002 she founded Queri (www.queri.com), a qualitative research consulting firm. With over 25 years of experience in qualitative research design, data collection, analysis, reporting, and stakeholder relations, she is an expert in a diverse array of qualitative methodologies. She also has extensive experience in large-scale and small-scale team research and evaluation research. As Chair of the Special Interest Group (SIG) on Digital Tools for Qualitative Research at the International Congress of Qualitative Inquiry, she continues to cultivate decades of collaborative, international relationships with a wide range of stakeholders in the Qualitative Data Analysis Software (QDAS) community. Her theoretical frames tend to be sociological, and her research interests include conceptualizations of qualitative research transparency and the constantly changing spaces where qualitative researchers and technologies meet.

ORIENTATION

Learning to do qualitative analysis with NVivo does not mean *learning how to operate the program really well*. Instead it means *learning to harness NVivo powerfully*. These two objectives could not be more different, and this orientation prepares you for what is to come.

Orientation means *finding one's location in an environment*. Orientations are common in the business world to socialize new employees in an organization, with activities to gain their commitment, reduce their anxiety, and let them know what they should expect from the organization. Only then are employees trained for their specific jobs. It is in this sense that we provide this orientation. The purpose is to alleviate your concerns and enlist your patience for what is to come by telling you why this book is written in the way that it is.

Three areas require orientation. The first is what kind of program NVivo is and what it means to harness it powerfully. The second area is the best way to learn to do this. We have drawn on our combined 40 years of teaching experience to develop an approach to learning that is not what is generally expected in software training. The third area concerns the differences between using NVivo in solo research projects and in research teams. The orientation ends with a roadmap through the book.

NVivo Is Not an Analysis Program

Some researchers expect—or hope—that NVivo will somehow do the analysis and reduce the hard mental work of qualitative analysis. Others are fully aware that this is not the case, yet they unconsciously expect that NVivo will make at least some contribution to the analysis. Part of the problem is the names for these types of programs—Computer-Assisted Qualitative Data AnalysiS (CAQDAS), or qualitative data analysis software (QDAS), or simply qualitative analysis software. All have *software* and *analysis* in them, which inevitably suggests that the software performs analysis. (See Box 0.1 for more on the history of acronyms for these dedicated software packages).

The idea that the software does some kind of analysis can be hard to overcome. The natural assumption is that NVivo is a qualitative cousin to statistical software packages like SPSS or SAS. But programs like Scrivener or Microsoft Word that support the writing process offer a more useful comparison. Microsoft Word is never called a computer-assisted writing program—it is not a writing program at all. It just displays characters corresponding to the keys you press, with bells and whistles to move text around and format text to make it look appealing. There are no

---

BOX 0.1 WHY WE USE THE ACRONYM CAQDAS

Several acronyms are used for a group of dedicated software programs that qualitative researchers use to assist them in conducting their analysis. Some writers use QDAS for these programs, which stands for Qualitative Data Analysis Software (e.g., Bazeley & Jackson, 2013; di Gregorio & Davidson, 2008). We prefer not to use this acronym because it can be misunderstood to mean software that performs analysis, which none of the writers who use the acronym intend it to mean. Other writers use CAQDAS, which stands for Computer-Assisted Qualitative Data AnalysiS (e.g., Friese, 2014; Paulus, Lester, & Dempster, 2014). We also prefer to use CAQDAS, the original term for this software, because of its historical roots and more general use and acceptance in the field.

The acronym CAQDAS was first coined by Raymond Lee and Nigel Fielding in their 1991 book *Using Computers in Qualitative Research*, which was published following the first conference on qualitative software that they convened in 1989, the *Surrey Research Methods Conference* (Fielding & Lee, 1991). This conference brought together pioneers in the field to discuss the issues for the first time. Their debates revealed that use of computers for qualitative analysis was a thorny issue, and Lee and Fielding wanted to reflect this in the acronym, so they intentionally designed the acronym CAQDAS to evoke a big thorny plant—the cactus. Another reason for the acronym is that at the same time other technology-based methodological innovations, such as CAPI (Computer-Assisted Personal Interviewing) and CATI (Computer-Assisted Telephone Interviewing) were using "computer-assisted" in their acronyms, so Lee and Fielding felt it made sense to follow this trend. In 1994 Fielding and Lee went on to establish the CAQDAS Networking Project (CNP) at the University of Surrey, UK, which became an internationally reputed and independent source for practical support, training, information, and debate in the use of these technologies. The establishment of the CNP had the effect of 'fixing' the acronym. Originally the second S stood for 'software,' but in response to suggestions that it is illogical to have both the term "computer-assisted" and "software" in the same acronym, over time the second S has come to refer to the second S in AnalysiS, and this is now the way the CNP uses the acronym. For more information about CNP and the origins of the CAQDAS acronym, see www.surrey.ac.uk/sociology/research/researchcentres/caqdas/support/choosing/caqdas_definition.htm.

---

buttons or menus for writing tasks like *compose short story*, or *outline critical essay*, or *write novel in Russian*. Similarly, NVivo has no buttons for *identify themes* or *compare the meaning of a statement in one context rather than another*. There is no menu for *grounded theory* or *discourse analysis*. Where Microsoft Word is essentially a character display program, NVivo is essentially a program for managing concepts. You provide concepts, and NVivo provides many bells and whistles to organize, display, and work with them according to your instructions. You as the researcher do 100 percent of the intellectual work.

NVivo therefore makes no analytical contribution to your research. We hope this does not make you sad. If it does and you wonder if you have made the right decision to learn to harness NVivo powerfully, think analogously about Microsoft Word. Just because Microsoft Word can't actually write by itself, would you want to go back to writing by hand, if you have ever done such a thing? We imagine you would agree that time spent learning how to take advantage of Microsoft Word was time well spent. We are confident you will feel the same about NVivo.

What It Means to Harness NVivo Powerfully

Since the early 1990s we have taught hundreds of workshops for many thousand novice and highly experienced researchers on using NVivo to conduct qualitative data analysis. Our experience is that simply learning how to operate NVivo—learning what happens when each button is clicked and each menu item is selected—does not lead to powerful use of the program. This book is the result of observing how experienced researchers who have become expert users of NVivo use the program. We saw that they learned for themselves how to take full advantage of the program in every stage of a project while remaining true throughout to the emergent spirit of qualitative research. This is what we call *harnessing NVivo powerfully*, and learning how to do this is the purpose of this book.

Taking full advantage of NVivo throughout a project is highly efficient. There is no need to switch back and forth between programs or between software and manual methods, unless there is a compelling reason to do so. However, many researchers do not use NVivo in every stage of their projects because they are uncertain if the software is unduly influencing the conduct of their analysis. In other words, can you conduct qualitative analysis using software and remain true throughout to the emergent spirit of qualitative research? This leads to the central issue in harnessing NVivo powerfully: the basic contrast between the nature of qualitative analysis and the nature of computer software. The purpose of the *Five-Level QDA* method is to resolve this contrast. (QDA stands for qualitative data analysis. For brevity we use the term *qualitative analysis*, or simply *analysis*.)

Qualitative analysis is a systematic process in the dictionary sense of doing something *according to a careful plan and in a thorough way*. At the same time, most styles of qualitative analysis are, to various extents, open ended, organic, and unpredictable in the way they develop. As a shorthand we refer to qualitative analysis as *emergent*. This word comes with a lot of baggage, which we discuss further in Chapter 1. At this point it is enough to say that although qualitative analysis is systematic, it is not intended to proceed in a predetermined, step-by-step manner. Imagine being a painter with a definite idea of what you want to paint. Each brushstroke has an effect, leading to a fresh consideration of the progress of the entire picture. Certainly the next 20 brushstrokes cannot be planned out in advance and applied without modification one by one, regardless of the newly apparent and unpredictable effects of each one. Qualitative analysis is similarly emergent.

Computer software works in the opposite way: it is more like painting by numbers. The software features work in a predetermined and predictable way—when we press a button or choose a menu option, something specific always happens because it has been preprogrammed this way. We refer to this as being *cut and dried*. We have observed thousands of researchers—novice and experienced alike—struggle to use a cut-and-dried software package that appears to bear little resemblance to the emergent practice of qualitative research. Some researchers decide not to use NVivo after all, or they use it for the first stages of a project, before the more subtle aspects of the analysis emerge. They then continue the project on paper, or with yellow stickies, or on a whiteboard, or in a more generic program like Microsoft Word or Excel, just when NVivo could be helping the most. Worse is the opposite situation, when less experienced researchers change the character of the analysis to more easily fit the software, thereby suppressing the more emergent aspects of a qualitative analysis.

None of these alternatives is necessary, and by proceeding systematically through this book, they can be avoided. The key is to recognize that harnessing NVivo powerfully is a skill *in addition* to the ability to conduct qualitative analysis and to operate the software, one that allows you to transcend the contrast between emergent qualitative analysis and cut-and-dried software. Learning this skill is the focus of this book. We will continue to use the longer phrase *harness NVivo powerfully* to describe this skill. We don't want to start abbreviating it to *use NVivo* because that inevitably sounds like *operate the software*, which is the least important of the needed skills.

Is harnessing NVivo powerfully relevant to your own work? Are you an academic researcher planning to use NVivo for a particular style of analysis? Or are you doing applied work, such as program evaluation or public-sector consultations? Or are you using NVivo for a purpose not generally thought of as research, whether you are an author needing to organize a vast and disparate body of source materials, or a student undertaking a literature review, or a physician planning to organize or analyze patient records? There are no typical NVivo users and no typical NVivo projects—every kind of project calls for a somewhat different way of using the program. But underlying these disparate projects is a common feature: we all work with unstructured data. The *structure* of data refers to its degree of organization. *Fully structured data* are preorganized in numeric categories, ready for statistical analysis. *Unstructured data* are not preorganized in numeric categories. Unstructured data are often in the form of speech, audio-recorded and then transcribed, or notes or videos taken while observing others, or archival materials of all kinds—audio and video recordings; images like photographs, drawings, or diagrams; websites, blog posts, or social media interactions; and PDF files, which may have a mix of text and graphic data. All these forms of data come with some degree of preorganization or structure—for example, a transcript of free-flowing conversation may be structured according to who is speaking. But we call them all unstructured because they do not cross the line of being organized numerically.

All our approaches to working with such data share the same goal: making sense of or giving meaning to a mass of unstructured data. For some, the approach is prescribed in a research methodology, so the conclusions can be justified and evaluated in a recognized way. Others, who do not see their projects as academic or even as research at all, will simply choose the analytic approach or procedure that fulfills the purpose of collecting the data. All these activities are to some extent emergent, even if you do not use that word to describe your work. Harnessing NVivo powerfully is relevant to all of these projects because they all require making sense of a body of unstructured data.

One caveat: using NVivo throughout a project may include activities other than data analysis such as project planning, preliminary or pilot study activities, data collection, or representation of results. This book is focused only on data analysis. But we hope you will draw analogies for using the *Five-Level QDA* method in other phases of your project.

How to Learn to Harness NVivo Powerfully

Experts in any field have mentally "automatized" what they do so that it has become unconscious. Experts just know what to do in each new circumstance, but they have difficulty describing how or why they do what they do (Sternberg & Frensch, 1992). This describes the skills of expert users of NVivo. The purpose of this book is to unpack this black box of expert performance. We make the process explicit so that you can learn this skill more easily.

Learning to harness NVivo powerfully is not like learning the finer skills of Microsoft Word, which are best learned independently of learning how to write—because these skills and writing skills are independent. With NVivo, however, learning to use the program in a sophisticated way is intricately bound up with the specific analytic task that is being executed in the software. Yet there is a contradiction between the emergent nature of qualitative analysis and the step-by-step nature of computer software. The *Five-Level QDA* method is a way of managing this contradiction.

Over two decades of teaching, we saw that the *Five-Level QDA* approach is most effectively learned when the principles come first and hands-on use of the software comes last. Many of our students say they prefer learning by doing from the outset, but our experience has been that this does not work—beginning with hands-on learning unconsciously establishes a step-by-step software mind-set. We delayed opening the computers for hands-on learning until later and later in the workshops, and our participants quickly realized the benefit of this approach (Silver & Woolf, 2015). And that is what we do in this book.

A natural reason to prefer immediate hands-on learning is the misunderstanding that some NVivo features are basic and some are advanced, so that it makes sense to first jump into the basic features hands-on and later move on to learning more advanced features if they seem to be needed. We have noticed that qualitative researchers tend to humility and assume that their own projects are "basic" and only call for "basic" software features—only other people's projects are "advanced" and call for "advanced" software features. Distinguishing between basic and advanced features is neither true nor helpful. In reality all the features taken together are like a single palette containing all the colors that a painter has available to use. For any particular painting, some colors would be used and others not. But at the outset you still need *all* the colors to be known and available. And just as there are straightforward and more sophisticated ways to use all the paints on a palette, there are straightforward and sophisticated ways to use *all* the software features.

In summary, we do not begin right away with hands-on learning of "basic" features of the program and move on to the "advanced." We instead adopt a layered approach, moving from abstract to concrete learning, beginning with the principles of the *Five-Level QDA* method in Part I, moving on to the application of those principles in Part II, and finally to hands-on learning in Part III. Each layer is a prerequisite for making sense of the next and takes for granted all that comes before. We therefore appeal to your patience in moving through the chapters in the sequence presented.

Learning to Operate NVivo

We mentioned earlier that this book is not about learning the basics of operating NVivo. You may wonder how and when you are supposed to learn to operate the program.

Because the *Five-Level QDA* method sits between research methods and software operations, use of the method requires that you know your research methodology and how to mechanically operate the software. If you already use NVivo and are familiar with its features, you are ready to learn to use it in a more powerful way. If you are not yet familiar with the program, the best time to gain that skill is immediately after reading Chapter 5 in Part II of this book.

Learning to operate NVivo is best accomplished in two phases. First is understanding how the program has been designed and how it works. We call this the architecture of the program. It is a great advantage to understanding this before learning hands-on operation. The second phase is hands-on experience of manipulating or operating the software, including how to manage the computer files, open and use the various windows, locate menus and buttons, enter information, and so on.

The first phase is ideal to present in narrative form in a book. We teach this in Chapter 5. This chapter thoroughly explains the architecture of NVivo—the design of the program and the intended purpose of each of its features. We also provide short orientation videos on the companion website to make the abstract instruction in Chapter 5 concrete. These videos are only for orientation purposes and do not comprise hands-on instruction in operating the program.

Learning to operate NVivo is independent of learning the *Five-Level QDA* method. We recommend face-to-face instruction, online webinars, or online videos for learning to operate the program. NVivo is updated frequently and automatically with bug fixes and new and improved ways to carry out tasks, and so face-to-face or online instruction ensures you will be seeing the exact same, most recently updated version of the software that also appears on your own computer screen. We therefore invite you after reading about the architecture of the program in Chapter 5 to take advantage of the numerous free online resources or fee-based face-to-face workshops offered by the NVivo developer at www.qsrinternational.com. This site also provides an up-to-date listing of independent training companies offering their own courses. These learning resources vary in their approach to using NVivo for qualitative analysis, but all include the basic skills of operating the software, which is all that is needed as a companion to this book.

Working in Teams

Conducting research in teams is very different from researching alone. Team research adds two new tasks: deciding *who does what* and on that basis deciding *how each team member's contributions will be integrated*. These are significant decisions for the successful progress of a project. How they affect your use of NVivo depends on whether you use a standalone version of NVivo or NVivo for Teams. When using the standalone versions each team member works independently in NVivo on their own assigned analytic tasks, just as if they were working on a solo research project. Then periodically each team member's work is merged together in NVivo with the other team members' work. This task is unrelated to *Five-Level QDA* principles, but it does affect how NVivo is used. We discuss *who does what* in Chapter 4 and the technical aspects of *integrating team members' work* in Chapter 5—for both the single-user versions and NVivo for Teams.

A Roadmap Through the Book

This book has three parts. Each part is a layer of learning that assumes knowledge of what has been covered in the prior layers. Part I covers all the *Five-Level QDA* principles. Part II illustrates the practical mechanics of the method in preparation for hands-on practice. Part III provides full-case and mini-case illustrations of real-world research projects. These cases are demonstrated in videos on the companion website.

Part I: The Principles of the Five-Level QDA Method

Part I sets the stage for what is to come with an explanation of the principles behind the *Five-Level QDA* method and a description of each of the five levels. Chapter 1 begins with the core principle: the difference between strategies and tactics. We then explain why there is a contradiction between the nature of the analytic strategies of a qualitative analysis and the nature of the software tactics that we use to accomplish the strategies. There is more than one way to reconcile this contradiction, and we contrast three approaches that we call One-Level QDA (which involves not addressing the contradiction), Three-Level QDA (which involves introducing a compromise), and our own preferred approach, the *Five-Level QDA* method, which involves going beyond, or transcending, the contradiction by keeping the strategies and tactics distinct and separate and "translating" back and forth between them.

Chapter 2 focuses on Levels 1 and 2, which are concerned with the strategies. This means the objectives or research questions of a project and the analytic plan to fulfill the objectives. This is the area of research methods, and this book does not teach research methods. But because clear, coherent strategies are an essential prerequisite to successfully putting the *Five-Level QDA* method into practice, we discuss these areas in some detail so that you know what is needed to write clear, coherent objectives; to select a methodology; and to develop an analytic plan. We also suggest resources for further guidance in these areas.

Chapter 3 focuses on Levels 3, 4, and 5, the mechanics of translating between analytic strategies and software tactics. This leads to operating the software in either a straightforward or a more sophisticated way in order to accomplish each analytic task. Our layered approach to learning requires the complete exposition of all five levels before moving on to describing the architecture of NVivo in terms of these principles. We therefore illustrate the process of translation at this early stage using an everyday activity rather than an NVivo research project. This also serves to focus attention on the translation process rather than the specifics of a research project. The situation changes in Parts II and III, and all further illustrations are in terms of real-world research projects.

Part II: The Five-Level QDA Method in Practice

Part II describes the architecture of NVivo and provides in-depth instruction in the mechanics of the *Five-Level QDA* translation process.

Chapter 4 is a short orientation to NVivo. If you have recently upgraded to Version 11 or plan to upgrade soon, we are happy to report that the basic functions of the program have not changed and do not need to be relearned. This chapter also introduces all the versions of NVivo: the three Windows editions, NVivo for Mac, and NVivo for Teams.

Chapter 4 also contrasts the use of NVivo by a sole researcher with use by a member of a research team. Chapter 4 discusses the human side of working in a team—*who does what.*

Chapter 5 introduces the design or architecture of NVivo in terms of *Five-Level QDA* principles. This means focusing on what we call NVivo's *components* rather than its *features.* Focusing on components is a much simpler way to describe how the program works, and components play a significant role in the *Five-Level QDA* translation process. This chapter takes each component in turn and describes its purpose and how it works. Many users of NVivo are not aware of much of this information, and it is often the missing link in a researcher's understanding of how best to take advantage of the software. This is more important than learning how to operate the program— what buttons to click and which menu items to use. We provide *Component Orientation* video demonstrations of each component on the companion website, but we do not provide complete training in operating NVivo in the book. Chapter 5 also deals with the technical issues of working in teams—*integrating team members' work.*

If you are not already familiar with operating NVivo, we indicate in Chapter 5 that this is the time to learn to operate the program by taking advantage of either the free or fee-based workshops offered by the software developers and independent training companies.

Chapter 6 builds on all the earlier layers of understanding about the translation of strategies into tactics. This chapter describes and illustrates the mechanics of translation in a practical manner in terms of real-world research tasks. Following Chapter 6 you will be ready to learn from the case illustrations and video demonstrations of the translation process in Part III and conduct your own project using *Five-Level QDA* principles.

Part III: Case Illustrations

According to educational researchers, people learn best in the context of doing something personally meaningful, which facilitates the *transfer* of what they have learned in one context to their own very different context (Merriam & Leahy, 2005). Learning through real-world activities is perhaps the best approach to making learning personally meaningful (Woolf & Quinn, 2009). Because of the great variety of qualitative methodologies, styles of analysis, research contexts, and disciplines, we illustrate a wide variety of case illustrations to serve as analogies to transfer to your own projects. The variety is also intended to emphasize that there is no "correct" way to use NVivo.

Chapter 7 is an orientation to the case illustrations and how to access the accompanying video demonstrations on the companion website. These are case illustrations, not case studies. A case study is concerned with the *content* of a case. Our case illustrations demonstrate the *Five-Level QDA process*, and so we focus on how NVivo was harnessed rather than on the content or conclusions of the studies. We provide two sets of case illustrations: full cases and mini-cases.

For the full cases we have chosen two research studies. The first is a more straightforward project. This serves as a starting point for those with little or no experience in qualitative research or for those with no experience in using NVivo. The second is a more sophisticated project. This is intended for those who already have experience in both qualitative research and NVivo and as a second step of learning for those who have watched the videos of the first full case. Both projects are described in full in Chapters 8 and 9 in a standard *Five-Level QDA* format. Chapter 8 is a literature review for a PhD dissertation, contributed by Elizabeth Pope at the University of Georgia. Chapter 9 is a program evaluation contributed by Dr. Kristi Jackson, President of Queri, an independent research consultancy, based in Denver, Colorado. An important feature of the two full cases is that the analysis process is not sanitized to save space, as in a journal article. Rather, they include the detours and messiness that are part and parcel of real-world qualitative analysis. The objective is to illustrate how an NVivo project actually progresses.

No two projects can illustrate all uses of NVivo. We have therefore included a variety of mini-cases to illustrate additional or unusual uses of NVivo not illustrated in the two full cases. The mini-cases are described in an abbreviated *Five-Level QDA* format and are available for download on the companion website.

Both the full cases and the mini-cases have accompanying video demonstrations on the companion website, described in the next section.

The Companion Website

The companion website contains the three sets of video demonstrations: *Component Orientation* videos, *Case Illustration* videos, and *Harnessing Components* videos.

The *Component Orientation* videos provide a concrete orientation to each component as a supplement to the instruction in Chapter 5. These videos assume that you have read the associated section in Chapter 5 that describes that component, as they are not intended as meaningful standalone instruction. Prompts in the text suggest the most helpful time to view these videos.

The *Case Illustration* videos demonstrate the full-case illustrations in order to show the progress of real-world projects that use NVivo, and include videos that demonstrate how selected analytic tasks were fulfilled using NVivo. Videos of the more sophisticated full case in Chapter 9 include dialogue with the case contributor about the pros and cons of alternative ways in which NVivo could have been harnessed.

The *Harnessing Components* videos are the culmination of the instruction in this book. They contain a variety of demonstrations of the translation of individual analytic tasks and focus on the contrasting ways that components can be harnessed. These videos assume knowledge of the entire *Five-Level QDA* process contained in Parts I and II, and they assume that the videos for at least one of the two full-case illustrations have been viewed.

To register and log in to the companion website go to www.routledgetextbooks.com/textbooks/5LQDA and follow the on-screen instructions.

We hope you enjoy the book!

References

Bazeley, P., & Jackson, K. (2013). *Qualitative analysis with NVivo* (2nd ed.). Thousand Oaks: Sage.

di Gregorio, S., & Davidson, J. (2008). *Qualitative research design for software users*. Maidenhead, UK: McGraw Hill/Open University Press.

Fielding, N., & Lee, R. M. (Eds.). (1991). *Computing for qualitative research.* London: Sage.

Friese, S. (2014). *Qualitative analysis with ATLAS.ti* (2nd ed.). Thousand Oaks, CA: Sage.

Merriam, S. B., & Leahy, B. (2005). Learning transfer: A review of the research in adult education and training. *PAACE Journal of Lifelong Learning, 14*(1), 1–24.

Paulus, T. M., Lester, J. N., & Dempster, P. G. (2014). *Digital tools for qualitative research.* Thousand Oaks, CA: Sage.

Silver, C., & Woolf, N. H. (2015). From guided instruction to facilitation of learning: The development of *Five-Level QDA* as a CAQDAS pedagogy that explicates the practices of expert users. *International Journal of Social Research Methodology, 18*(5), 527–543.

Sternberg, R. J., & Frensch, P. A. (1992). On being an expert: A cost-benefit analysis. In R. Hoffman (Ed.), *The psychology of expertise* (pp. 191–203). New York: Springer-Verlag.

Woolf, N. H., & Quinn, J. (2009). Learners' perceptions of instructional design practice in a situated learning activity. *Educational Technology Research & Development, 57*(1), 25–43.

PART I

The Principles of the *Five-Level QDA* Method

Mastering the *Five-Level QDA* method means first learning the principles before hands-on use of the software. Part I contains all the principles. Chapter 1 lays the groundwork with the central principle: the contradiction between strategies and tactics when using NVivo to conduct qualitative analysis and the alternative ways to reconcile the contradiction. Chapters 2 and 3 flesh out each of the five levels. Chapter 2 deals with the first two levels of strategy: the objectives of a research project and the analytic plan to fulfill it. Chapter 3 deals with translating those strategies into the tactics of software operations.

1

STRATEGIES AND TACTICS

This chapter describes the principles behind our approach to harnessing NVivo powerfully. The central issue is the contradiction between the nature of qualitative analysis and the nature of software used to conduct the analysis. The way these contradictions are reconciled determines the approach to harnessing the software. Experienced researchers have learned to reconcile these contradictions unconsciously, but our intention is to make this transparent in order to facilitate learning. In this chapter we compare three possible approaches to reconciling the contradiction in order to highlight the reasons why this book takes the approach that it does.

A word about the illustrations used in this chapter. Because of the need to discuss the principles before we can demonstrate or provide hands-on instruction in NVivo, we use analogies in this chapter that have nothing to do with qualitative research but refer to everyday experiences we can all relate to. The variety of qualitative methodologies is so great that a single example of research would risk misleading you if you are using a different approach, and it would be cumbersome to offer multiple illustrations at this early stage. Bear with us—we will soon get on to using illustrations from real-world research projects.

The Contradictions Between Strategies and Tactics

This section describes how the nature of qualitative analysis is contradictory to the nature of software. Recognizing this contradiction is the first step in learning to harness NVivo powerfully.

Over many years of teaching we have tried to get to the bottom of what holds people up from quickly learning to harness NVivo powerfully. Our conclusion lies in the difference between strategies and tactics. They are often confused with one another or thought of as two ways to say the same thing. Understanding the relationship between strategies and tactics is the key to harnessing NVivo powerfully.

In any endeavor, strategies refer to *what you plan to do*, and tactics refer to *how you plan to do it*. It makes sense to *first* be clear about what you plan to do and *then* to be clear about how you plan to do it, but often people start with the tactics and hope for the best. A good example is pruning a fruit tree, which requires finding the right tool and then cutting the branches. If the only tools in the shed are a tree lopper and some shears, you may choose the shears and start cutting, but give up when you reach branches that are too thick near the trunk. Next year the results may be disappointing if you were hoping to encourage healthy growth and maximize the number of large, juicy apples. You then decide to read up on how an apple tree should be pruned—the strategies—rather than just start cutting again—the tactics—and you discover there are very different pruning strategies for apple trees of different varieties, ages, and states of health. Sometimes you might cut back whole branches, trim the length of others, or remove shoots, and so on. Once the strategies have been decided, the best tool can be selected for each task, whether saw, shears, or small clippers, and no task is particularly difficult because the tactics fit the strategies. The moral is that strategies and tactics are different in nature, and the tactics are made to fit the strategies, not the other way around.

In qualitative research the strategies—*what you plan to do*—are matters like deciding the purpose of the study, determining what kind of data will be required, and choosing methods for analyzing the data. Each of these areas calls for tactics to be considered and put into effect, but the strategies are largely independent of whether the tactics are going to be highlighter pens, general-purpose software like Microsoft Word or Excel, or special-purpose software like NVivo. Our contention is that when using software to conduct a qualitative analysis, the underlying nature of the strategies is contradictory to the underlying nature of the tactics to fulfill them.

The high-stakes area of computer security, such as for online banking, provides an example of contradictory strategies and tactics. Successfully encrypting your password and financial information as it moves around the Internet so that it is safe from prying eyes requires the computer to generate random numbers. This is what needs to happen—the strategy. However, computers are deterministic, meaning that they can only follow rules and procedures, referred to as algorithms, which always give the same answer to the same question. Computers cannot function in a truly random way and cannot generate truly random numbers. They can only generate pseudo-random numbers that have an underlying pattern, even though this is not discernible by the average person or computer program. So, the tactics available do not fit the needs of the strategy.

How do computer security people deal with this contradiction between the nature of what they want to do and the nature of the software with which they want to do it? First, they are consciously aware of the issue and do not ignore it. Second, they have decided that for most uses the encryption provided by even pseudo-random numbers provides adequate security. They do not need to find a way to generate truly random numbers. They have reconciled the contradiction between the need for random numbers and the nonrandom nature of computers with a conscious compromise: pseudo-random numbers are good enough (Rubin, 2011).

A similar situation arises when using software in qualitative research, and we are certainly not the first to wonder how software can be used successfully for such an open-ended process as qualitative analysis (e.g., Gilbert, Jackson, & di Gregorio, 2014; Tesch, 1990). Everything about a computer program has been predetermined by its developers to work in the same standard way, regardless of the purpose a researcher has in mind for using the software. Choosing an option from a menu or clicking on a button always has the same predetermined effect, and it is natural to assume that the features of the software are independent and are intended to be used one at a time for their most apparent purpose: in other words, that there must be a correct way to use the software in every analysis. In fact many researchers who are experienced with NVivo come to our workshops to ensure that they are using the software "correctly." But most kinds of qualitative analysis do not proceed in a predetermined way, following the same steps in the same sequence, and so NVivo is not used in remotely the same way in every project, and certainly not in a "correct" way.

Qualitative projects are, to varying degrees, *iterative* and *emergent*, with unique strategies evolving from moment to moment as the analysis unfolds. *Iterative* refers to the continual reconsideration of what is being done in light of what has just been done and what is anticipated to come next so that the individual parts of a qualitative analysis develop together as a whole. In an *emergent* system the whole is more than the sum of the parts, but the qualities of the whole are not predictable from the parts (Kauffman, 1995). The results or findings of a whole qualitative research project therefore

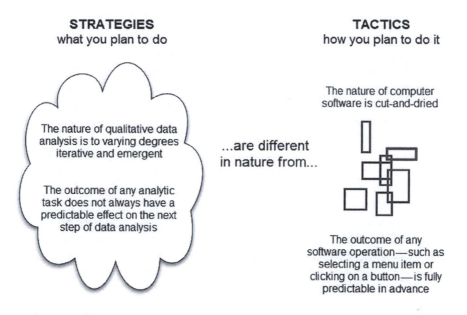

FIGURE 1.1   The contradictory nature of qualitative data analysis and computer software

emerge as the parts develop in an iterative manner. Whereas many qualitative research projects are only somewhat iterative or emergent, many are highly so, and in later chapters the case illustrations of more or less iterative and emergent types of projects will make these qualities come to life.

The contradictions between the predetermined and step-by-step processes of software, which we refer to simply as *cut and dried*, and the iterative and emergent processes of qualitative analysis that we refer to simply as *emergent*, are illustrated in Figure 1.1. Box 1.1 provides a deeper look into the relationship between cut-and-dried and emergent processes.

BOX 1.1 A DEEPER LOOK: CUT-AND-DRIED VERSUS EMERGENT PROCESSES

One way to think about the contrast between the cut-and-dried nature of computer software and the emergent nature of qualitative data analysis is by considering the contrast between *well-structured* and *ill-structured* activities more generally. These two kinds of activities are at opposite ends of a spectrum and can be considered contradictory. Taking an intentional approach to reconciling the contradiction is the rationale for the *Five-Level QDA* method.

Well-Structured Activities

A structure is an arrangement of the parts of something. Everything—a building, a problem to be solved, a society, a qualitative analysis—has a structure. One characteristic of structure common to all these examples is the *degree* of structure that something has. Churchman (1971) proposed two main classes of problems or activities: well structured and ill structured. In well-structured activities everything is known: there are clear goals, a single correct outcome or purpose, and clear criteria for knowing when the activity is successful or complete. It is a matter of going through a process or a series of steps to complete the activity. Chess is a good example. It is challenging to play well, but everything about it is well structured: how each piece moves, a single result, and a single way of knowing who has won—by the capture of the opposing king. It is therefore amenable to being represented by algorithms, or step-by-step procedures, which explains why computers do it so well.

Computer software is an example of a well-structured domain. Every aspect about using it is definite and always works in the same way (unless there is a bug in the program, but that is a different matter). For example, if you wish to copy and paste in Microsoft Word, selecting some text and pressing the Copy button will always reliably copy those lines of text. Pressing the Paste button at a different location will always reliably paste in the exact same lines. Operating computer software is a step-by-step activity predetermined by the software developer, like following a recipe. And like chess, it is not necessarily easy to learn or use. But each act of using it is a well-structured activity.

Most important is the mind-set involved in using software. Cognitive psychologists have proposed that we create *schema*—mental templates—whenever we do an activity, so that next time we meet a similar set of circumstances we have a preorganized set of expectations and blank mental *slots* already prepared to quickly interpret the new situation in terms of our previous experience of a similar activity (Shank & Abelson, 1977). Most people have been using computer software for quite a while and have what we call a well-developed "software schema." When using software we have expectations that everything we do with the program follows a step-by-step procedure, with each task broken down into a set of clear-cut steps that will work in the same way each time. There is nothing iterative about using software, because the outcome of an action is always the same. There is nothing emergent about using software, because we know what that outcome will be in advance. The "software schema," or mind-set, we have all developed sets up a high expectation for an extremely well-structured activity.

Ill-Structured Activities

Activities that lack structure are quite different. Goals are vague, there is incomplete information available, there are many possible outcomes or problem solutions, and many possible criteria for knowing if the activity is complete or the problem solved. They are not called ill structured because there is anything wrong with them, they just lack structure—they are uncertain, and information is incomplete in various ways. For example, "solving for x in an algebraic equation" is a well-structured activity, but "judging the adequacy of a theoretical proposition" is ill structured (King & Kitchener, 2004, p. 11). Reitman (1964) and Simon (1973) conducted the pioneering work on how people deal with the ill-structured activities that make up most of everyday life, and Jonassen (1997) summarized the major characteristics of all ill-structured problems. King and Kitchener (2004) developed a program for assessing how people respond to ill-structured problems, focusing on the cognitive skills necessary to work successfully in ill-structured domains. They described seven levels of development of a skill they call "reflective judgment."

Qualitative analysis is certainly an ill-structured activity according to the descriptions of these scholars. Reitman (1964) described how well-structured and ill-structured problems form a continuum, which is helpful when thinking about the degree of emergence in a qualitative research methodology. Schön (1983) described professional practice in many fields as an ill-structured design skill in which a "reflective practitioner . . . must make sense of an uncertain situation that initially makes no sense . . . we *name* the things to which we will attend and *frame* the context in which we will attend to them (p. 40, italics in original). Schön (1983) was describing professional practice generally, but he could be describing qualitative analysis. In our field no piece of data has a single correct meaning, no research question has a single correct finding, and there is no single criterion to evaluate findings that have been proposed or an obvious ending point at which the analysis is complete.

The consequences of the ill structure of qualitative analysis are to require varying degrees of iteration and emergence, in contradiction to the step-by-step, recipe-like procedures of well-structured computer software. *Iteration*, with its reconsideration and modification of what we had done previously in the light of new perspectives, leads to an evolving relationship between the developing parts—the individual analytic tasks we undertake and their outcomes—and the whole—the overall picture that emerges with each iterative adjustment of one or more of the parts, a process sometimes called entering the *hermeneutic circle* (Packer & Addison, 1989). This is in contradiction to the relationship of parts and wholes in the well-structured nature of computer software, in which describing the whole adds nothing new to describing the individual parts of the whole. To say "cut and paste" is functionally identical to saying "select text, copy, move cursor, paste." *Emergence*, a much-abused term that is often used for anything vaguely qualitative, does have a specific meaning regarding parts and wholes. In general, emergence refers to the properties of any complex system (Kauffman, 1995). A system is a general term for any collection of things that are related to one another in some way—the bones in a body, the members of an organization, the atoms in a molecule, the concepts in a qualitative analysis, are all systems. When the number of parts in a system and their interconnections reach a certain point, the system is called complex and has emergent qualities in which the whole has characteristics not predictable for any of the parts. Each qualitative project is emergent to greatly different degrees, from very little to a great deal, depending on the guiding methodology and on practical matters such as the time available to bring a project to conclusion.

In summary, the well-structured features of computer software—predetermined and step by step—are at the opposite end of Reitman's (1964) spectrum of ill structure from the iterative and emergent features of qualitative analysis. An iterative process cannot be accomplished in a step-by-step fashion, and a step-by-step process cannot be emergent. It is in this sense that the nature of computer software and the nature of qualitative analysis are contradictory, and when dealing with contradictory circumstances, some resolution has to occur to be able to function effectively. Intentionally deciding what approach to take in the face of these contradictions is the underlying principle of this book.

Contradictory strategies and tactics suggest various possible solutions. Imagine you are an architect with a set of building blocks that come in standard shapes and sizes: perhaps square bricks and rectangular bricks with tongues and grooves that fit together in predetermined ways. Some construction projects in this imaginary world might call for exactly these shaped bricks stacked up in various ways just as the tongues and grooves provide for. But many projects might not. They might include circular designs or call for bricks that stack together differently from how the predetermined tongues and grooves connect. An expert architect would find a way to make the standard bricks work; she would overcome the apparent inconsistency between the angular shape of the bricks and the circular designs. A novice architect is more likely to decide that a circular building is impossible to design with these bricks, or she may refuse to use bricks at all, as they are simply the wrong shape. Remember these architects: we'll come back to them.

In qualitative analysis such contradictions between strategies and tactics are in no way a barrier to harnessing NVivo powerfully. Most qualitative researchers neither want nor expect the cut-and-dried operations of the program—the tactics—to play a role in the emergent strategies of the analysis or to contribute to the interpretive process. It is commonly said that in qualitative research the instrument of research is the mind of the researcher, in which an entire lifetime of accumulated human experience and learning is brought to bear on the interpretation of data in a systematic and justifiable manner. In the language of the *Five-Level QDA* method, the *strategy* levels of qualitative methods are fundamentally the province of the researcher's mind. In contrast, the mechanical levels of *tactics* are the province of the cut-and-dried software operations. The researcher decides how to harness the tactics in the service of her strategies, and developing this skill is the focus of this book. No software program remotely approximates the sophistication of the human brain in finding meaning in a body of data—at least not yet—and the potential misuse of rudimentary automated features that may be introduced in the future are concerning. But that is not the concern of this book.

Different Ways to Reconcile Contradictions

This section describes three different ways to reconcile the contradiction between the nature of qualitative analysis and the nature of software. Each way leads to a different approach to using software for qualitative analysis.

When two things are contradictory, like darkness and light, each one precludes the other: on the face of it you cannot have both. There is more than one way to deal with such a contradiction: first, by avoiding the contradiction; second, by compromising; or third, by going beyond or transcending the contradiction. We begin with a discussion of the first two ways as a context for describing why we choose the third way.

The first way is simply to avoid the contradiction—for example, by ignoring the darkness and stumbling around knocking things over in the middle of the night on the way to the bathroom. A second way is to find a compromise between the contradictory things, which partially satisfies each one. Perhaps a door can be opened to let in a sliver of moonlight: not enough light to read or do anything useful, but just enough to avoid knocking things over, yet still dark enough to let others sleep. A workable compromise. In situations of contradictory demands this might be the best we can hope for, a compromise that works well enough, as it did for the computer security engineers who decided that pseudo-random numbers are good enough for their data encryption process.

A third way is to transcend the contradiction so that you do not have to sacrifice the full integrity of either side. This is generally accomplished by seeing the situation in a larger context so that the contradiction is no longer there. The invention of night-vision goggles allowed night to be day. Before this invention, darkness and light referred only to the frequencies of light visible to humans, which are only a small portion of the electromagnetic spectrum. When this limited perspective is expanded to include the much higher (ultraviolet) and much lower (infrared) frequencies that humans cannot see unaided but that can be seen through the goggles, the contradiction between darkness and light is transcended and no longer exists.

Similarly, these different ways to deal with the contradiction between our strategies and tactics lead to different approaches to using NVivo. Each of the three ways differs regarding what happens in between the two extremes, in the middle area between the strategies (the emergent qualitative analysis) and the tactics (the cut-and-dried features of the software). The first approach of avoiding the contradiction between qualitative analysis and software does not require anything in the middle, because there is no middle: the situation is treated as a single, unproblematic task of *doing-qualitative-data-analysis-with-software*. We call this One-Level QDA. The second approach recognizes that there is indeed a difference between qualitative analysis methods and the software features, and it addresses the difference by creating an analytic process in the middle that becomes a compromise between the emergent nature of qualitative analysis and the cut-and-dried software features. This leads to three separate processes, and so we call this approach Three-Level QDA. The final approach, which we take in this book, transcends the contradiction in order to see it in a larger context. We call this approach the *Five-Level QDA* method. Before saying why we call it *Five-Level QDA*, it is necessary to describe One-Level QDA and Three-Level QDA a little more fully in order that you can appreciate why it is well worth the effort to learn the principles of the *Five-Level QDA* method.

One-Level QDA

Sadly, many people do not harness NVivo powerfully. Many experienced researchers never try CAQDAS packages at all, having read the unwarranted concerns in the academic literature. For example, they fear that using these programs will impose a particular style of qualitative analysis, or distance the researcher from the data, or that they are a kind of qualitative equivalent to statistical analysis programs that will take over or do the analysis. These largely theoretical concerns were written about in the 1980s or 1990s when few researchers had gained experience in using these programs. Several authors have convincingly refuted these concerns (e.g., Davidson & di Gregorio, 2011; Gilbert, 2002; Gilbert et al., 2014; Jackson, 2017; Nathan & Jackson, 2006).

Many researchers who do embrace the use of software use it superficially. A common approach is to use CAQDAS packages for the initial straightforward stages of a project, but then switch to another program, often Microsoft Word or Excel, or even back to paper and pencil, to complete the analysis (e.g., Ose, 2016). Another approach is to continue using NVivo in a simplistic or step-by-step way, which can have the effect of suppressing some of the emergent aspects of the analysis. Using NVivo in a superficial way may be intentional as part of a larger plan for conducting a research project. But more commonly this superficial use is not intentional but an unconscious avoidance of the contradiction between the emergent nature of qualitative analysis and the cut-and-dried nature of software. Avoiding or denying a contradiction is particularly easy for humans—we have a remarkable ability to maintain contradictory ideas at the same time without feeling the need for any resolution (Fitzgerald, 1945, p. 13; Kurzweil, 2012, p. 197). This is helpful in many situations, especially humor, which relies on seeing contradictory ideas occupying the same space (Koestler, 1964).

It's true that many qualitative researchers have a good sense of humor, but nevertheless, avoiding or leaving unresolved the contradictions surrounding the use of software in qualitative analysis does not lead to harnessing NVivo powerfully. Avoiding the inherent contradictions amounts to considering qualitative analysis and the operations of software as a single process. That means that the strategies and tactics are thought of as a single activity. We could call that *what-you-plan-to-do-and-how-you-plan-to-do-it*, or as we refer to it, One-Level QDA. Strategies and tactics are not differentiated, and if they do not match in the mind of the researcher, then the process grinds to a halt.

In the world of standardized bricks a circular building is simply impossible to design with the available bricks. If only square and rectangular bricks were available, then square and rectangular buildings could be designed; if a circular building is required, then curved bricks must be provided. This is not the reality of expert architects, who find a way to resolve these differences. We now consider two different approaches to resolving these differences in qualitative analysis.

Three-Level QDA

One approach to handling the incompatibility between cut-and-dried software and the emergent nature of qualitative analysis is to organize the analysis into a more structured set of tasks in order to make them more amenable to being executed on a computer, a kind of compromise. This is in some ways the most natural thing to do, so we need to dwell on the consequences of this approach in order to describe why we take the approach that we do.

Everyday life requires compromises of all kinds, and this is generally considered a good thing. Neither side gets everything they want, but enough that both sides can live with it. Compromising allows people with very different outlooks to peacefully live together. But the suitability of a compromise depends on the context.

In the earlier example of a darkened bedroom in the middle of the night, partially satisfying each side of the contradiction by opening the door just a little avoided the need to choose between either extreme, complete darkness or complete light—a good thing in this example, as the compromise in the middle is far better than either extreme pole. But in other contexts a compromise that does not fully satisfy either pole may be *less* desirable than choosing between them, and is thus a bad thing. Here's a very different example about a compromise between darkness and light.

A few minutes into the very funny play *Black Comedy* (Shaffer, 1967), there is an electrical short circuit, and the action continues in total darkness for most of the play until near the end when the electricity is restored and it finishes in normal light. That is the plot of the play. In reality, in the theater, there is a reversed lighting scheme. To the audience, the play opens in total darkness but the actors are performing (invisibly to us) as if they are in normal light. When the short circuit happens in the play, the stage lights come on, so we can finally see what is happening on stage. But the actors are acting as if they have now been plunged into total darkness, and they continue acting as if in the dark, which we see under normal lighting. It's very funny. Then toward the end when the electricity is supposedly restored in the play, the stage lights go off again, while the actors finish up the play as if in normal light, we—and they—can see nothing!

What if the theater director had said that this was too complicated and decided to scrap the reverse lighting? According to such a director, at one extreme the reverse lighting is too challenging for the actors to convincingly pull off, but the other extreme of normal lighting—dark on stage when it is dark in the play, and light on stage when it is light in the play—eliminates the humor. Neither extreme is good, so perhaps very dim light throughout would be a workable compromise? The audience would get the general idea that the main part of the play is supposedly taking place in pitch blackness, because the light would be very dim, but the actors would have enough light to be able to see their way around the stage. And when the action was supposedly in full light, rather than the stage being completely dark, there would be at least some light for the audience to watch how the actors were managing to act out in the play in darkness, although it wouldn't be complete darkness but very dim light. Not perfect, but a workable compromise.

Would this be better than either of the poles of full light or full darkness? We hope you'll agree it would not be; the play would never have been the award-winning success it was if staged throughout in very dim light. In this context, a compromised, watered-down strategy of acting in very dim light that gives the idea of darkness to the audience is the worst choice. It leads to the unnecessary outcome that the play ceases to be funny.

Which context is more like using software for qualitative analysis? In the going-to-the-bathroom-at-night context, the compromise was not greatly inferior to either pole. Moving around in a sliver of moonlight is just slightly easier than in darkness, basically the same kind of activity, and if the sleepers are wakened by the sliver of moonlight they would likely get back to sleep pretty quickly in the almost darkness. But in *Black Comedy* the compromise of running the whole play in dim light would eliminate the plot and thus the humor, which is created by the inability to see anything in the dark. We suggest that qualitative analysis is more *like Black Comedy*, in which a compromise is not the best choice.

We refer to the addition of a compromise position between the analytic strategies of a qualitative analysis on one side and the software tactics to fulfill them in NVivo on the other side as Three-Level QDA. This is illustrated in Figure 1.2. What does Three-Level QDA look like in practice? The strategies—*what you plan to do*—are at a more abstract level, expressed in conceptual terms:

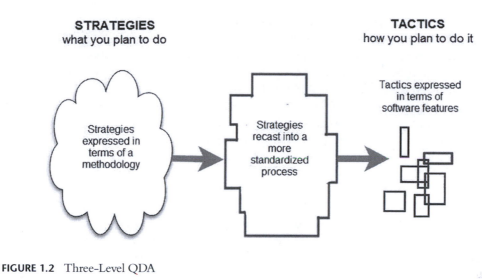

STRATEGIES
what you plan to do

Strategies
expressed in
terms of a
methodology

Strategies
recast into a
more
standardized
process

TACTICS
how you plan to do it

Tactics expressed
in terms of
software features

FIGURE 1.2   Three-Level QDA

identifying kinds of leadership behaviors in an organizational leadership study, *describing degrees of community support* in a community-based public health initiative, or whatever the project involves. The tactics—*how you plan to do it*—are necessarily at a more concrete level. If NVivo is used for the tactics, this will involve such things as using different colors on screen to represent different types of leadership that are being considered as possible candidate types of leadership, or searching for different keywords to explore for possible examples of a kind of community support that is not yet clearly defined. At the strategy level of deciding *what you plan to do*, tasks such as these vary greatly. They vary in how definite or exploratory their purpose is or how settled or interim the result is expected to be, depending on the research methodology being used. In summary, they vary in how emergent the tasks are. Even if the tasks in your project are very different from the tasks in these examples, they will have a degree of emergence, or your projects would not be qualitative. However, at the tactics level these tasks become extremely cut and dried: select a color, find the instances of a word. At the tactics level there is a cut-and-dried way of thinking that is very different from an emergent way of thinking.

Taking a Three-Level QDA approach means bridging this chasm in ways of thinking with a workable compromise between thinking in a fully emergent manner and thinking in a fully cut-and-dried manner. And just in the same way that the compromise of having very dim light throughout *Black Comedy* would spoil the basic rationale for its humor, a compromise is not the best approach for conducting qualitative analysis using NVivo. Here's what this Three-Level QDA thinking might look like in the example of *identifying kinds of leadership behaviors*.

First, the emergent way of thinking at the strategy level that you might write about in an analytic memo to yourself might be:

> If I understand my methods text correctly as it applies to my project, at this point in my analysis it wants me to read my interviews again. I'll be looking for signs of those leadership behaviors I have been reflecting on and name them in a conceptual way based on what the respondents actually say. That's the first step of a multistep conceptualizing process. Hmm. I think I'll start by looking for different types of leadership behaviors that are very different from one another and see where that gets me.

Looking ahead, it may well be that many steps down this process the idea of "types of leadership" turns out to be a dead end. The reason is that you discover that the different so-called "types of leadership" you were naming are actually only subtly different manifestations of one of two main kinds of leadership already well understood, "transactional" rather than "transformational" leadership (e.g., Hartog, Muijen, & Koopman, 1997). Transformational leadership seeks to bring about major change, whereas transactional leadership focuses on promoting adherence to the current organizational goals and procedures. However, the various transactional leadership behaviors you discovered varied greatly depending on the size of the organization that the respondent works at, and so that became a very interesting new way forward. The idea of multiple "types of leadership" is ditched as a new direction emerged.

In contrast, the cut-and-dried way of thinking might go like this:

> I have already named and represented seven types of leadership in NVivo using seven differ-ent colors, which I then took several steps further in the software because certain software features made this easy and natural to do. Cancelling the idea of "types of leadership" is basi-cally too late; they are already built in to the analysis as now represented in the software, and that is the path the analysis is taking, even though it doesn't quite fit what the respondents were saying.

This is very far from the ideal of qualitative research. Is there an alternative?

One alternative is a Three-Level QDA way of thinking—to adopt a compromise between the emergent and the cut-and-dried ways of thinking. For example, rather than adopting the suggested strategy in the methods textbook for the leadership study, it might be replaced with a simpler, more general, and concrete approach that can be readily executed in the software: *identify how respondents talk about their leadership behaviors, gather together similar examples, represent each group in the software, and think of a way of working further with these groups of examples in ways the software provides*. This does not fully reflect the intentions of the methods text, and although it is not expressed in software terms, it can be directly executed in the software. It is a compromise. However, it is a compromise of the same kind as the very dim light in *Black Comedy*: it weakens the intentions of the methods text to the point that the analysis is no longer in the emergent spirit of qualitative research.

We are not suggesting that Three-Level QDA is a method of analysis that is proposed by any methods writers. It is rather a way of thinking about doing qualitative analysis with software that in our view should be guarded against. Although it may seem like the natural thing to do, our experience suggests that it leads to an unsatisfactory compromise. Texts that aim to assist qualitative researchers in using CAQDAS packages can be easily misinterpreted in the way described earlier. If a text you are using appears to be suggesting a generic, one-size-fits-all approach for conducting analysis, we suggest that you assume that you are misinterpreting the intentions of the writer and that you look for ways to take advantage of their advice that does not amount to a compromise between the emergent nature of your strategies and the cut-and-dried nature of the software.

Five-Level QDA

The key difference between Three-Level QDA and the *Five-Level QDA* method is what happens at the middle level, in between the strategies and the tactics. In our years of teaching and using NVivo for different kinds of projects, we became convinced that harnessing NVivo powerfully involves a process of *translation* between the emergent strategies of a qualitative analysis and the cut-and-dried tactics involved in using the software. When researchers harness NVivo successfully, translation is put into effect in a different way for every project by going back and forth between strategies and tactics without having to compromise either to match the nature of the other. This translation is a separate skill from research or analytical skills. It is the skill of *harnessing* the software rather than simply operating it. The translation process is in no way a complex skill; it is simply a separate skill that has to be recognized, learned, and put into practice.

The *Five-Level QDA* method amounts to transcending the contradictions between the nature of the strategies and the nature of the tactics by placing both in a larger context so that the contradiction between them is unproblematic. This is a standard way of dealing with contradictions that seek a "both/and" rather than an "either/or" solution. Placing them in a larger context means maintaining, distinguishing, and attending to each of the five levels in their own terms, according to their own nature. As a first introduction to the five levels, there are two levels of strategy and two levels of tactics, with an additional level of translation that comes between them.

The principles of the *Five-Level QDA* method developed gradually over many years of teaching and using CAQDAS packages, but its formulation in five formal and related levels is greatly informed by Edward Luttwak's description of five general levels of military strategy (Luttwak, 2001). Some qualitative researchers find military strategy a distasteful metaphor for qualitative data analysis, yet this is the one field in which the contradictions between strategies and tactics have been thought through in most detail. We do not need to dwell on the similarities between the levels of military strategy and qualitative analysis strategy, but we do wish to acknowledge Edward Luttwak's contribution to our thinking (Box 1.2 provides more information about Edward Luttwak's levels of strategy).

An important aspect of the *Five-Level QDA* method is that it is not something new. It is neither a new research method nor a new way of conducting qualitative analysis. It is our way of describing what expert users of NVivo already do, but generally unconsciously and automatically when harnessing NVivo through every phase of a project while remaining true throughout to the emergent spirit of qualitative research. Our aim is to make the process explicit so that the process of becoming an expert user can be sped up.

BOX 1.2 A DEEPER LOOK: EDWARD LUTTWAK'S FIVE LEVELS OF MILITARY STRATEGY

We knew that expert users of NVivo had learned to unconsciously keep separate their strategies from their tactics and to successfully move between them without having their emergent analytic strategies unduly influenced by their cut-and-dried software tactics. But we did not initially know how to unpack the black box of this expertise in order to help others do the same. Nick searched for guidance in other fields but was mightily disappointed. Various books and articles encouragingly included strategy and tactics in the title, but then used the terms interchangeably as if synonyms or discussed them separately without relating them together. He found only one field—military studies—that offered a helpful guide. This is the one field in which the contradictions between strategies and tactics have been thought through in detail, most notably by the military strategist Edward Luttwak.

Most writers on military strategy throughout history have prescribed strategic thinking relevant to the conditions and conflicts of their age (Luttwak, 2001, p. 267). Luttwak (2001) set out to describe universal principles of strategy that applied to any age or kind of conflict. Nick was amazed to find how the details of Luttwak's (2001) model so readily applied outside the domain of warfare. Luttwak (2001) identifies five interrelated levels of strategy, each with a different role and type of activity, that are uncannily analogous to the activities of a research project. At the most general level of military strategy are national goals and values—the level of *grand strategy*. Its various characteristics are closely analogous to the objectives and methodology of research projects, which we call Level 1 of the *Five-Level QDA* method. Luttwak's (2001) next level is *theater strategy*, the implementation of grand strategy in a specific, self-contained territory. The characteristics of theater strategy are highly analogous to the tasks of creating a specific analytic plan, our Level 2. For purposes of exposition it is now easiest to move to the end of the list. The fourth and fifth levels in Luttwak's (2001) model are the *technical* development of individual weapons, vehicles, and other equipment and their combined use in combat in *tactical units*. These are directly analogous to our Levels 4 and 5, the levels of selected and constructed software tools.

However, of greatest significance is the middle level between the two levels of strategy and the two levels of tactics. Luttwak (2001) calls this middle level the *operational level*. This is a coordinating level between strategies and tactics that is not directly involved in the activities of either. It is an abstract layer of activity consisting of adding or removing tactical units within a battle in response to the needs of the theater strategy. This is Luttwak's unique contribution, the identification of the separate "operational level of war" that is now a part of U.S. Army doctrine (Luttwak, n.d.). It is directly analogous to the abstract level of activity that we call translation, the additional skill that experienced qualitative researchers have unconsciously learned to use to manage the contradiction between their analytic strategies into their software tactics.

This overview is intended to give credit where credit is due, as these universal principles of strategy assisted greatly in our unpacking and describing what expert users of NVivo do. For more detailed information on the characteristics of Luttwak's' (2001) five levels of strategy and their close analogy to the levels of the *Five-Level QDA* method, see Woolf (2014).

References

Churchman, C. W. (1971). *The design of inquiring systems: Basic concepts of systems and organization*. New York: Basic Books.

Davidson, J., & di Gregorio, S. (2011). Qualitative research and technology: In the midst of a revolution. In N. K. Denzin & Y. S. Lincoln (Eds.), *The Sage handbook of qualitative research* (4th ed., pp. 627–643). Thousand Oaks: CA: Sage.

Fitzgerald, F. S. (1945). *The crack-up*. New York: James Laughlin.

Gilbert, L. S. (2002). Going the distance: 'Closeness' in qualitative data analysis software. *International Journal of Social Research Methodology, 5*(3), 215–228.

Gilbert, L. S., Jackson, K., & di Gregorio, S. (2014). Tools for analyzing qualitative data: The history and relevance of qualitative data analysis software. In J. M. Spector, M. D. Merrill, J. Elen & M. J. Bishop (Eds.), *Handbook of research on educational communications and technology* (pp. 221–236). New York: Springer

Hartog, D. N., Muijen, J. J., & Koopman, P. L. (1997). Transactional versus transformational leadership: An analysis of the MLQ. *Journal of Occupational and Organizational Psychology, 70*(1), 19–34.

Jackson, K. (2017). Turning against each other in neoliberal times: The discourses of otherizing and how they threaten our scholarship. In N. K. Denzin & M. D. Giardina (Eds.), *Qualitative Inquiry in Neoliberal Times* (pp. 151–165). New York: Routledge.

Jonassen, D. H. (1997). Instructional design models for well-structured and ill-structured problem-solving learning outcomes. *Educational Technology Research & Development, 45*(1), 65–94.

Kauffman, S. (1995). *At home in the universe: The search for laws of self-organization and complexity*. New York: Oxford University Press.

King, P. M., & Kitchener, K. S. (2004). Reflective judgment: Theory and research on the development of epistemic assumptions through adulthood. *Educational Psychologist, 39*(1), 5–18.

Koestler, A. (1964). *The act of creation*. London: Hutchinson.

Kurzweil, R. (2012). *How to create a mind.* New York: Viking.

Luttwak, E. N. (n.d.). In Wikipedia. Retrieved November 18, 2016 from https://en.wikipedia.org/wiki/Edward_Luttwak

Luttwak, E. N. (2001). *Strategy: The logic of peace and war* (2nd ed.). Cambridge, MA: Harvard University Press.

Nathan, M. J., & Jackson, K. (2006). *Boolean classes and qualitative inquiry* (WCER Working Paper No. 2006-3). Madison: University of Wisconsin-Madison, Wisconsin Center for Education Research. Retrieved from www.wcer.wisc.edu/publications/workingPapers/papers.php

Ose, S. O. (2016). Using Excel and Word to structure qualitative data. *Journal of Applied Social Science, 10*(2), 147–162.

Packer, M. J., & Addison, R. B. (1989). *Entering the circle: Hermeneutic investigation in psychology.* Albany, NY: SUNY Press.

Reitman, W. R. (1964). Heuristic decision procedures, open constraints, and the structure of ill-defined problems. In M. W. Shelly & G. L. Bryan (Eds.), *Human judgments and optimality* (pp. 282–315). New York: John Wiley & Sons.

Rubin, J. M. (2011). Can a computer generate a truly random number? *MIT School of engineering: Ask an engineer.* Retrieved from http://engineering.mit.edu/ask/can-computer-generate-truly-random-number

Schön, D. A. (1983). *The reflective practitioner: How professionals think in action.* San Francisco: Jossey-Bass.

Shaffer, P. (1967). *Black comedy.* New York: Samuel French.

Shank, R. C., & Abelson, R. P. (1977). *Scripts, plans, goals, and understanding.* Hillsdale, NJ: Erlbaum.

Simon, H. A. (1973). The structure of ill-structured problems. *Artificial Intelligence, 4,* 181–201.

Tesch, R. (1990). *Qualitative research: Analysis types and software tools.* London: Falmer Press.

Woolf, N. H. (2014). Analytic strategies and analytic tactics. Keynote address at ATLAS.ti User Conference 2013: Fostering Dialog on Qualitative Methods, Technische Universität Berlin. doi:http://nbn-resolving.de/urn:nbn:de:kobv:83-opus4-44159

2

DEVELOPING OBJECTIVES AND ANALYTIC PLANS (LEVELS 1 AND 2)

This chapter describes the two levels of strategy in the *Five-Level QDA* method: Level 1, the objectives of a research project, and Level 2, the analytic plan for meeting those objectives. This book does not teach how to write objectives or research questions or how to select a methodology or develop an analytic plan. But because these are prerequisites for putting the *Five-Level QDA* method into practice at Level 3, we do go into some depth in this chapter about the principles behind what needs to be done at Levels 1 and 2, and we suggest resources for more practical guidance in these areas.

Dealing with five levels of a qualitative analysis is not as daunting as it might seem. The first two levels are the strategies, the last two levels are the tactics, and the middle level translates between them. Translation simply means *transforming* the strategies into tactics. Later we take this further by showing what this transformation means in practice, but in this chapter we begin by introducing the principles behind just the first two levels, the strategy levels. Level 1 concerns the formulation of the objectives of a project, usually expressed as a research question and a research methodology. However, many people who use NVivo do not come from a formal research background, and they express their objectives in a less formal way. But one way or another, expressing the objectives has to be the first step, as it is in any successful endeavor, and Level 2 concerns the development of a plan to fulfill these objectives. These two levels of strategy are the prerequisites for harnessing NVivo powerfully. In this chapter we introduce you to what is needed for Levels 1 and 2, and then we guide you to further resources that you can consult for accomplishing this, if necessary.

Level 2 results in identifying a series of specific analytic tasks to be accomplished. Looking ahead, in the next chapter we begin discussing Level 3, the level of translation. This means transforming the analytic tasks identified in Level 2 into software operations that can be carried out in NVivo—Levels 4 and 5.

Figure 2.1 lays out the five levels of activity in an orderly way, and we discuss these levels one by one. However, if the layout of Figure 2.1 gives the impression that a research project *proceeds* in an orderly, linear, step-by-step way in practice, be assured that this is not the case. Qualitative research is, to varying degrees, an emergent activity. The whole emerges out of a series of developing parts—meaning a series of developing analytic tasks. It does not proceed in a linear, step-by-step manner, but in an iterative, cyclical, unpredictable manner. Inevitably there are detours and a good amount of messiness as a qualitative research project progresses. This messiness is not always apparent when

Two Levels of Strategy >>>>> Translated To >>>>> Two Levels of Tactics				
Level 1	*Level 2*	*Level 3*	*Level 4*	*Level 5*
Objectives	Analytic plan	Translation	Selected tools	Constructed tools
The purpose and context of a project, usually expressed as research questions and a methodology	The conceptual framework and resulting analytic tasks	Translating from analytic tasks to software tools and translating the results back again	Straightforward choice of individual software operations	Sophisticated use of software by combining operations or performing them in a custom way

FIGURE 2.1   The five levels of the *Five-Level QDA* method

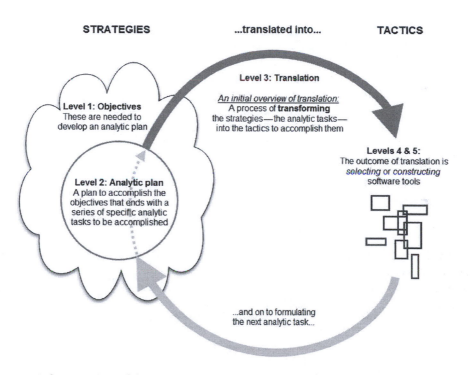

FIGURE 2.2   A first overview of the iterative process of the *Five-Level QDA* method

reading qualitative research articles. Space in academic journals is limited, and descriptions of the research process need to be concise and may appear more sanitized and orderly than what actually occurred. The portrayal of the *Five-Level QDA* method in Figure 2.1 should be seen as a convenient way of laying out and explaining each level of the process in an orderly manner. Figure 2.2 offers a more accurate portrayal of the iterative process that better reflects the detours and messiness of real-world projects, which will be on full display in the case illustrations in Part III. Figure 2.2 is a first overview of this iterative process. We will be adding more detail to this circular portrayal as we go more deeply into the process step by step.

But first, we now begin with Level 1—the objectives—and then move on to Level 2—the development of an analytic plan.

Level 1: Objectives

In this section we describe the first level of the *Five-Level QDA* method, the highest level of strategy. This consists of the project objectives, which describe the *purpose* of the project and the *context* in which it occurs, and a set of research methods for undertaking the various phases of the project—known as a *methodology*—that guides how the objectives will be fulfilled. Taken together these constitute the boundaries around a universe of interest, and they are the essential starting point of any research project.

It is common for beginning researchers to have vague, partially thought through, or unrealistically broad and ambitious research objectives. However, clear objectives are a prerequisite for harnessing NVivo powerfully, because the objectives that come out of Level 1 lead directly to Level 2—formulating an analytic plan—which leads directly to Level 3—transforming the plan into software operations in NVivo. If the process begins with vague or inconsistent objectives, these qualities will trickle all the way down to the use of the software.

Learning to formulate clear objectives is not the focus of this book. No single textbook can be a one-stop destination for every phase of qualitative research—the range of activities is too wide and disparate. It would be like having a single book about how to grow your own vegetables in all possible climates integrated with a cookbook for making every kind of dish from all the cuisines of the world. No author could be equally expert in all these topics. Yet the success of the menus in the cookbook depends on the quality of the gardening described in the gardening text.

In a similar way, although our focus is on harnessing NVivo, it is of great concern to us that your objectives are indeed clear, for otherwise the *Five-Level QDA* method will not accomplish its purpose. We therefore do introduce the subject later, to let you know what is needed. The objectives of a project are best thought about in the same way as the *Five-Level QDA* method as a whole—in other words, as having both strategies and tactics. *What* the objectives are comprise the strategies to be accomplished (generally, one or more research questions), and *how* they are to be fulfilled are the tactics (a guiding methodology). First, the strategy.

Clear Objectives

Many NVivo projects are academic studies in which the objectives are expressed as formal research questions, for example, *How do attitudes and responses to bullying vary across the different schools in a single school district?* But not all NVivo projects are of this kind. Many users of NVivo have quite different purposes in mind from answering a research question, such as researchers undertaking a literature review, management consultants studying an organization in order to propose changes to business strategy, authors categorizing or indexing their sources in preparation for writing a book, or physicians organizing and annotating patient records in an electronic system to make it easier to find or communicate information (Fielding & Lee, 2002). All these projects could be accomplished using NVivo, but they do not have formal research questions. For simplicity, we call all project purposes *objectives*. All these kinds of objectives must be *clear*, whether or not they are research questions, so that the actions inspired by the objectives actually move the project in the desired direction of fulfilling their purpose.

The criteria are the same for all successful objectives: they must be *coherent* (the parts fit together in a logical way and do not contradict one another), *unambiguous* (expressed in a way that makes it clear what is to be accomplished without having to guess what is meant), and *capable of being answered* with the available data or with data that are planned to be collected. It is quick and easy to write incoherent or ambiguous objectives, and usually several drafts are required before they become both clear and fulfillable.

TABLE 2.1 Selected resources for learning to write clear objectives

Miles, M. B. and Huberman, A. M. (1994). Qualitative data analysis: An expanded sourcebook. Thousand Oaks, CA: Sage.	Still the go-to text for a practical approach to qualitative analysis. Includes a helpful section on formulating research questions.
Patton, M. Q. (2015). Qualitative research and evaluation methods: Integrating theory and practice (4th ed.). Thousand Oaks, CA: Sage.	The best general text on qualitative evaluation methods. Includes sections on types of evaluation purposes and developing questions.
Marshall, C. and Rossman, G. B. (2016). Designing qualitative research (6th ed.). Thousand Oaks, CA: Sage.	Now in its sixth edition, this popular text discusses the fundamentals of valid and achievable research objectives and how to write research questions.
Maxwell, J. A. (2013). Qualitative research design: An interactive approach (3rd ed.). Sage. Thousand Oaks, CA: Sage.	Now in its third edition, this is another popular text with an excellent chapter on writing research questions.

Research studies from different traditions have very different approaches to formulating their research questions, and each has its own texts to offer guidance (Creswell, 2013). But regardless of your approach, research questions are ultimately questions, taking the form of *What . . .*, *How. . .*, or *Why. . .?* If you are not yet familiar with writing research questions and are just considering your approach, one good starting point is the chapter on qualitative research objectives by the anthropologist Harry Wolcott (Wolcott, 1994). The chapter clearly explains the differences between three kinds of objectives that are increasingly abstracted from the data: *describing what is there* (an objective that typically leads to a *What . . .* question), *analyzing how it works* (an objective that typically leads to a *How . . .* question), and *interpreting what it means* (an objective that typically leads to a *Why . . .* question). Wolcott goes on to recommend analytic approaches for beginning, intermediate, and more advanced researchers. Even if your project is not an academic study, you will likely still enjoy reading that chapter. If you do not plan to write formal research questions to express your objectives, you will still likely want to write out your objectives by starting with an action verb that indicates the action to be taken, such as *assess*, *identify*, *compare*, and so on.

Many resources are available if more guidance is needed in formulating objectives. If you are not following a prescribed methodology or do not know where to start, Table 2.1 provides an annotated bibliography of some popular authoritative texts that introduce the topic of research objectives.

Adopting a Methodology

Once an objective has been formulated—clearly articulating *what* you plan to do—the next issue is deciding how you will go about fulfilling it, which is the role of methodology. This book does not teach methodology, but we must be sure there are no weak links in the chain from clear objectives down to the use of the software. We therefore introduce several aspects of methodology to sensitize you to the issues to ensure that all the preliminaries are in place for learning to harness NVivo powerfully.

In the first section, "Methodology and Methods," we introduce the idea of methodology in a straightforward and practical way by contrasting it with research methods. The difference between the two is important to understand regardless of whether you conduct theoretical, interpretive, or mixed-methods research; or whether you conduct evaluations, policy studies, or other applied research; or whether you are harnessing NVivo for practical projects that you consider nonacademic or not research at all. Methodology applies to all these. In the second section, "Different

Ways of Knowing," we briefly introduce an aspect of methodology that is helpful to be aware of, as it is not completely obvious what it means "to know something." We end with a longer discussion of how researchers *adopt a methodology in practice*.

Methodology and Methods

A *methodology* is not a pretentious way of saying a *method*. A method describes exactly how a particular task should be accomplished, such as how to approach a senior manager in an organization to request an interview or how to write an interpretive rather than a descriptive memo. A methodology describes something much larger than how a particular task is to be performed. A methodology is often called a system of methods, in the sense that a system is something that has a set of interconnected parts. A methodology describes how an entire research project will be conducted and provides guidance for selecting the methods, the specific tasks to be undertaken. Methodology "can only offer general, not specific guidance. But offering guidance is its task" (Hammersley, 2011, p. 39).

For example, a researcher may be hired by an organization to evaluate why a new way of conducting employee performance reviews has been implemented more successfully in some departments than in others. The researcher concludes she is being asked to conduct an *implementation evaluation*, and she finds a suitable methodology text to guide her (e.g., Patton, 2008). She chooses one type of implementation evaluation in this text that matches her objectives, the *process evaluation*, which focuses on studying the actual operation of a program, or its process, in order to understand its strengths and weaknesses. The text instructs her to begin by gathering information from people who are "closest to the new program" (p. 325). This methodological guidance then has to be put into practice with a specific course of action, or research method that is relevant to her particular study, which, of course, the methodological textbook knows nothing about. The researcher might decide that for this project, the process of gathering data from those closest to the program should start with interviewing the head of each department, because they conduct the reviews in this organization. This in turn requires a method for approaching these individuals that is appropriate to the organization. In small organizations this might simply require an initial email and a follow-up phone call. But her client is a large organization, and she finds an article that describes a suitable method for approaching senior managers that involves first getting in the good graces of the gatekeeper, who might be a personal assistant or secretary (e.g., Bloor & Wood, 2006, pp. 5–9).

This very practical project may not sound anything at all like your own research, but the principles are the same. First a methodology is identified that fits the objectives. This describes the research process in general terms as guidance for choosing specific methods that fit the specific study. This gives confidence that the project is proceeding in a coherent manner, guided by the wisdom of many researchers who have been down a similar path and whose accumulated experience has been set down in a methodology text.

Different Ways of Knowing

There is one further aspect of methodology to be considered. Research of any kind is concerned with finding out something not yet known. This is obvious, but what it means to *know* something is not so obvious. The study of different ways of knowing is referred to as epistemology, a somewhat off-putting term. The methods writer Johnny Saldaña prefers the term "this is where I'm comin' from" (Saldaña, 2014, p. 977). In reality, the issue is not particularly esoteric. For example, does *knowledge* consist of what is known by authorities or experts in the field of study, in which case finding this knowledge is just a matter of asking them? Or is this only a distraction from gaining true or valid knowledge in a field, which can only really be *known* when everyday people describe from their perspective how they interact with the world in that particular context?

Some researchers think long and hard about the appropriateness of the epistemological assumptions underlying the methodology they consider adopting. But many do not, and they are satisfied to go along with whatever epistemological assumptions are built in to the methodology they have chosen. Others are not aware that there are alternative assumptions about knowledge and ways of knowing. For a deeper look at alternative ways of knowing, see Box 2.1.

BOX 2.1 A DEEPER LOOK: ALTERNATIVE WAYS OF KNOWING

This deeper look is intended to help you decide whether you want to look further into different ways of knowing, the field of epistemology. It is worth considering this topic because different assumptions about the nature of knowledge lead to different ways of going about gaining knowledge. Every research methodology necessarily has underlying assumptions about what it means to know something, whether the assumptions are explicit or simply implicit. These assumptions about knowledge affect the analytic strategies used to answer research questions, even if you are not really aware of what your "assumptions about knowledge" are. Next we give one practical example that may resonate with your own work and one academic example of two contrasting ways of knowing. Additionally, Carter and Little (2007) provide a concise introduction to epistemology in qualitative research.

A Practical Example

Many qualitative researchers conduct interview research. The way in which researchers conduct their interviews necessarily reflects their assumptions about knowledge, whether recognized or not. For example, one assumption about knowledge may be that you can discover your respondents' true attitudes on a topic by questioning them in an unbiased, depersonalized way, setting aside what you already know about the topic when formulating your follow-up questions. Doing this would ensure that other researchers in a similar context would reach similar conclusions; or in other words, ensure that your conclusions are reliable. Or, you may believe the opposite, that a respondent's words alone never give real access to their inner experiences. Therefore, only through interacting with them in a personal way during an interview and reflecting on your role in the interactions and the relationship can you and the respondent jointly create an understanding of the research topic that is valid in that particular context (e.g., Mischler, 1986). Brinkman and Kvale (2015) is also an excellent resource on the interconnectedness of interviewing and theories of knowledge.

An Academic Example

Emile Durkheim's (1951) seminal study of suicide and Jack Douglas's (1967) critique of the study illustrate how researchers' different epistemological positions greatly affect the way research is conducted. Durkheim's (1951) study was part of his effort to establish sociology as a science. His epistemological position, referred to as positivism, was that valid knowledge is only produced by measuring and testing empirical observations of human behavior to uncover what he called the social facts. In this case, the pressures of social structures that accounted for different patterns of suicide in different countries were considered a valid way to understand suicide, rather than studying individuals and what underlay their acts of suicide. In contrast, Douglas's (1967) criticism of Durkheim's conclusions is based on a different epistemological position, social constructivism, which believes that social reality is not a "fact" but is constructed consciously and actively by individuals. Therefore, to understand the social meaning of suicide, we must understand how individuals construe their social reality, for example, by talking with individuals who have unsuccessfully attempted suicide, reading the suicide notes of those who succeeded, or studying how coroners record deaths and thereby "create suicide."

Adopting a Methodology in Practice

How do you decide which methodology best fits your objectives? Methodology is more of a "craft [than] an abstractly formulated set of rules or techniques" that can be mechanically matched to objectives (Hammersley, 2011, p. 26). There is no standard list of methodologies with an index of what kinds of objectives are suitable for each. And there is unlikely to be a clear one-to-one match between your research objectives and the guidance of a single methodology text. It is more common that one methodology stands out as best fitting the research objectives generally, but some aspects or phases of a project are better matched to other similar or somewhat different methodologies. In practice, then, the methodology for a project is often put together, or constructed, rather than choosing a single methodology to follow step by step.

How do researchers choose or construct their methodologies in practice? Generally by striking a balance between complete neglect and excessive concern. Clearly there are drawbacks to neglecting methodology altogether, especially for new researchers, as this requires an unnecessarily risky reinventing of the wheel. A lack of fit between the methodology and the objectives may not make itself apparent until well into analysis, when it may be troublesome to go back to choose or construct a more appropriate methodology. On the other hand, an excessive concern with methodology "can be a diversion from real work," as the methods writer Clive Seale suggests, or as Freud put it, "Methodologists remind me of people who clean their glasses so thoroughly that they never have time to look through them" (both cited in Hammersley, 2011, pp. 17, 30). So a balance is best. There are three issues when choosing or constructing a methodology in practice: deciding which comes first, the objectives or the methodology; locating candidate methodologies; and finally, considering whether an "implicit methodology" is appropriate.

Regarding which comes first, objectives or methodology, in an ideal world one would formulate research questions and select a methodology as co-constituting activities. In theory, it would not be possible to properly formulate research questions for a project without knowing in advance the philosophical underpinnings of the methodology that would be used to answer them. But at the same time, there is no reason to choose or construct a particular methodology before having a project's specific objectives in mind. In practice, adopting a "co-constituting" approach is rather complicated, and many researchers take a more practical approach. One is to prepare research questions based on the researcher's (or the funder's) interests and then select the most appropriate methodology to answer that question. Another is to select a methodology that appeals or is already familiar and then formulate research questions that make sense for that methodology. A third, perhaps less laudable approach, is to formulate research questions based on your interests or those of the funder and then independently select a methodology because it appeals or because it is familiar or because it is acceptable to the funder and hope for the best.

The next issue is to locate a methodology. Many researchers have already studied certain methodologies and stick to those. If you are new to qualitative research or are looking forward to branching out, think of two broad classes of methodology: generic and specialized. *Generic* has a connotation of inferior or unsophisticated, but it is becoming a more common way to describe qualitative research that focuses on the basic exploratory and inductive purposes of qualitative research without being tied to a particular methodological position. Many researchers using CAQDAS packages describe their methodologies and methods in published articles in quite generic terms, such as a "qualitative design" or a "qualitative, exploratory study" (Woods, Paulus, Atkins, & Macklin, 2016, p. 9). "Generic" refers to all manner of approaches that are in the inductive or emergent spirit of qualitative research. Sharon Merriam is a methods writer who since the 1980s has never shied away from the "generic" label to describe high-quality approaches to methodology (e.g. most recently, Merriam & Tisdell, 2016, p. 23). Other methods writers have now begun to describe generic approaches in more detail (e.g., Kahlke, 2014; Thorne, 2008) or have made proposals for ensuring the quality of generic approaches (e.g., Caelli, Ray, & Mill, 2008; Cooper & Endacott, 2007). If you decide that a generic approach is to your taste, one of the best standard texts for a generic methodological approach is still *Qualitative Data Analysis: An Expanded Sourcebook* by Miles and Huberman (1994).

Of course, much qualitative research is more specialized, and innumerable texts offer guidance in a multitude of approaches. The variety is so great that there is not even a standard scheme for categorizing the range of approaches. One useful resource is Graham Gibbs' helpful webpage at the University of Huddersfield that lists and explains 26 different methodologies, with several textbooks to choose for each (Gibbs, 2011). Another useful text that focuses on the analysis procedures associated with 10 different methodologies is *Analyzing Qualitative Data: Systematic Approaches* by Bernard, Wutich, and Ryan (2017).

Finally, even if there is no explicit methodology chosen or constructed to guide a study, there is always an *implicit* methodology at work, the unconscious or taken-for-granted ideas or principles that underlie the process of accomplishing a project's objectives. This could have been absorbed by osmosis from working in an academic institution, or from working in an organization with a community of researchers, or simply as a result of doing what makes sense based on the sum total of your life experiences. Even though (by definition) you are not consciously aware of your implicit methodology, you would not be able to decide what to do next without it. Later in the chapter we describe an implicit methodology to illustrate how it can guide the progress of a project.

At this point you may have your objectives clear and be aware of the guiding principles for how you will go about your analysis, either from an established methodology described in a textbook or a methodology you have constructed for your specific objectives, or your implicit methodology that you have now reflected on and decided is appropriate for your project. But if not, it is a good idea to pause until you have settled on these two outcomes of Level 1 before continuing to read the next section, which involves turning objectives into an analytic plan.

If the basic idea of a methodology for fulfilling an objective is still not coming alive, the more concrete everyday illustration that we use for the remainder of Part I may help.

An Everyday Illustration

For the remainder of Part I we use as our primary illustration an everyday activity with clear, achievable objectives and an implicit methodology—the preparation of a gourmet meal. Using an illustration of a meal preparation rather than a qualitative research project ensures that you do not treat an illustrative research project representing one methodology as the "correct way" to do qualitative research. The essence of the *Five-Level QDA* method is the relationship between *tasks* and *tools*. Explaining this process for the first time in terms of an everyday activity focuses attention on the process rather than on the content of the illustration. Box 2.2 provides a deeper look into the rationale for using an everyday example.

We will compare the steps of the meal preparation process to the levels of the *Five-Level QDA* method as we go along, but we recommend you do not try to relate the principles you are learning to your own research project. The best approach is to temporarily put aside thoughts of qualitative research and your current project in order to focus on the relationship between tasks and tools.

Now on to the illustration.

BOX 2.2 A DEEPER LOOK: WHY WE USE AN EVERYDAY ILLUSTRATION

There are three reasons we use an everyday activity as an illustration in Part I. First is to overcome the problems with using a single example of a research project. The second is that we have not yet introduced the workings of NVivo, a consequence of the layered sequence of instruction. Finally, we initially want to focus attention on the underlying process to be learned—the relationship of tasks to tools—rather than the context of the illustration. Using an everyday activity rather than a research project at this early stage facilitates that goal.

The Problem With Single Illustrations

Qualitative research methodologies vary so widely, from positivist to constructivist approaches, that some researchers consider these in opposition to one another. If the methodology represented by the one example was quite different from your own, you might be misled into thinking that the *Five-Level QDA* method is inapplicable to your style of research and read no further.

But at a deeper level, qualitative analysis is an example of an *ill-structured activity*, a kind of activity with incomplete information, no correct conclusion, and no one way to evaluate answers (Jonassen, 1997). Oversimplifying instruction in these ill-structured domains, particularly by using single illustrations, promotes the misunderstanding that they are well structured, which in our case suggests that there is a correct way to conduct qualitative analysis with NVivo. In order to promote effective learning in ill-structured domains, cognitive flexibility theory proposes "criss-crossing the conceptual landscape" using multiple illustrations (Spiro, Coulson, Feltovich, & Anderson, 1988, p. 6), and in Part III we follow this guidance by using contrasting examples of harnessing each component of NVivo. In Part I we avoid the pitfalls of single examples by using an everyday activity that cannot be misinterpreted as the one correct way to conduct a qualitative analysis.

The Layered Sequence of Instruction

A second reason for using an everyday activity is a consequence of our layered instruction. This creates a chicken-and-egg quandary for what should be learned first. It is not possible to learn to translate real-world analytic tasks into software operations until you understand the full capabilities of the software that can be harnessed. But conversely, learning to operate the software first without knowing the principles of translation in the *Five-Level QDA* method encourages students to jump in and implement their data analysis in a step-by-step manner, driven by the capabilities of the software. This does not lead to using the software powerfully. We therefore begin with the principles of the *Five-Level QDA* method in Part I without reference to the capabilities of NVivo. One alternative is to illustrate a qualitative data analysis conducted with a software program that we are all sure to know, such as Microsoft Word or Excel. These are obviously not CAQDAS programs and would not allow us to properly illustrate the principles of the *Five-Level QDA* method. We therefore use an everyday activity to initially illustrate the principles.

Focusing on the Relationship Between Tasks and Tools

The final reason for using an everyday activity is that the subject matter of the book is not research methods, but the relationship between tasks and tools. Initially using an illustration that does not involve qualitative research focuses attention on the process of translation of tasks into tools rather than on the subject matter of the illustration. Using a qualitative research project would inevitably distract from focusing on the relationship between tasks and tools in this initial illustration. After the principles of the *Five-Level QDA* method have been learned in Part I, we focus exclusively on multiple examples of real-world research projects.

Christina is looking for a way to relax after a hard day at the keyboard writing a textbook. First comes Level 1, sufficiently clarifying her objectives so that they can be transformed into a plan at Level 2. As in research projects, this very large goal of *ways to relax* has to be narrowed down to a single purpose or objective, and she narrows it down to *cooking gourmet food*. This objective must now be better specified to be both clear and fulfillable. She decides that her purpose is to cook a meal for the whole family within 90 minutes using ingredients already available in her kitchen, because she does not want to take the time to go shopping. In working through the clarification process with her family, she discovers that they are hungry and they are not prepared to wait a full 90 minutes, and 60 minutes is the outside boundary of what they would find acceptable. With the family's agreement, Christina settles on a clear objective: *promptly prepare a gourmet family meal with what's already available in the kitchen*. She decided that *promptly* sufficiently clarifies the boundary of the activity's time dimension, and in the present context *promptly* means 60 minutes or less.

For this project the methodology is implicit, based on Christina's prior experience with many informal cooking projects for her family. She gives a name to what she will be doing, *recipe-inspired improvisation*, to remind herself of her approach as she is planning the steps, just as we will later be naming implicit research methodologies when planning the analysis. Her implicit methodology could be summarized as: *based on a recipe that stimulates enthusiasm in the chef, adjust every aspect of the recipe in any way desired in order to align the adjusted recipe to the constraints of available time, space, and ingredients*. However, a methodology does not specify the methods of each phase of the project—the particular courses of action—but serves as the framework or guide for selecting and executing methods appropriate to the context.

Christina has now formulated the objectives and the implicit methodology for preparing the meal—a good start.

Level 2: Analytic Plan

This section describes Level 2 of the *Five-Level QDA* method, the second level of strategy (Figure 2.3). This involves converting the objectives of Level 1 into an analytic plan, which includes a conceptual framework and a set of analytic tasks that need to be performed. After explaining this process, we illustrate it by developing a plan of action for Christina's gourmet meal.

Level 1	*Level 2*	*Level 3*	*Level 4*	*Level 5*
Objectives	Analytic plan	Translation	Selected tools	Constructed tools
The purpose and context of a project, usually expressed as research questions and a methodology	The conceptual framework and resulting analytic tasks	Translating from analytic tasks to software tools and translating the results back again	Straightforward choice of individual software operations	Sophisticated use of software by combining operations or performing them in a custom way

FIGURE 2.3 Level 2 of the *Five-Level QDA* method

Plans of action are referred to in the research literature as *research methods*. This includes how to do all the tasks in a project, including how to gain access to research sites, collect the data, analyze the data, and organize and write the final product of the research, whether a report, an article, book, or a thesis or dissertation. Listing the activities of a research project in this way implies that they are separate and undertaken in sequence. Obviously gaining access to a research site has to come well before a final report can be written, and data have to be collected before they can be analyzed, but there is a surprising amount of overlap between analysis phases, and many adjustments to the sequence of activities and tasks in a qualitative research project. For example, the grounded theory methodology calls for an alternation of data collection, analysis, and then further data collection based on the outcome of the first round of analysis (Glaser & Strauss, 1967). Other methodologies, such as qualitative content analysis, require all data to be collected before a systematic analysis of their content can begin. But writing occurs throughout a project, not just in the phase of the final write-up. Analytic writing begins at the very start of a project, as part of the formulation of clear objectives, and continues throughout data collection in order to document the context of the data and to record immediate reflections, whether conducting interviews, visiting research sites, or studying archival data. These informal reflections constitute the first round of analysis, and in this way data collection and analysis overlap.

Qualitative analysis, our primary concern in this book, is not a fixed phase of activity in the middle of a project, between data collection and write-up of findings. It occurs throughout with varying degrees of formality. For example, undertaking a literature review is a form of analysis, and writing up a research report or journal article is also an analytic act. Methods of analysis are often referred to with the general-purpose term *analytic strategies*. To avoid ambiguity with our own terminology, we do not use this general-purpose term. Instead, we call Level 2 the *analytic plan* for the project. Analytic plans consist of a general plan for the whole project and an evolving set of analytic tasks that are the individual action steps.

We refer to the general plan as the *conceptual framework* for the project, which we discuss in detail in the next section. Every qualitative research project has a conceptual framework, whether it is explicit or simply implied. In the *Five-Level QDA* method, we make it explicit. The individual analytic tasks, or action steps, that develop out of the conceptual framework are the central building blocks of the *Five-Level QDA* method. They are what are translated into software operations. From this point on ANALYTIC TASK is printed in SMALL CAPS to be clear we are referring to entities with specific characteristics in the *Five-Level QDA* method.

The relationship of the conceptual framework to an ANALYTIC TASK is like the relationship of a map to a journey. A map displays locations, their spatial relationships, and possible routes of traveling. You plan a journey by studying the map to see which route makes the most sense according to the objectives of that journey. For some journeys, the most efficient route makes most sense; for others, the most scenic route is best; and for others, it is the route that passes the most friends with an available spare room: it all depends on the objectives. Remember, though, that once a journey starts there will likely be unexpected circumstances—a road closure, some bad weather, or a friend who gets sick—which may lead to modifications to the travel plan. Such modifications are accomplished by consulting the map as well as by making sure that the new plan is still consistent with the objectives. This is just what it feels like to be working at Level 2, the level of the analytic plan, when undertaking a qualitative analysis. The conceptual framework—like a map—provides the possibilities for the next ANALYTIC TASK. The ANALYTIC TASK that makes the most sense at any given moment depends on the project's objectives. This also illustrates what we mean when we say that qualitative research projects are both iterative and emergent.

The Conceptual Framework

Nick well remembers the first time he heard the words *conceptual framework* in his first research methods class. The words sounded just right, just what he looked forward to constructing for himself—but how? What would one look like? The professor was so steeped in conceptual frameworks that he had long ago lost all awareness that others did not yet live with them day and night, and it was assumed everyone in the class knew what they were.

For our purposes, a conceptual framework is a set of concepts that are related to one another. Think of concepts in the most general way possible. A concept is the name and meaning of any collection of things, such as seats, or unconscious racial biases, or effective teachers, or positive emotions. To say something is a seat is to say a great deal. It implies membership of a collection of things that has a definition—does it mean it has four legs and some kind of platform to sit on and a back? Or would anything that can be sat on be included, like a rock? It depends on the context. A rock is not generally a seat in a natural history museum, but often is in a campground. In everyday life the meaning of a concept is usually obvious from the context and does not need to be stated. Saying "have a seat" to a visitor in your home does not have to be qualified by adding *that means on one of the chairs, not on that low table or the cabinet ledge please.* But in qualitative research the purpose and meaning of each concept are made explicit. For a good introduction to the creation and use of concepts in qualitative research, see Morse (1995).

A conceptual framework is a set of named concepts that are related to one another. It could take the form of a diagram, a list, a table, or a narrative. We use diagrams in this book as an easy way to communicate concepts. In a research project, using diagrams to illustrate your conceptual framework lets you compare earlier versions as they evolve through the life of the project. Miles and Huberman (1994) discuss and illustrate the use of visual conceptual frameworks in research (pp. 18–22). Also see Maxwell's (2013) excellent chapter on the use of concept maps for visually exploring conceptual frameworks. However, you may prefer writing a narrative to think through the concepts in a project and to represent their relationships as a conceptual framework. How a conceptual framework is represented is a matter of preference.

We now illustrate the narrative development of a conceptual framework, followed by its representation as a diagram, in Christina's planning for her gourmet meal. For her objective to *promptly prepare a gourmet family meal with what's available,* she might identify these concepts as relevant: *60-minute recipes, available ingredients, dietary preferences of family members, complexity of preparation process, degree of relaxation needed,* and *promptly.* In most styles of qualitative research the concepts we create and name are intended to be malleable. Consider *promptly*: as it turned out, despite the family's need to be fed quickly, it became impossible to produce a gourmet meal in 60 minutes. Christina felt confident in justifying that a redefinition of *promptly* up to 75 minutes was quite sufficiently prompt in the context of her need to relax after a long day at the keyboard writing a textbook and the expected excellence of the meal. Similarly, in qualitative research, concepts only have meaning within a certain context (Morse, 2000, p. 335).

Christina decides to draw a diagram of her meal preparation process and put it in a Meal Planning Worksheet along with her objectives, implicit methodology, and the overall plan for what to do next: *review recipe books for suitable recipes*. The worksheet has two purposes—to *manage* the progress of the meal to help it efficiently get completed on deadline and to *document* the process in case it is a great success and she wants a record of what she has done. Figure 2.4 displays the first iteration of the worksheet. This is a simplified version of a similar worksheet, called the ANALYTIC PLANNING WORKSHEET, that we begin illustrating in Part II to manage and document the progress of real-world *Five-Level QDA* projects.

Analytic Tasks

Just as a map is not a journey, but the resource with which to select a journey, a conceptual framework is not an action plan. How the conceptual framework is transformed into a set of ANALYTIC TASKS depends on the dictates of the chosen methodology; or in the case of an implicit methodology, it depends on your intuition or established habits of working that substitute for a chosen methodology.

In qualitative research projects, ANALYTIC TASKS are individual, self-contained steps of action. They are generated by the researcher from the conceptual framework. Rarely can *all* ANALYTIC TASKS be generated in one fell swoop, as qualitative projects are, to some degree, emergent. Initial ANALYTIC TASKS are generated and executed by the researcher, and based on the outcome another set of ANALYTIC TASKS is generated, possibly accompanied by changes to the analytic plan. This is the meaning of iterative. Level 2 is thus traversed in a series of iterative cycles in the light of "what the data are telling us."

In the gourmet meal we will carefully identify each TASK in the process in the same way we do in *Five-Level QDA* research projects, and so we will SMALL CAP the term TASK to be clear we are thinking about these individual activities in an equivalent way. The first TASK can be easily determined now that Christina has a conceptual framework: *find all suitable 60-minutes-or-less recipes*, in which "suitable" means evaluating them against the dietary preferences of the family (which she already knows). Just because the methodology is implicit does not mean that the TASKS cannot be represented formally.

Once Christina has identified the 60-minutes-or-less recipes, she might notice a theme—that many tempting recipes call for fresh ginger. A second and unanticipated TASK might therefore emerge: *check for fresh ginger*. Finding none, she has to decide what to do next. A quick check of the Meal Planning Worksheet reminds her that she already decided to prepare the meal only with what's available to avoid having to go out shopping. Similarly, in qualitative research, referring back to research questions at tricky moments during analysis is a frequent activity that keeps the research on track, and as we will see in Part III, having these written out on the ANALYTIC PLANNING WORKSHEET is a big help in managing the progress of a project.

But back to the need for fresh ginger. Christina could look up the culinary characteristics of fresh ginger in one of her numerous recipe books or search Google for an alternative ingredient with the same characteristics and then check if she has any of that. If she unfortunately found none, she could search Google again for related culinary characteristics and then look up ingredients that have those characteristics. This is an iterative process, but time is short, and this degree of iteration is beyond what Christina had in mind for tonight's relaxing activity. So she adjusts her plan by generating a third TASK: *discard recipes requiring fresh ginger*. Figure 2.5 displays the next version of

MEAL PLANNING WORKSHEET – Version 1

**Level 1:
OBJECTIVES**

OBJECTIVES

To relax after a long day, promptly prepare a gourmet family meal with what's already available in the kitchen

GUIDING METHODOLOGY: Recipe-inspired improvisation

Based on a recipe that stimulates the chef's enthusiasm, adjust every aspect as needed to the constraints of the context

CURRENT CONCEPTUAL FRAMEWORK

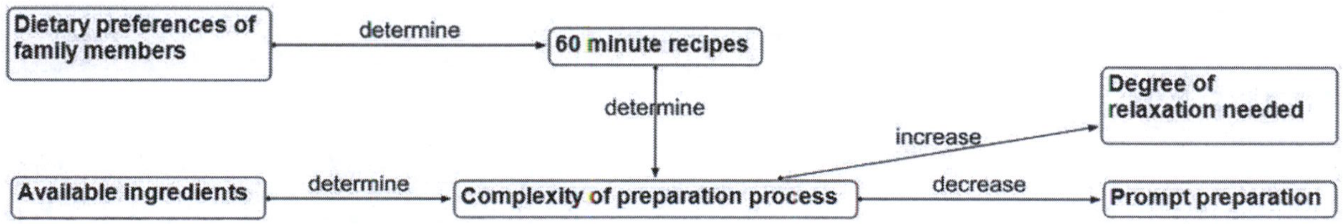

**Level 2:
OVERALL PLAN**

FIGURE 2.4 Meal Planning Worksheet —Version 1: Objectives and initial plan

MEAL PLANNING WORKSHEET – Version 2

Level 1: OBJECTIVES

OBJECTIVES
To relax after a long day, promptly prepare a gourmet family meal with what's already available in the kitchen

GUIDING METHODOLOGY: Recipe-inspired improvisation

Based on a recipe that stimulates the chef's enthusiasm, adjust every aspect as needed to the constraints of the context

CURRENT CONCEPTUAL FRAMEWORK

Level 2: OVERALL PLAN

| Dietary preferences of family members | —determine→ | **75 minute recipes** *Originally 60 minutes, but adjusted to 75 due to unsufficient 60 minute recipes and the reasonableness of 75 minutes constituting "prompt"* |

75 minute recipes —determine→ Complexity of preparation process

Available ingredients —determine→ Complexity of preparation process

Complexity of preparation process —increase→ Degree of relaxation needed

Complexity of preparation process —decrease→ Prompt preparation

Level 2: TASKS

| Find all suitable one hour or less recipes |
| Check for fresh ginger |
| Discard recipes requiring fresh ginger |

FIGURE 2.5 Meal Planning Worksheet—Version 2: The first three tasks

the Meal Planning Worksheet with highlighted updates: the first three TASKS, and a new version of the conceptual framework with the 75-minute recipes and the redefinition of "prompt."

This example of suppressing a degree of iteration is quite appropriate for tonight's cooking methodology—one that is guided by *improvisation*. Similarly in qualitative research projects it is never possible to iterate to the fullest extent possible, or the projects would never end. Some methodologies indicate when enough is enough, such as the idea of *saturation* in grounded theory methodology which, to put it informally, lets you know that you have done enough to understand a concept when further data collection and analysis are telling you nothing very new (Glaser & Strauss, 1967).

Knowing What You Plan to Do Next

We have not yet discussed the appropriate size for an ANALYTIC TASK, meaning its level of detail. In the gourmet meal a TASK can be more general, such as *prep all the ingredients*, or more detailed, like *open refrigerator door*. In the *Five-Level QDA* method, identifying the level of detail of ANALYTIC TASKS that will most easily TRANSLATE into software operations plays a central role. This is a central skill of the expert qualitative researcher, as it reflects the facility to work at different levels of abstraction of concepts. We elaborate further on this in Chapter 6, and in preparation we consider the underlying principles in more detail at this stage.

Any task can be described with any level of detail. *Prep all the ingredients* is an economical way—a brief way—to start a recipe. But this might not contain enough information for you to know exactly what to do with the ingredients. At a greater level of detail, a recipe could begin with *open the refrigerator door*. This level, however, lies at the other extreme, providing unnecessary information. Something between the two will strike a better balance between economy of expression and informativeness.

Humans have evolved to perceive and describe the world at a middle level, striking a balance between very economical and very informative. For example, everybody says *Is that chair comfortable?* Nobody says *Is that object comfortable?*, which is less informative, but more economical as the speaker could use that question for any number of surfaces a person might sit on. And, in the other direction, nobody says *Is that green, wicker-backed garden seat comfortable?*, which is highly informative but not an economical way of asking generally about the chair's comfort. We naturally organize and describe the world at what psychologists call the *basic level*, a roughly middle level of detail. In this example the basic level is *chair*, the level of detail that is the best balance of economy and informativeness in the context of inquiring about its comfort. The basic level of categorizing things was first proposed by Rosch, Mervis, Gray, Johnson, and Boyes-Braem (1976), and Lakoff (1987) provided a comprehensive discussion of all aspects of basic-level categories.

The basic level of detail comes naturally to the human mind in normal, everyday communication, and is almost always the briefest way to describe something. However, deciding on the best level of detail to describe something also depends on the context. Whereas you might respond to a four-legged animal in the street that barks continuously by saying I *wonder what's the matter with that dog?*, a vet in her office surgery surrounded by animals is more likely to say I *wonder what's wrong with that terrier?* Your basic level of description and the vet's basic level of description are different in these two contexts. The situation is similar with ANALYTIC TASKS. There is no "correct" level of detail for every ANALYTIC TASK: it depends on the context. Instead there is a principle that determines the best level of detail. It is the golden rule of decision making in the *Five-Level QDA* method that will come up over and over again: *what you plan to do next*. A TASK is too large if it does not easily refer to the next TASK. For example, in the gourmet meal the very large TASK of *prep all the ingredients* does not have a natural next step that sufficiently assists in the cooking process. There are several types of ingredients, and so matching the next step at the same level of detail, like *cook all the ingredients*, would be lamentably uninformative. So expressing that very large TASK as a set of somewhat smaller TASKS is better, like *chop salad ingredients evenly*, *cut up fish*, and *wash vegetables*, because each has a natural next step. For example, if a later TASK requires placing each person's portion of fish in a parchment pouch, then it is clear how to accomplish the earlier TASK of *cut up fish*—it is not a matter of just cutting the fish into generic pieces, but rather of allocating it in advance for each of the pouches, knowing the appetites of the various family members. Similarly, at the other end of the spectrum, a tiny and self-evident TASK like *retrieve the largest cutting board* is also not helpful as an individual TASK, as it does not have a natural next step by itself—the next TASK will involve using the cutting board for something, and so will require other prior tiny TASKS to also have been completed—perhaps finding a certain kind of knife, certain ingredients, and so on. The TASKS *chop salad ingredients evenly*, *cut up fish*, and *wash vegetables* seem to be at a helpful level of detail, because each conveniently leads on to the next TASK.

Determining the best level of detail of an ANALYTIC TASK in a research project comes with experience; it cannot be turned into a neat and tidy procedure. Our purpose in this chapter is to highlight the principle to help create a mind-set that hastens gaining this experience once we are using NVivo to fulfill ANALYTIC TASKS in Part III. The principle is that we generate ANALYTIC TASKS from conceptual frameworks based on *what we plan to do next* rather than simply at the basic or middle level of detail that comes naturally, because we want the outcome of fulfilling an ANALYTIC TASK in the software to easily refer to the next ANALYTIC TASK that can also be performed in the software. It is true that *what you plan to do next* is never known with certainty, as the process is emergent to varying degrees. The best we can do as qualitative researchers is to plan the current ANALYTIC TASK with an eye to the likely next ANALYTIC TASK. Using the ANALYTIC PLANNING WORKSHEET when learning these skills allows us to see the whole picture when planning the next course of action—including the objectives and methodology. This process will become clear in the ANALYTIC PLANNING WORKSHEETS that accompany the illustrations in Parts II and III.

We have now introduced what is needed at Levels 1 and 2 as preparation for harnessing NVivo powerfully. We can now move on from these strategy preparations to where the detailed instruction in this book begins: Level 3 of the *Five-Level QDA* method, the translation of ANALYTIC TASKS into the tactics for fulfilling them by using NVivo.

References

Bernard, H. R., Wutich, A. Y., & Ryan, G. W. (2017). *Analyzing qualitative data: Systematic approaches* (2nd ed.). Thousand Oaks, CA: Sage.

Bloor, M., & Wood, F. (2006). *Keywords in qualitative methods: A vocabulary of research concepts.* Newbury Park, CA: Sage.

Brinkman, S., & Kvale, S. (2015). *Interviews: Learning the craft of qualitative research interviewing* (3rd ed., pp. 55–82). Thousand Oaks, CA: Sage.

Caelli, K., Ray, L., & Mill, J. (2008). 'Clear as mud': Toward greater clarity in generic qualitative research. *International Journal of Qualitative Methods*, *2*(2), 1–13.

Carter, S. M., & Little, M. (2007). Justifying knowledge, justifying method, taking action: Epistemologies, methodologies, and methods in qualitative research. *Qualitative Health Research*, *17*(10), 1316–1328.

Cooper, S., & Endacott, R. (2007). Generic qualitative research: A design for qualitative research in emergency care? *Emergency Medicine Journal*, *24*(12), 816–819.

Creswell, J. W. (2013). *Qualitative inquiry and research design: Choosing among five approaches.* Thousand Oaks, CA: Sage.

Douglas, J. D. (1967). *The social meaning of suicide.* Princeton: Princeton University Press.

Durkheim, E. (1951). *Suicide: A study in sociology* (J.A. Spaulding & G. Simpson, Trans.). Glencoe, IL: Free Press. (Original work published 1897).

Fielding, N., & Lee, R. M. (2002). New patterns in the adoption and use of qualitative software. *Field Methods*, *14*(2), 197–216.

Gibbs, G. (2011). University of Huddersfield, UK, Retrieved from http://onlineqda.hud.ac.uk/methodologies.php

Glaser, B. G., & Strauss, A. L. (1967). *Discovery of grounded theory*. Chicago: Aldine.

Hammersley, M. (2011). *Methodology: Who needs it*. Thousand Oaks, CA: Sage.

Jonassen, D. H. (1997). Instructional design models for well-structured and ill-structured problem-solving learning outcomes. *Educational Technology Research & Development, 45*(1), 65–94.

Kahlke, R. M. (2014). Generic qualitative approaches: Pitfalls and benefits of methodological mixology. *International Journal of Qualitative Methods, 13*, 37–52.

Lakoff, G. (1987). *Women, fire, and dangerous things*. Chicago: University of Chicago Press.

Maxwell, J. A. (2013). *Qualitative research design: An interactive approach* (3rd ed.). Los Angeles: Sage.

Merriam, S. B., & Tisdell, E. J. (2016). *Qualitative research: A guide to design and implementation* (4th ed.). San Francisco: John Wiley.

Miles, M. B., & Huberman, A. M. (1994). *Qualitative data analysis: An expanded sourcebook*. Thousand Oaks, CA: Sage.

Mischler, E. G. (1986). *Research interviewing: Context and narrative* (pp. 52–65). Cambridge, MA: Harvard University Press.

Morse, J. M. (1995). Exploring the theoretical basis of nursing using advanced techniques of concept analysis. *Advances in Nursing Science, 17*(3), 31–46.

Morse, J. M. (2000). Exploring pragmatic utility: Concept analysis by critically appraising the literature. In B. L. Rodgers & K. A. Knafl (Eds.), *Concept development in nursing: Foundations, techniques, and applications* (2nd ed., pp. 333–352). Philadelphia: W. B. Saunders.

Patton, M. Q. (2008). *Utilization-focused evaluation* (4th ed.). Los Angeles, CA: Sage.

Rosch, E., Mervis, C. B., Gray, W. D., Johnson, D. M., & Boyes-Braem, P. (1976). Basic objects in natural categories. *Cognitive Psychology, 8*, 382–439.

Saldaña, J. (2014). Blue-collar qualitative research: A rant *Qualitative Inquiry, 20*(8), 976–980.

Spiro, R. J., Coulson, R. L., Feltovich, P. J., & Anderson, D. (1988). *Cognitive flexibility theory: Advanced knowledge acquisition in ill-structured domains*. Paper presented at the Proceedings of the 10th Annual Conference of the Cognitive Science Society. Montreal, Quebec, Canada.

Thorne, S. (2008). *Interpretive description*. Walnut Creek, CA: Left Coast Press.

Wolcott, H. F. (1994). *Transforming qualitative data: Description, analysis, and interpretation*. Thousand Oaks, CA: Sage.

Woods, M., Paulus, T., Atkins, D. P., & Macklin, R. (2016). Advancing qualitative research using qualitative data analysis software (QDAS)? Reviewing potential versus practice in published studies using NVivo and NVivo 1994–2013. *Social Science Computer Review, 34*(5), 597–617.

3

TRANSLATING ANALYTIC TASKS INTO SOFTWARE TOOLS (LEVELS 3, 4, AND 5)

This chapter focuses on the principles of translating analytic strategies into software operations of NVivo. In Chapter 1 we said that translation means *transforming* strategies into tactics. Now we will describe the process in more detail as the *matching* of ANALYTIC TASKS to software operations. This requires *framing* ANALYTIC TASKS and features of the software in a way that facilitates matching one to the other. The outcome of this matching is to either *select* an existing software tool or *construct* a custom tool for oneself.

This chapter completes Part I—the principles of the *Five-Level QDA* method. Parts II and III of the book build on these principles by demonstrating the practice of translation in the context of real-world research projects.

Level 3: Translation

This section describes how to frame ANALYTIC TASKS and how to frame the features of the software in order to match one to the other.

Translation between analytic strategies and software tactics is required in order to go beyond, or transcend, their contradictory natures. Rather than trying to make the strategies more cut and dried than they really are or trying to think of the software features as more emergent than they really are, we view the strategies and tactics as entirely separate and contrasting elements in the larger *Five-Level QDA* process and translate between them (see Figure 3.1).

Level 1 Objectives	Level 2 Analytic plan	Level 3 Translation	Level 4 Selected tools	Level 5 Constructed tools
The purpose and context of a project, usually expressed as research questions and a methodology	The conceptual framework and resulting analytic tasks	Translating from analytic tasks to software tools and translating the results back again	Straightforward choice of individual software operations	Sophisticated use of software by combining operations or performing them in a custom way

FIGURE 3.1 Level 3 of the *Five-Level QDA* method

We express this contrast between strategies and tactics in how each of them is *framed*. A frame is a way of focusing on some aspects rather than others. For example, organizations can be framed in different ways that lead to different ways of understanding how they work, how they should be managed, or how they can be changed (Morgan, 2006). An organization can be framed as a machine with clearly defined parts that are intended to work together, such as divisions or departments. Alternatively, the same organization could be framed as a political system to help understand how and why people in the organization attempt to advance their different interests or agendas. Framing things in different ways leads to entirely different ways to think about them.

We must now consider how ANALYTIC TASKS and the features of NVivo are framed in the *Five-Level QDA* method. Sometimes the two contrasting frames happen to match, and the translation process is simple and obvious. But sometimes they do not, and there has to be a reframing or transformation between them in order to use the software features powerfully. Reframing means seeing something in a different way (Bolman & Deal, 1997).

The Framing of Analytic Tasks

There could be innumerable ways to frame ANALYTIC TASKS. One way could be to express them in terms of the *purpose* of each task in relation to the objectives of the project; another could be in terms of their *complexity*, such as how well defined or ill defined a particular task is. For purposes of the *Five-Level QDA* method, we frame ANALYTIC TASKS in terms of their building blocks. These are generally referred to as their units of analysis, or simply units.

The idea of a unit is central to research. Some of the more interpretive styles of qualitative research do not use the word "unit," as it has a reductionist connotation of breaking the whole into separate pieces. Yet units *are* central to the process of all styles of research, even if described in a different way, and we do need to identify units when harnessing NVivo powerfully.

A unit describes the types of things that you are interested in, the kinds of things that are being analyzed. They could be individual people, or particular groups of people, or factors that are perceived as barriers or facilitators to the accomplishment of something, or as one textbook says, they may be "newspapers, folk tales, countries, or cities" (Bernard, Wutich, & Ryan, 2017). All parts of the analysis are expressed in units that are unique to each project. Much of qualitative analysis is about finding instances in the data of these units.

A project as a whole may be thought of as having a major unit, such as *school*, if the project's primary objective is to compare attitudes and responses to bullying in different schools of a school district. There may be additional units that reflect additional or secondary objectives. For example, if a secondary objective of the study is to explore how different attitudes or responses to bullying found in different schools reflect the socioeconomic characteristics of the neighborhood, an additional unit may be *location*.

It is not likely that you will identify all relevant units at the start of your study. The first reason is that most styles of qualitative research are "grounded" to a greater or lesser degree. "Grounded" means, in general, that the concepts of the study and the units they are expressed in are found in the data as part of the process of analyzing them, rather than being predetermined and brought into the study at the outset. However, even for grounded styles of analysis there will be a research question that is necessarily expressed in units, that is, in terms of the kinds of things that are being studied, so there will be at least one major unit at the outset.

Regardless of how grounded the study is, new units will likely emerge as the analysis continues and new ANALYTIC TASKS are undertaken. In the bullying study you may notice that an unexpected response to bullying seems to be coming up more frequently in teachers who teach a particular subject area. You decide to follow up this surprising observation with an ANALYTIC TASK that looks for examples of this response across all schools in the study, but separating the examples by the teachers' subject area in order to interrogate the data for these differences. Later a new unit might be *teacher* if another objective emerges to understand different responses to bullying by, say, male and female teachers.

It is not standard practice in qualitative research to explicitly identify and name the units of each ANALYTIC TASK. But for purposes of understanding what experienced qualitative researchers who use NVivo have come to do intuitively and unconsciously, thinking more consciously about units is essential. For example, an ANALYTIC TASK in our bullying example may be *identify and name types of responses by male teachers to provoked and unprovoked bullying behaviors.* Here there are two units: *teacher response* and *bullying behavior.* If there had been an intention at the outset to distinguish the responses of male and female teachers, perhaps to follow up a finding from earlier research, then the ANALYTIC TASK might have been larger: *identify and name types of responses by male and female teachers to provoked and unprovoked bullying behaviors.* Now we need to capture differences in behavior of male and female teachers, and there would be three units in a single ANALYTIC TASK: *teacher response, bullying behavior,* and *teachers.* That is fine. Identifying an ANALYTIC TASK to work on at any moment is driven by the needs of the analysis at the strategy levels, as we have just described. It is never driven by the convenience or ease of working in NVivo on an ANALYTIC TASK with more or fewer units.

The Framing of Software Features

What corresponds in NVivo to these units of the ANALYTIC TASK? Recall that a *frame* is a way of seeing something that focuses on some aspects rather than others. Framing ANALYTIC TASKS in terms of their units is not in any way unusual to researchers. However, the way we frame software features is not the standard way to think about software. We need to go into this in detail as it is central to the translation process.

A "software feature" is not a technical term. The Institute of Electrical and Electronics Engineers defines a "feature" very generally as "a distinguishing characteristic of a software item" (Feature, n.d.). The idea of a software feature can therefore be framed in many ways: in terms of how simple or complex the feature is, or how useful, or how unique compared with other programs, and so on. But the default or automatic way for a user of computer software to unconsciously frame its features is through its *affordances.* We therefore drop the term feature, which doesn't have a specific meaning, and focus on affordances, which does.

One meaning of *afford* is to *make available,* as in *a large tree affords plenty of shade.* The psychologist James Gibson invented the word *affordance* to refer to things that you would automatically know how to do because information about them is directly available in the environment (Gibson, 1979). The standard example is the handle on a door. A thin vertical bar as a door handle affords opening the door toward you because your hand and arm are configured for pulling when you grasp the bar, whereas a flat horizontal plate on a door affords pushing the door away from you (Norman, 1988).

Psychologists and industrial designers have applied this principle of affordances to computer software (e.g., Gaver, 1991; Hartson, 2003; Norman, 1999). Software developers now try to present information on the screen so that the affordances of their programs are correctly perceived, so that users intuitively and effortlessly use the program based on how the developers believe we want to use the software. In the case of CAQDAS packages, the variety of ANALYTIC TASKS is so great that it is impossible to predict every one in advance and provide affordances for each—that is, visible and obvious ways to use the software for each detailed ANALYTIC TASK. The developers therefore create affordances for more general categories of task than the detailed project-specific ANALYTIC TASKS we identify in the *Five-Level QDA* method.

In our experience, the affordances of NVivo—the intuitively obvious things to do based only on information on the screen—are sometimes exactly what we want to do and sometimes mask what we want to do or would like to do in a different way. This has not prevented us or any of the numerous expert users of NVivo from happily accomplishing what we need to accomplish with the program. Our explanation is that experts have learned unconsciously not to frame the software in terms of its affordances—the directly perceivable information on the screen about the program's action possibilities. Instead they unconsciously frame NVivo in terms of its "components", the *things* in the program that can be acted on. Separating the "components" of the program from the actions that can be taken on them is a different way of thinking about software. It is not difficult or complicated—quite the opposite. It is just different.

In Part II we provide a list of NVivo's 14 components. As we have not yet introduced the architecture of NVivo, we cannot use it to provide a meaningful example of the difference between framing software in terms of its components rather than its affordances. Instead we give an example from a program we all know and use: Microsoft Word. The principle is the same.

A less experienced user of Microsoft Word can produce unexpected and unwanted effects when just relying on the program's *affordances*, whereas a more experienced user who is aware of the software's *components* does not. One affordance of Microsoft Word is to be able to "drag" a section of text with the mouse button held down. When you let go of the mouse button, the text moves to wherever you "drop it." However, if you drag text that is formatted in one way to a location that is formatted in another way, sometimes the result may not be what you want. Figure 3.2 illustrates this situation.

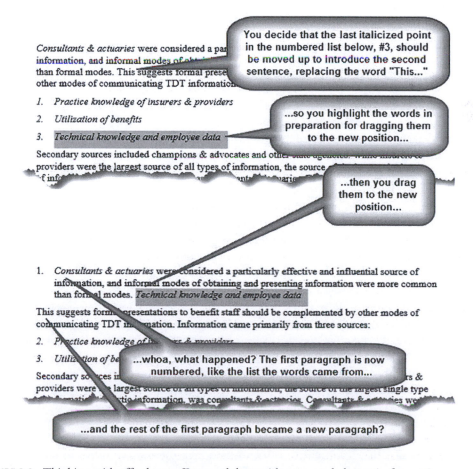

FIGURE 3.2 Thinking with affordances: Drag and drop with unwanted change in formatting

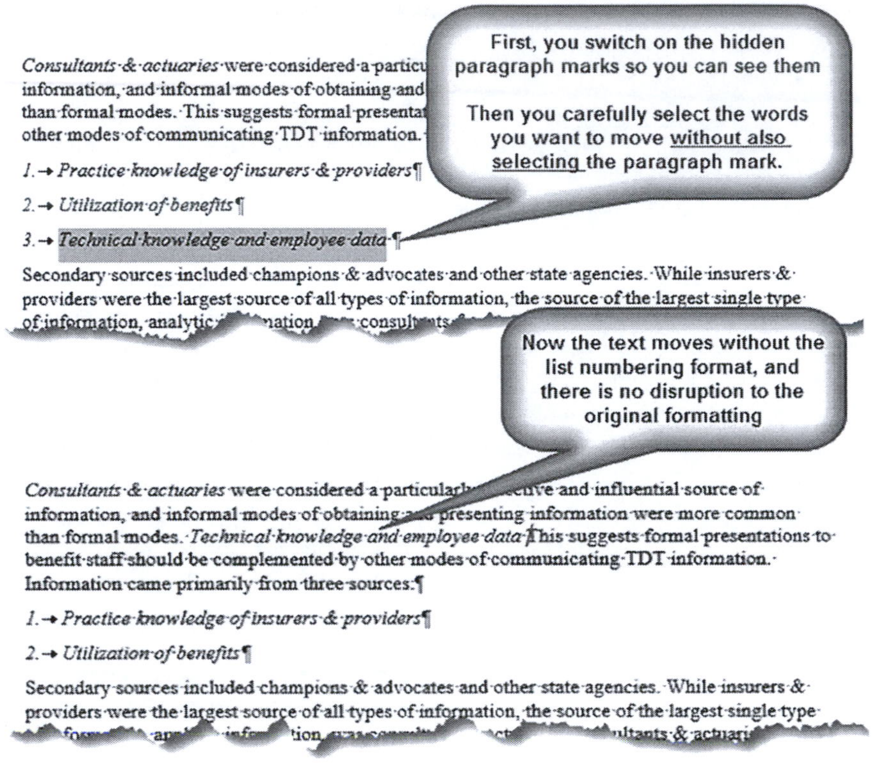

FIGURE 3.3 Thinking with components: Drag and drop with the desired effect

An alternative way to think about Microsoft Word is not in terms of its affordances—the apparently correct way to accomplish something—but in terms of its components. Experienced users of Microsoft Word know—perhaps without thinking of it in this way—that the affordance to drag and drop text involves two components. One component is *text*, and a second component is the *hidden paragraph mark* that comes at the end of each paragraph. They also know that the hidden paragraph mark contains the formatting instructions for that paragraph. If the hidden paragraph mark is unintentionally selected and dragged along with the text, which is what inadvertently happened in Figure 3.2, the formatting gets copied as well, changing the appearance of the whole paragraph it is dropped into. In Figure 3.2 the formatting that inadvertently got copied was automatic list numbering. One easy way around this is to select and drag only the *text*—one component—without including the *hidden paragraph mark*—the second component. Then the drag-and-drop operation does not change the formatting in the new location, and we get the outcome we wanted. This is illustrated in Figure 3.3. (If you are unfamiliar with Microsoft Word and would like a demonstration of this example, see the video on the companion website *Illustration of components in Microsoft Word*.)

Thinking in terms of components of Microsoft Word allows a more powerful use of the program, and the principle is exactly the same when thinking in terms of components of NVivo.

The Process of Translation

As we have now seen, we frame ANALYTIC TASKS in terms of their units, and we frame NVivo in terms of its components. We now put the term COMPONENT in SMALL CAPS as we are giving it a

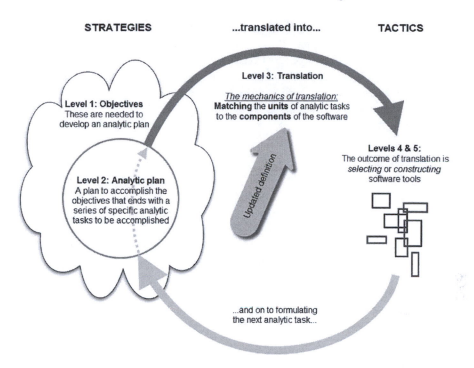

FIGURE 3.4 The mechanics of TRANSLATION

special meaning. In Chapter 2 we described translation rather generally as the *transformation* of strategies into tactics. We can now describe the mechanics of translation more specifically as *matching* the units of an ANALYTIC TASK to a COMPONENT of the software. See Figure 3.4 for this updated depiction.

First, to avoid confusion we print the word translation in regular type when referring to translation in general, but use SMALL CAPS when referring specifically to TRANSLATION of units of ANALYTIC TASKS to COMPONENTS of NVivo.

Consider the translation of books from one language to another. This highlights two major ways that a process of translation can occur. If you read a translated book you expect the translated version to be in some way *equivalent* to the original. *Formal equivalence* means a word-by-word translation from one language to the other, regardless of the idioms and natural sound of the second language. *Dynamic equivalence* is very different. It is not a word-by-word translation, but a translation that sounds to native speakers of the second language as if it had been written in that second language in the first place, so that both the original and the translated versions have roughly the same effect on their respective readers. Clearly there can be many different versions of a translation, and no single translation can be considered right or wrong (Nida & Taber, 1969).

In the same way, TRANSLATION means first looking for a straightforward match—a *formal equivalence*—between the units of an ANALYTIC TASK and a COMPONENT of the software. If there is one, we use the program to act on that COMPONENT in the obvious way. If there is not a workable match, then rather than change the ANALYTIC TASK so that it matches the software, we reframe the process: we look for *dynamic equivalence*, using COMPONENTS of the program in combination or in an unusual way, as if trying to find *just the right word* in a language translation. Just as there is no single correct dynamically equivalent translation of a book, there is often more than one way to do something more sophisticated in NVivo. The important issue is that different ways to do something more sophisticated may lend themselves to *different next steps*. Therefore, when deciding on which way to do something more sophisticated, the best criterion for deciding will be *what you plan to do next*.

We now move on to the different outcomes of TRANSLATION when there is a straightforward match between the units of an ANALYTIC TASK and a software COMPONENT, or when there needs to be a more sophisticated match.

Level 4: Selected-Tools

This section describes the situation when there is a straightforward match between the units of an ANALYTIC TASK and a COMPONENT of the software, resulting in what we call a SELECTED–TOOL.

The outcome of any translation process is something new. In our case of TRANSLATING units to COMPONENTS, the outcome is a software tool. In general, the nature of software tools is different from other kinds of tools. We are all familiar with physical tools and learning to use them, but software tools are different. According to the educational researcher John Seely Brown, software tools can only be described and learned through their use (Brown, Collins, & Duguid, 1989).

A tool in everyday language is a physical thing, like a knife, or a process, like a checklist. It is easy to describe how to use these kinds of tools. But thinking of software as a set of tools is different. John Seely Brown studies the use of computers as tools. He emphasizes that the use of software as a tool cannot be explicitly described. Learning to use them can only arise out of their use and is a process of enculturation into the community of those that use the tools—learning is "situated" in the context in which it occurs. This resonates well with our experience of NVivo. This is because the affordances of NVivo—the visible and obvious ways to use the program as designed by the developers—do not explicitly describe how researchers use software in their varied and idiosyncratic research projects. Each researcher seems to use the software differently, even for similar tasks, and passes on these ways of using the programs to their colleagues and students.

We refer to a TOOL as a way of acting on COMPONENTS of the program, by clicking buttons, selecting menu items, and so on. A TOOL, as we are using the term, is therefore a combination of a COMPONENT and an action. We print TOOL in SMALL CAPS when referring to this specialized use of the term and in regular type when talking generally about tools.

There is a comprehensive list of COMPONENTS—the *things* in the program to be acted on—but it makes no sense to have a comprehensive list of TOOLS to pick from, because TOOLS come into being in the course of using the software when the TRANSLATION process has determined a set of action steps that is specific to an ANALYTIC TASK. There would be many hundreds of TOOLS if we tried to create such a list, and it would serve no purpose. Think of the affordances of the program as frozen—they come fully formed, designed as the software developer thought best. In contrast, think of TOOLS as emergent—we create them, and they only exist in the context of use.

It is most helpful to think of a TOOL as a way of thinking about how to fulfill an ANALYTIC TASK, rather than as an established course of action that resides in the software. TOOLS are driven by and are specific to ANALYTIC TASKS. They come into being in the course of use, as John Seely Brown describes (Brown et al., 1989).

When an ANALYTIC TASK has a single unit, and the unit directly matches a COMPONENT of the software so that acting on the COMPONENT accomplishes the task, then this results in what we call a SELECTED–TOOL, the most straightforward way of using the software. This is Level 4 (see Figure 3.5).

It is not yet practical to illustrate Level 4 with real-world ANALYTIC TASKS to be accomplished in NVivo because we have not yet introduced the architecture of the program. We also do not want to use a single research project or methodology to exemplify this process, for the reasons we provided in Chapter 2. We therefore continue with the gourmet meal, in which TRANSLATION to

Level 1	Level 2	Level 3	Level 4	Level 5
Objectives	Analytic plan	Translation	Selected tools	Constructed tools
The purpose and context of a project, usually expressed as research questions and a methodology	The conceptual framework and resulting analytic tasks	Translating from analytic tasks to software tools and translating the results back again	Straightforward choice of individual software operations	Sophisticated use of software by combining operations or performing them in a custom way

FIGURE 3.5 Level 4 of the *Five-Level QDA* method

a SELECTED-TOOL can be easily illustrated in concrete, everyday terms. The only change required is to replace the term ANALYTIC TASK with the word TASK to represent in an equivalent way the meal preparation activities at a level of detail that Christina identifies as most convenient based on what she plans to do next.

You recall from the Meal Planning Worksheet in Chapter 2 (page 40) that we listed Christina's first three TASKS of the meal preparation process. The first task is to *find all suitable 75-minute-or-less recipes* by finding all possibilities and evaluating them against the dietary preferences of the family. The second task, *check for fresh ginger*, was prompted by the fact that many of these recipes happened to call for fresh ginger. After finding none and referring to the objectives on the Planning Worksheet, which reminded her of the decision to prepare the meal only with what is available, she generates a third TASK: *discard recipes requiring fresh ginger*.

In Chapter 2 we had not yet discussed the mechanics of TRANSLATION and so had not fully completed the Meal Planning Worksheet. We will now go back and complete the Meal Planning Worksheet in the same way that we will in the *Five-Level QDA* method. Figure 3.6 illustrates the completion of the first two TASKS, with the TRANSLATION process highlighted. The TRANSLATION column identifies the unit of the TASK, then the kitchen COMPONENT that could potentially match the unit, and finally a summary of the TRANSLATION that describes the matching process. The final column describes the SELECTED-TOOL—in other words, the action that will be taken on an available kitchen COMPONENT to fulfill the task. That is always what we mean by a TOOL—a particular action taken on a COMPONENT. It may not be completely realistic to think that Christina would fill out this Meal Planning Worksheet when preparing a gourmet meal, TASK by TASK. But it is worth studying the highlighted area of Figure 3.6 in this simple example, which identifies the UNITS and COMPONENTS, because this is exactly what we learn how to do in Parts II and III in more complicated research examples.

Figure 3.6 illustrates both of the first two tasks completed, but remember that in reality this is an iterative process carried out TASK by TASK. Only when the outcome of the first TASK is known—in this case, discovering that many recipes called for fresh ginger—does the second TASK become apparent—in this case, *check for fresh ginger*. So in reality the first highlighted line for the first TASK would have been completed and its outcome known before the second TASK had even been identified.

Having completed the second task and determined there is no fresh ginger available, and having reminded herself that the objectives call for only using what is already available in the kitchen, Christina identifies the third task as *discard all the recipes calling for fresh ginger*. She must now find an accurate and—she hopes—efficient way to accomplish this. Unfortunately, there is no kitchen COMPONENT on which an action could be taken to accomplish this, such as recipe books that already

MEAL PLANNING WORKSHEET – Version 3

Level 1: OBJECTIVES	*OBJECTIVES*
	To relax after a long day, promptly prepare a gourmet family meal with what's already available in the kitchen
	GUIDING METHODOLOGY: Recipe-inspired improvisation
	Based on a recipe that stimulates the chef's enthusiasm, adjust every aspect as needed to the constraints of the context

CURRENT CONCEPTUAL FRAMEWORK

Level 2: OVERALL PLAN	

Dietary preferences of family members —determine→ **75 minute recipes**

Originally 60 minutes, but adjusted to 75 due to unsufficient 60 minute recipes and the reasonableness of 75 minutes constituting "prompt"

75 minute recipes —determine→ **Complexity of preparation process**

Available ingredients —determine→ **Complexity of preparation process**

Complexity of preparation process —increase→ **Degree of relaxation needed**

Complexity of preparation process —decrease→ **Prompt preparation**

Level 2: TASKS	Level 3: TRANSLATION of TASKS into TOOLS	Levels 4 & 5: SELECTED or CONSTRUCTED TOOLS
Find all suitable one hour or less recipes	*UNITS* Individual recipes *COMPONENTS* Pages of recipe books *EXPLANATION* The recipe books are already organized sequentially by recipes, so there is a direct match between the unit and the component	*SELECTED-TOOL* Read through each recipe on each recipe book to identify one hour or less recipes
Check for fresh ginger	*UNITS* Pieces of ginger *COMPONENTS* All containers in every location of kitchen *EXPLANATION* Each container either does or does not contain a piece of ginger, so there is a direct match	*SELECTED-TOOL* Inspect every container on every surface and in every draw or shelf for pieces of ginger

FIGURE 3.6 Meal Planning Worksheet—Version 3: SELECTED-TOOLS

exclude recipes with fresh ginger. She has to somehow construct a TOOL from what is available in the kitchen.

Level 5: Constructed-Tools

This section describes the outcome of TRANSLATION when there is no direct match between the units of an ANALYTIC TASK and a COMPONENT of the software, resulting in what we call a CONSTRUCTED–TOOL.

Sometimes there is a direct match between a unit of an ANALYTIC TASK and an affordance of NVivo such that the ANALYTIC TASK can be fulfilled with a single operation of the software, in other words, a SELECTED–TOOL. But it is more common to either require a sequence of software operations or to use the software in a customized way, which requires creating a CONSTRUCTED–TOOL. The skill of harnessing NVivo powerfully could be described as a facility in using CONSTRUCTED–TOOLS. This is Level 5 (see Figure 3.7). When limited to SELECTED–TOOLS the software is not used powerfully, missing the opportunities for undertaking tasks that may be unrealistically cumbersome without NVivo.

Coming back to the gourmet meal, Christina is working on her third TASK, to find an accurate and efficient way to *discard recipes requiring fresh ginger*. There is no available COMPONENT in the kitchen for automatically hiding or eliminating some recipes in a physical recipe book, so she has to construct a way to do this.

Looking around the kitchen, Christina seeks TOOLS she could harness for this purpose. She could use a marker to cross out the unneeded recipes, use scissors to cut them out of the recipe book, use paper clips to temporarily indicate where they are, or prepare a list of them on a separate piece of paper, noting the recipe book and page number. All would work, but which TOOL best matches the task? The criteria for choosing, as always, is *what you plan to do next*. In an emergent activity like recipe-inspired meal improvisation—not to mention qualitative analysis—this can never be known in advance and therefore requires reflection. Christina reflects on two issues: the need to continue reviewing and choosing among suitable recipes for tonight's meal, but also not to ruin the recipe book for future meals. This requires thinking more about what it means to *discard* in the context of tonight's TASK. (Stopping to investigate the meaning of a concept in a particular context is also a common activity in qualitative analysis.) One of the many dimensions of *discard* is *how long lasting* the discarding should be, which could vary a lot. Christina only needs to discard recipes in order to more easily focus on those that are feasible within her objectives. The discarding is therefore not intended to be long lasting, let alone permanent, and so she does not want to cut the unwanted recipes out of the book with scissors and make them unavailable in the future.

Another dimension of *discard* is how *abstract or concrete* the discarding needs to be in order to be effective in the context. The most abstract way to discard recipes would be to remember which ones had been discarded while flipping back and forth among them; more concrete would be a

Level 1	Level 2	Level 3	Level 4	Level 5
Objectives	Analytic plan	Translation	Selected tools	Constructed tools
The purpose and context of a project, usually expressed as research questions and a methodology	The conceptual framework and resulting analytic tasks	Translating from analytic tasks to software tools and translating the results back again	Straightforward choice of individual software operations	Sophisticated use of software by combining operations or performing them in a custom way

FIGURE 3.7 Level 5 of the *Five-Level QDA* method

visual indication that lets Christina see the ones previously discarded; and the most concrete would be the physical removal of the pages with discarded recipes, an option already rejected. Because what Christina *plans to do next* is to revisit the ginger-less recipes many times back and forth while focusing on other aspects of the recipes besides ginger, a visual indication for the duration of the meal preparation seems to best serve the purpose. It looks like using paper clips to visually signify the temporarily feasible ginger-less recipes is the best way to go, reminding Christina which ones are suitable candidates as she flips back and forth through the recipe books without having to remember them all. This is a *custom* use of the kitchen COMPONENT paper clip. Everyone knows that paper clips are designed to secure together a number of sheets of paper, the number depending on the size of the clip. The paper clips in the junk drawer in Christina's kitchen are medium-sized and offer the affordance *attach together up to about 20 sheets of paper*. However, that means that attaching a paper clip to a single piece of paper is also afforded, but there wouldn't be much point unless you were using the paper clip for a different purpose—not for *attaching together* but for *visually marking a single piece of paper*. This use is perfect in the recipe selection context to serve as a temporary indicator. This unusual or at least less common use of the paper clip becomes a CONSTRUCTED-TOOL. The highlighted area of Figure 3.8 illustrates this translation of the third TASK.

Clearly this laboriously elaborated thinking process would be entirely unconscious and experienced as a single quick task in the case of deciding how to *discard recipes requiring fresh ginger*. But it is a realistic model of the thinking that occurs for complicated ANALYTIC TASKS in real-world qualitative research studies using NVivo. Expert NVivo users perform this thinking process quickly and unconsciously, just like Christina would do in the kitchen with her paper clips. But when initially learning to harness NVivo powerfully, this needs to be thought through consciously in order to shortcut the long process of trial and error, and this is what we will be doing in Parts II and III.

The Sequence of Tasks

We have now completed the principles of the *Five-Level QDA* method and introduced each of its levels. Figure 3.9 displays the five levels of the process. A final point to dwell on is the one-way circular path of action depicted in Figure 3.9 and the question of where one starts on this circular path. It is important to recognize the difference between a fixed sequence of activities—which is *not* the nature of qualitative research and not intended in the *Five-Level QDA* method—and a one-way direction around the five levels—which is intended.

Unlike quantitative or statistical research, qualitative research does not have a fixed sequence of activities. The logic of quantitative or statistical research calls for a predetermined sequence: developing a hypothesis, then gathering data to test it, and finally performing the statistical analysis of the data. After the results are in, there is no revisiting and modifying the hypothesis or collecting more data in order to fine-tune the results. But qualitative research has a different logic based on iteration and emergence, and so emergence does not have such a fixed sequence of activities. The specifics depend on the guiding methodology, but as a general principle if you recognize partway through a qualitative study that the data are "telling you" something different from what you thought you were investigating, it would not violate the underlying logic of qualitative research to modify the research question appropriately, provided it still meets the needs of the study objectives or the funders.

The *Five-Level QDA* method is no different—there is no predetermined sequence of activities that is the same in every project. But there *is* a one-way-only direction around the circular path of five levels that serves the iterative and emergent spirit of qualitative research. This is because the iterative process of qualitative research takes place at the strategy levels—Levels 1 and 2—inside the cloudlike area of Figure 3.9 in which there is no set sequence of activities other than

MEAL PLANNING WORKSHEET – Version 4

Level 1: OBJECTIVES

OBJECTIVES
To relax after a long day, promptly prepare a gourmet family meal with what's already available in the kitchen

GUIDING METHODOLOGY: Recipe-inspired improvisation
Based on a recipe that stimulates the chef's enthusiasm, adjust every aspect as needed to the constraints of the context

CURRENT CONCEPTUAL FRAMEWORK

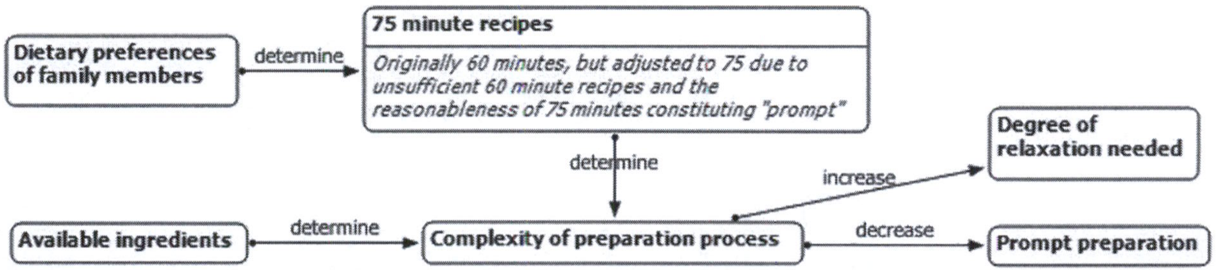

Level 2: OVERALL PLAN

[Dietary preferences of family members] — determine → [75 minute recipes]

75 minute recipes: Originally 60 minutes, but adjusted to 75 due to unsufficient 60 minute recipes and the reasonableness of 75 minutes constituting "prompt"

[Available ingredients] — determine → [Complexity of preparation process]

[Dietary preferences of family members] / [75 minute recipes] — determine → [Complexity of preparation process]

[Complexity of preparation process] — increase / decrease → [Degree of relaxation needed]

[Degree of relaxation needed]

[Prompt preparation]

Level 2: TASKS

- Find all suitable one hour or less recipes
- Check for fresh ginger
- Discard recipes requiring fresh ginger

Level 3: TRANSLATION of TASKS into TOOLS

UNITS Individual recipes
COMPONENTS Pages of recipe books
EXPLANATION The recipe books are already organized sequentially by recipes, so there is a direct match between the unit and the component

UNITS Pieces of ginger
COMPONENTS All containers in every location of kitchen
EXPLANATION Each container either does or does not contain a piece of ginger, so there is a direct match

UNITS Individual recipes
COMPONENTS Paperclips and pages of recipe books
EXPLANATION Use paper clips in custom way by marking a single page rather than attach multiple pages together

Levels 4 & 5: SELECTED or CONSTRUCTED TOOLS

SELECTED-TOOL
Read through each recipe on each recipe book to identify one hour or less recipes

SELECTED-TOOL
Inspect every container on every surface and in every draw or shelf for pieces of ginger

CONSTRUCTED-TOOL
1. Identify a recipe not requiring ginger
2. Attach a paper clip to the first page of the recipe

FIGURE 3.8 Meal Planning Worksheet—Version 4: CONSTRUCTED–TOOLS

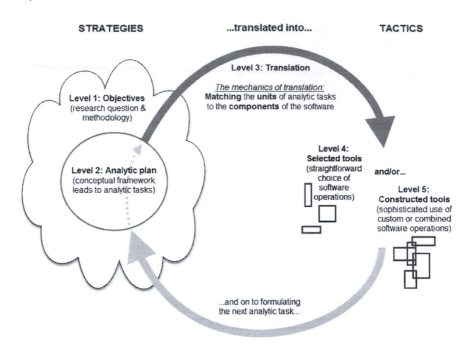

FIGURE 3.9 The five levels of the *Five-Level QDA* method

what the guiding methodology suggests. But once an ANALYTIC TASK has been identified, it emerges from the cloud and is on its way, first to Level 3, to be TRANSLATED to either a Level 4 SELECTED-TOOL or a Level 5 CONSTRUCTED-TOOL. When the outcome of those software operations is known, the activity journeys back to the ANALYTIC PLAN at Level 2 until the next ANALYTIC TASK is produced *in terms of the conceptual framework* of the project, not in terms of the COMPONENTS of the software.

In contrast, the first sign of using NVivo superficially is the use of an abbreviated process in the opposite direction: first learning how to operate the software in the most straightforward way at Level 4 and then looking around for ways to make use of it in the analysis, at Level 2. This is intuitive, not unreasonable, and a common way of engaging with NVivo, but it means letting the tactics determine the strategy. This often leads to dead ends because the ANALYTIC TASKS grow out of the software's capabilities rather than the conceptual framework that has been honed from the objectives of the project.

In summary, qualitative analysis means working at the strategy levels, Levels 1 and 2. Once an ANALYTIC TASK has been identified and expressed in its own units, *then* it begins its cyclic one-way-only journey around the *Five-Level QDA* process. This is the essence of harnessing NVivo powerfully.

References

Bernard, H. R., Wutich, A. Y., & Ryan, G. W. (2017). *Analyzing qualitative data: Systematic approaches* (2nd ed.). Thousand Oaks, CA: Sage.

Bolman, L. G., & Deal, T. E. (1997). *Reframing organizations.* San Francisco: Jossey-Bass.

Brown, J. S., Collins, A., & Duguid, P. (1989). Situated cognition and the culture of learning. *Educational Researcher, 18*(1), 32–42.

Feature. (n.d.). In Wikipedia. Retrieved November 4, 2016 from https://en.wikipedia.org/wiki/Software_feature

Gaver, W. W. (1991). Technology affordances. In S. P. Robertson, G. M. Olson, & J. S. Olson (Eds.), *Proceedings of the SIGCHI conference on Human Factors in Computing Systems* (pp. 79–84). NY: ACM.

Gibson, J. J. (1979). *The ecological approach to visual perception.* Boston: Houghton Mifflin.

Hartson, R. (2003). Cognitive, physical, sensory, and functional affordances in interaction design. *Behaviour & Information Technology, 22*(5), 315–338.

Morgan, G. (2006). *Images of organization* (Updated ed.). Thousands Oaks, CA: Sage.

Nida, E. A., & Taber, C. R. (1969). *The theory and practice of translation.* Leiden: E. J. Brill.

Norman, D. A. (1988). *The psychology of everyday things.* New York, NY: Basic Books.

Norman, D. A. (1999). Affordance, conventions, and design. *Interactions, 6*(3), 38–43.

PART II

The *Five-Level QDA* Method in Practice

Part II applies the principles of Part I in describing how NVivo works and how translation is accomplished in practice. Chapter 4 provides an orientation to NVivo for those upgrading to Version 11 of the program and for those who work in research teams. Chapter 5 describes in depth how NVivo works in terms of *Five-Level QDA* principles, meaning in terms of its components rather than its features. Chapter 5 is accompanied by videos on the companion website for each component. Chapter 6 describes in depth the five steps of the translation process, with examples from a variety of research projects.

4

ORIENTATION TO NVivo

The Different Versions and Editions of NVivo

There are three versions of NVivo 11: NVivo for Windows, NVivo for Mac, and NVivo for Teams. NVivo 11 for Windows has three editions: Starter, Pro, and Plus. The *Five-Level QDA* method described in this book can be easily adopted by users of any version. Table 4.1 summarizes the versions and editions to serve as an initial orientation to the differences. Chapter 5 provides more detail about the differences in relation to the COMPONENTS of NVivo. All versions are continually being developed and new features are added regularly, so it is important to install updates when they

TABLE 4.1 The different versions of NVivo

NVivo 11 Starter Edition (Windows)	• Provides features for managing and analyzing textual materials: text documents (e.g. Microsoft Word files) and PDFs. • Includes simple text search, word frequency, and coding queries. • Includes selected charts and diagrams for data visualization.
NVivo 11 Pro Edition (Windows)	*All the features provided by the Starter Edition and additionally:* • Work with audio, video, images, and spreadsheets. • Integrate information from bibliographic and referencing software (e.g. Endnote, RefWorks). • Use more powerful querying tools, including matrix coding queries. • Create maps to show associations in data. • Use NCapture to capture social media content for analysis.
NVivo 11 Plus Edition (Windows)	*All the features provided by the Pro Edition and additionally:* • Automatic identification of themes and sentiments. • Automatic creation of social network visualizations from social media or other data.
NVivo 11 for Teams (Windows)	Enables geographically dispersed team members to work on the same NVivo project at the same time. Each team member needs a license for the NVivo for Windows, so that license affects the functionality available when using NVivo for Teams.
NVivo 11 for Mac	Almost equivalent to the Pro edition of NVivo 11 for Windows, but with some differences. For example, at the time of writing the Mac version does not include all the types of queries, maps, and charts that the Pro edition does.

are available. The QSR International website provides detailed information about the differences in specific functionality between versions—www.qsrinternational.com.

Working in Teams

Conducting research in teams is very different from researching alone. In a solo project every role and task are conducted by the same person. Team projects are different and involve two additional issues: *who does what* and *integrating each team member's contribution*. These are, respectively, the human aspect and the technical aspect of working in teams. This chapter describes the human aspect of *who does what*, which is a necessary preparation for learning about the technical aspect of *integrating each team member's contribution* in Chapter 5.

There are several versions of NVivo. All the NVivo 11 for Windows editions (Starter, Pro, and Plus) and NVivo 11 for Mac are not multiuser programs. NVivo for Teams is a multiuser program, which allows team members to work on the same NVivo project at the same time. It connects to all editions of NVivo 11 for Windows. At the time of writing there is no NVivo for Teams for the Mac.

In the single-user versions of NVivo, team members work independently in NVivo on their own assigned analytic activities, just as they would if each were working on a solo research project. Then periodically each team member's work is merged in NVivo with the other team members' work. Team members' work does not need to be merged when using NVivo for Teams, but the principles of the *human aspects of team working* are the same.

Once a team member has an assigned task, she harnesses the program powerfully using the *Five-Level QDA* method in the same way as if working alone. There are therefore no separate or different *Five-Level QDA* principles when working in a team and no separate chapter in this book. However, there are important issues to be considered in determining *who does what*. Even though this has nothing directly to do with the *Five-Level QDA* method, we discuss some important aspects *of who does what* before going on to discuss how NVivo has been designed to *integrate team members' work*.

Deciding *who does what* raises a number of questions, and the answers vary greatly from team to team. Here we discuss four questions: Can some tasks be delegated to less experienced team members? Is the style of leadership more democratic or centralized? Are constraints needed on team members' freedom of action? And finally, how frequently should team members' work be integrated for single-user versions?

Delegation

Does the style of analysis lend itself to delegating some tasks to less experienced researchers? Some leaders of qualitative research projects have had an earlier career in quantitative research and are accustomed to delegating tasks such as running experiments or the data entry of a large number of survey responses to less experienced research assistants or clerical staff. Qualitative research has few, if any, comparable tasks, and managing a qualitative project similarly to a quantitative study can lead to anomalous situations if a critical part of a study—for example, the initial reading of texts and the generation of data-driven codes or categories—is considered to be humdrum work and assigned to the least experienced research assistant. Some methodologies do include phases of less interpretive activities—such as a period of use of predetermined and well-defined codes or categories to accumulate examples in the data for subsequent interpretation—and these methodologies accommodate delegation of these tasks to less experienced team members. But other methodologies do not, particularly those in which interpretation is to the fore. For these projects it is difficult to escape the conclusion that there are no lesser or more junior analytic activities, and to a large extent every team member has the same analytic status in the team. The underlying issue is whether the inevitable compromises in any research project with limited time and funding have to extend to delegating core or critical analytic activities to less experienced team members.

Leadership Style

Is the team more of a democratic venture, with each researcher's contribution having similar weight, or more centralized, with one or more Principal Investigators serving as decision makers in a group of contributing researchers? Our experience is that qualitative researchers are generally democratic, but they sometimes underestimate the significant increase in time required to incorporate and integrate the conceptual contributions of multiple researchers. Centralized projects involve a Principal Investigator receiving the contributions of each team member in each round of analysis, making all decisions about what to accept and how it is to be integrated, and then providing explanations of her decisions to inform the next round of analysis. This is a much faster and more streamlined process. Before deciding on a leadership style, consider the purpose of conducting the research in a team. In some projects the rationale is to investigate a phenomenon from the perspective of different disciplines, and so the contributions of each discipline's representative need to have equal or at least significant weight. In this case, the data analysis must proceed in a more democratic fashion. In other projects, the purpose of having a team is to meet a tight completion deadline that a single researcher could not accomplish. Time constraints lend themselves to a more centralized approach. In other teams personalities play an undeniable role. But we are surprised that many teams are unclear about why their project is being conducted with multiple researchers in the first place. When planning *who does what* in a team project, the best question to ask first may be: *Why are we conducting this project in a team?*

Constraints

Are constraints needed on team members' freedom of action? When working alone, each ANALYTIC TASK is individually TRANSLATED into a SELECTED- or CONSTRUCTED–TOOL with reference to what is coming next—no predetermined constraints are needed. But when working in a team, the actions taken by a team member can have unexpected outcomes. This is the case when working with the NVivo single-user versions and projects are merged together and also when working with NVivo for Teams. At the most general level there are only three possible actions: to *add* something, to *modify* something, or to *delete* something.

Adding something is in principle no problem. This, in fact, is what we want team members to do, whether identifying new meaning units of data, adding new codes, adding new analytic writing, adding new visual representations, or adding something to another team member's work. Certainly policies are needed so that each team member knows what is expected of them. This is all part of designing their assigned tasks. But there is nothing technically problematic about a team member adding something in NVivo.

Deleting something intuitively feels like something we need to control. If an inexperienced team member deletes something important, such as a code or a piece of analytic writing, this might be expected to cause a problem. When merging single-user projects, deleting unexpectedly is not problematic. If at least one other team member has not also deleted that same thing, it will reappear when every team members' work is merged together. However, we do not want to encourage team members to feel free to delete things willy-nilly. Deleting has an indirect effect because the team member who deletes something—for example, a code—will continue her work under the mistaken assumption that the code no longer exists, but her subsequent coding will then be subtly different from everyone else's. A policy is therefore needed for deleting things. This could be flagging something with a comment suggesting it be deleted, rather than actually deleting it, or simply bringing it to the team's attention at the next team meeting. Appropriate policies will vary depending on the stage of the project and the relationships, status, or physical proximity of the various team members. When working with NVivo for Teams deleting is more problematic because there is only one project—so if one member deletes something, it really is gone. Policies for deleting are therefore even more important when working with NVivo for Teams.

Modifying or changing things is almost always problematic. For example, if we have a code named *hard and invigorating*, a team member decides that a better code name would be *stressful*, so that it could also apply to respondents' experiences that had a tinge of stress. This effectively broadens the meaning of the code. Consider what happens on merging each team member's project file, which in the single-user versions of NVivo is called a PROJECT. The original code *hard and invigorating* still exists on everyone else's PROJECTS, so it appears in the merged PROJECT. But the new code *stressful* also appears in the merged PROJECT. This new code contains all this team member's newly coded segments of data to his newly renamed code, but it also contains all the segments originally coded to *hard and invigorating* in all earlier rounds of work coded by all team members. These segments are therefore now attached to both codes in the merged PROJECT. There is now overlap and a degree of incoherence in the coding scheme, particularly if other team members have been coding respondents' stressful experiences to an entirely different code. What happens next depends on the policies for dealing with newly appearing codes. In the best case, all new codes are routinely brought to the team's attention and discussed. This would lead to a decision about whether or not to integrate the new code *stressful* into the conceptual framework and perhaps remove the earlier *hard and invigorating* codings now mistakenly double-coded to the new code *stressful.* In the worst case, teams do not establish a policy for making modifications or they allow team members free reign. As with deleting, modifying something with NVivo for Teams is particularly problematic because there is only one project—so if one member modifies something, it changes for everyone. Policies for modifying are therefore even more important when working with NVivo for Teams.

In summary, the cause of conceptual coherence in the emerging analysis is best served if policies are thought through for *adding*, *deleting*, and *modifying* and appropriate constraints put on the freedom of action of each team member. In our consulting practice we give team members free rein to *add* things, but we prohibit *deleting* and *modifying*. We instead decide on a workable method for team members to communicate their proposed deletions and modifications and for these to be put into effect immediately following the next merge of all PROJECTS when using the single-user versions and by the project manager at specified times when using NVivo for Teams.

Frequency of Integration When Working With the Single-User Versions of NVivo

If working with the single-user versions of NVivo, the question arises as to how frequently you should merge team members' work. NVivo is unconcerned about this because each merge operation is independent. But from the human point of view, an intentional plan is best. Think in terms of merge cycles. After each cycle of work, all team members must stop work while their PROJECTS are collected and merged, and so they must not continue until the merged PROJECT is redistributed to each team for the next round of work. How often should this occur? There is no typical or recommended plan. We have worked with team projects in which each team member analyzes all the data separately from their disciplinary perspective, followed by a single integration or merge of all members' contributions at the end. And we have worked with a multinational team at the opposite end of the spectrum, in which researchers in vastly different time zones merged all their work nightly so that everyone could see the next day what everyone else had done the previous day. This was unusual and challenging to accomplish on the human side but unproblematic on the technical side regarding NVivo procedures. In practice most projects fall somewhere in the middle, with smaller projects merging their work on an ad hoc basis at turning points in the analysis or whenever the currently assigned tasks are completed. Larger or longer-term projects with many researchers conducting different parts of the analysis on different schedules often have a more structured plan, such as merging every Friday afternoon.

Using NVivo for Teams

Merging projects is not necessary when working with NVivo for Teams because all team members can work on the same project—at the same time or at different times. The program must be installed on a server, and each team member must have access to the same edition of NVivo for Windows. NVivo projects created using NVivo for Teams are therefore called SERVER-PROJECTS. Even though no merging of projects is required, the human aspects of team working in terms of *leadership style*, *delegation*, and *constraints* are just as relevant when using NVivo for Teams as with standalone versions and the merging of PROJECTS.

Each team member's Windows user profile is used in NVivo for Teams, which allows all the work they do on the SERVER-PROJECT to be tracked. Each SERVER-PROJECT has a Project Owner who assigns team members to different "user groups." There are three types of user groups, each providing different levels of access to the SERVER-PROJECT:

- **Readers**. This is the lowest level of permissions, allowing team members to view the SERVER-PROJECT but not make any changes to it.
- **Contributors**. This is the middle level of permissions, allowing team members to view and modify a SERVER-PROJECT but not undertake any project management tasks, such as modifying SERVER-PROJECT properties or managing user access.
- **Project owners**. This is the highest level of permissions, allowing full access.

Each team member can see each other's changes as they work on a SERVER-PROJECT. In order to avoid potential conflicts, NVivo for Teams has protocols for which team member's changes take precedence. For example, if one team member is editing data, other team members are locked out, meaning they can view the data but cannot make changes while the other team member is in edit mode. However, if two team members attempt to code a slightly different segment of data using the same code at the same time, the coding undertaken by the team member who completes the process first will be implemented. This means that some work may not be added to the SERVER-PROJECT. This is why protocols for *who does what* are needed.

Chapter 5 discusses the technical aspects of combining team member's work when working with the standalone versions of NVivo.

5

THE ARCHITECTURE OF NVivo

This chapter describes the architecture of NVivo 11, focusing on the design and purpose of each COMPONENT rather than the nuts and bolts of operating the software. The purpose is to provide a comprehensive understanding of the program. If you are not already familiar with operating NVivo, then immediately after reading this chapter is the time to take advantage of the free online resources or fee-based workshops offered by the software developers at www.qsrinternational.com. This site also provides an up-to-date listing of independent training companies offering their own courses.

The Different Versions of NVivo

As discussed in Chapter 4, there are three versions of NVivo 11: NVivo for Windows, NVivo for Mac, and NVivo for Teams. NVivo for Windows has three editions: Starter, Pro, and Plus. This chapter covers all versions, but illustrations are taken from the Plus Edition of NVivo 11 for Windows. The exception is Figure 5.2, which illustrates the interface for NVivo for Mac. As all versions of the software are continually being developed, we do not discuss the detailed differences. However, COMPONENTS that are not contained in all versions at the time of writing are indicated in Table 5.2. Up-to-date information about versions is available on the QSR International website: www.qsrinternational.com/product/product-feature-comparison.

Component Orientation Videos

After reading about each COMPONENT in this chapter we invite you to view a short orientation video of that COMPONENT at the Companion Website. These videos make the abstract learning about each COMPONENT concrete, but they are not hands-on instruction in operating the program. We recommend that you read about a COMPONENT and watch the corresponding video before moving on to the next one. To register and log in to the companion website go to www.routledgetextbooks.com/textbooks/5LQDA and follow the on-screen instructions.

The Organization of the Program

There are many ways to describe how NVivo is organized. As discussed in Chapter 3 we do not focus on the features of the software. "Feature" is a common term to describe generally what a

TABLE 5.1 The four clusters of components

Providing data	Providing the data to NVivo and everything to do with organizing, managing, and using data files.
Conceptualizing data	Most commonly accomplished by using NODES to represent the concepts in a study, by linking them to REFERENCES, or by grouping them to represent more general concepts. Other COMPONENTS may be harnessed for these conceptualizing purposes, and NODES may be harnessed for purposes other than conceptualizing data.
Writing	Writing can be captured in MEMOS, in ANNOTATIONS (comments linked to REFERENCES), in Descriptions that are attached to COMPONENTS, and by directly editing SOURCES inside NVivo.
Visualizing	COMPONENTS can be displayed and worked with visually in an NVivo display called a MAP. In addition, the associations between COMPONENTS can be visually displayed in different types of CHARTS.

program can do. Developers try to make the features visible on the screen so that it is as obvious as possible how to operate the program according to their assumptions about how the software will be used. In our experience, it is not helpful to focus on features when learning NVivo, because simply knowing what the program can do does not result in harnessing the software powerfully. We therefore do not go through NVivo feature by feature. Instead we think separately about NVivo's COMPONENTS and the actions that can be taken on those COMPONENTS in order to select and construct TOOLS. Explicit awareness of COMPONENTS facilitates powerful harnessing of the program.

Regarding terminology, for terms with specific NVivo meanings, such as Detail View, we capitalize them to indicate these are terms you will see on the screen. When we use terms with specific *Five-Level QDA* meanings, we continue to present them in SMALL CAPS.

Components

For convenience we discuss the COMPONENTS in this chapter in four clusters. There is no significance to the clusters themselves—this is simply a way to divide the information so that it's easier to digest. The four clusters are listed in Table 5.1, and the COMPONENTS are listed and defined in Table 5.2.

Components Are Not the Same as Project Items

NVivo uses the term Project Items to refer to all the things created and worked with in the software. COMPONENTS are things that can be *acted on*, and they are not the same as Project Items. Not all Project Items can be acted upon, and therefore not all Project Items are COMPONENTS, but all COMPONENTS are Project Items. Examples of Project Items that are not COMPONENTS are Classifications, Attributes, and Relationship Types. From now on we concentrate on COMPONENTS.

Actions

The *Five-Level QDA* method describes NVivo in terms of these COMPONENTS—the things that can be acted on. This chapter describes the COMPONENTS and how they work. The next chapter focuses on the TRANSLATION process—taking the UNITS of ANALYTIC TASKS and matching them to these COMPONENTS of the software. At that point we have to know what actions we can take on each COMPONENT. In the next chapter we therefore list these actions—one set of actions common to all COMPONENTS and one set specific to each COMPONENT. Focusing on how the COMPONENTS work first and listing the actions that can be taken on them later is the easiest way to master the *Five-Level QDA* process.

TABLE 5.2 The 13 components of NVivo

Components		*Definition*
Providing data	SOURCE	A data file in the NVIVO-PROJECT
	FOLDER	A storage location for COMPONENTS
	CASE	CASES represent the units in an analysis and can have ATTRIBUTE-VALUES linked to them
	ATTRIBUTE-VALUE	A factual characteristic about the units in an analysis (e.g., respondents, organizations, events, artifacts, etc.) that can be linked to SOURCES or CASES
Conceptualizing data	REFERENCE	A defined segment of data that can be linked to NODES to produce a CODED-REFERENCE, commented upon in an ANNOTATION, and linked to other REFERENCES
	NODE	A named concept that can be linked to other COMPONENTS for either analytic or housekeeping purposes
	CODED-REFERENCE	A REFERENCE linked to one or more NODES
	QUERY-RESULT	The saved result of a query
	SETS & SEARCH-FOLDERS★	A shortcut collection of COMPONENTS. They can be created manually, as a result of running a query, or by searching for components that meet specified criteria
Writing	ANNOTATION	A comment linked to a REFERENCE
	MEMO	A piece of writing that can be standalone or linked to SOURCES, NODES, or REFERENCES
Visualizing	MAP★	A graphical space to display and work visually with COMPONENTS
	CHART★	A graphical display showing QUERY-RESULTS or the association between COMPONENTS

★At the time of writing, the Starter Edition of NVivo 11 for Windows does not include MAPS, and NVivo 11 for Mac and the Starter Edition of NVivo 11 for Windows do not include SEARCH-FOLDERS. In addition, the range of CHARTS available varies according to platform and NVivo edition.

Tools

In the *Five-Level QDA* method a TOOL is the combination of a COMPONENT and an action appropriate for a specific ANALYTIC TASK. There is no definitive list of TOOLS because there are so many ways of acting on each COMPONENT and so many possible ANALYTIC TASKS and contexts. No benefit would be served by attempting to list hundreds of TOOLS, even if such a list were possible.

The NVivo Interface

We begin with the program interface as a whole. The NVivo interface is modeled on Microsoft Outlook and is therefore familiar to Windows users. The Mac version looks similar. The NVivo screen has four main elements:

1. ***Navigation View.*** This groups the elements of your project into areas. Each area provides access to the COMPONENTS stored in that area.
2. ***List Views.*** The contents of the area within the Navigation View that is currently selected are listed. Each List View has columns showing information about COMPONENTS.

3. **Detail View.** Opening a COMPONENT from the List View displays its content in tabbed windows. These can be undocked and then moved around the screen as convenient.
4. **Menu tabs and associated ribbons.** The ribbon displays the relevant toolbar for whichever menu tab is selected. Additional menu tabs appear when particular COMPONENTS are open in the Detail View.

There is enormous flexibility in arranging the screen to suit your preferences and the needs of any project, and it is simple and intuitive to open and arrange the screen elements. In general there are two main ways to take actions: First, by clicking on a main menu tab to reveal its ribbon, and then choosing an option. Second by right-clicking anywhere on the screen. If a context menu comes up, options will be available to take an action on whatever you right-clicked on. In addition, when content is displayed in a Detail View, there are tabs down the right-hand side where content can be visualized in different ways.

Figure 5.1 illustrates the four main elements of the screen for NVivo for Windows, and Figure 5.2 illustrates the four main elements of the screen for NVivo for Mac. Now that we have introduced you to NVivo, we invite you to go to the companion website to view the first *Component Orientation* video: *The NVivo interface.* This video demonstrates how to work with the four main elements and navigate around the screen.

The NVivo Project

All the work that you do within NVivo on a research project is contained within a single file. The only exception is when linking to files or websites or when working with large multimedia files that are stored in a location of your choice outside the program, which NVivo accesses separately. Other than this exception, NVivo takes care of everything from within the program.

You begin by opening NVivo, and on the opening screen you see all the projects you have been working on. From this screen you have the opportunity to do several things:

- Create a blank project
- Open a sample project
- Copy a project to back it up
- Change or reset Application Options
- Access the Help Menu and online content provided by the developers

Once you open a project or create a new one, you enter the NVivo main screen to view your project, as illustrated in Figure 5.1 for the Windows editions and Figure 5.2. for the Mac version. Throughout the book we use the term "project" for your research study, which means your project at the strategy levels. NVivo also uses the term "project" for your NVivo project at the tactics levels, which you work on within the program. We therefore call this the NVIVO-PROJECT. The NVIVO-PROJECT file is stored wherever you choose to save it when you create it.

The next three sections describe several other aspects of an NVIVO-PROJECT. The NVIVO-PROJECT is not a COMPONENT in its own right, but the container for all the other COMPONENTS. There is therefore no *Component Orientation* video for this topic on the companion website.

Importing Data to an NVIVO-PROJECT

When you import data such as a Microsoft document or a PDF file into your NVIVO-PROJECT, NVivo makes a copy of it within the NVIVO-PROJECT. Your original copy of the data file is unaffected by this, and it remains where it is, unchanged and no longer needed by NVivo.

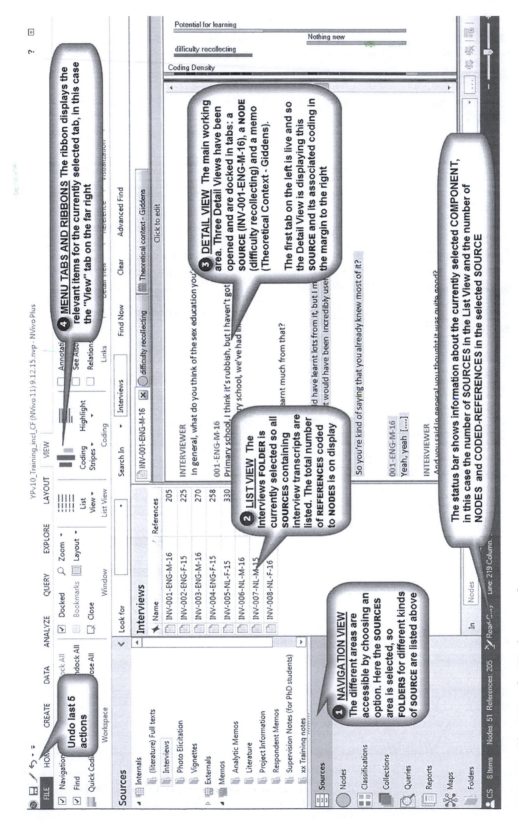

FIGURE 5.1 The NVivo for Windows interface

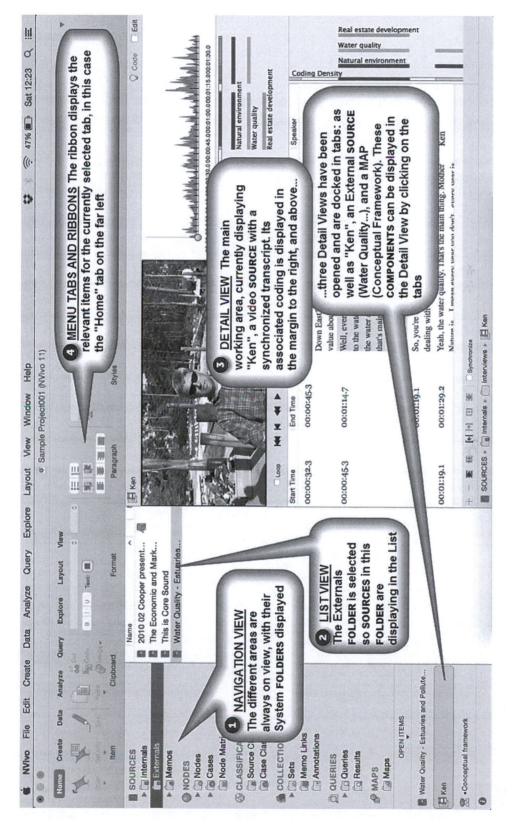

FIGURE 5.2 The NVivo for Mac interface

One exception to the usual practice of importing data is asking NVivo to *link* to any large multimedia files stored on your hard drive, rather than *copy* enormous files into the NVIVO-PROJECT. If you do link multimedia documents to an NVIVO-PROJECT, you must be sure not to move these files or edit them outside NVivo; otherwise, the program will no longer be able to find and display them in its workspace. This is the same commonsense principle that applies to other external links within your data files, such as webpages and other files on your computer. If the link is changed or broken, naturally NVivo cannot access it. Further details about preparing data files and importing them into the NVIVO-PROJECT are discussed in the section "Providing Data."

Backing Up an NVIVO-PROJECT

You may be concerned with backing up your NVIVO-PROJECT. As it is just one file, this is straightforward. You can either find it on your computer hard drive and then copy and paste it into a new location and change its name, or you can use NVivo's Copy Project feature, which will do the same. If you have linked to external files, however, you will need to ensure that those files are also copied to the same new location if you need the links to work when opening the copied NVIVO-PROJECT. Further details about backing up and moving NVIVO-PROJECTS appear in the section "The NVIVO-PROJECT as a Whole."

One NVIVO-PROJECT per Research Project

Each NVIVO-PROJECT is self-contained and does not communicate with any other NVIVO-PROJECT. It is therefore not possible to conduct any analytic activities across different NVIVO-PROJECTS. The usual way to proceed is to have one NVIVO-PROJECT for each research project, no matter how large it is or how many different people are working on the project. If a research project has several separate parts, there are many ways inside NVivo to focus on just a part of the project or temporarily hide parts. It rarely makes sense to divide a project into parts and create a separate NVIVO-PROJECT for each part. Very little would be gained, and potentially a lot of opportunity to review other parts of the project while working on a different part would be lost. Likewise, the opportunity to later compare or cross-analyze between parts of the project, something you might not have anticipated at the beginning, would be lost.

Unless you are working with NVivo for Teams, NVivo is a single-user program. This means that in team projects each team member has their own copy of the NVIVO-PROJECT to work on in their own copy of the program, and these copies are periodically merged. Each team member will be assigned certain tasks, which we discussed in Chapter 4 as the human aspect of working in teams—*who does what*. Even though it is likely that each team member will be analyzing only part of the data, it still makes sense in almost all circumstances to have a single NVIVO-PROJECT for the entire research project. This is because NVivo makes it easy to focus on just some parts of an NVIVO-PROJECT, and there is no reason to sacrifice a view of the whole project in a single NVIVO-PROJECT just because each team member is working on only a part. The technical aspects of working in teams—*integrating each team member's contribution*—are discussed in detail in the final section of this chapter, "Working in Teams."

Providing Data

When some or all of the data are available to be analyzed, it is time to provide it to the NVIVO-PROJECT. Four of the 13 COMPONENTS are most closely associated with this activity, displayed in Table 5.3.

TABLE 5.3 Components most associated with providing data to an NVIVO-PROJECT

Components	Definition
SOURCE	A data file in the NVIVO-PROJECT
FOLDER	A location where COMPONENTS are stored
ATTRIBUTE-VALUE	A factual characteristic about the units in an analysis (e.g., respondents, organizations, events, artifacts, etc.) that can be linked to SOURCES or CASES
CASE	CASES represent the units in an analysis and can have ATTRIBUTE-VALUES linked to them

Sources

SOURCES are the data that you work with inside an NVIVO-PROJECT. NVivo uses the term "document" to refer to text files that originate as Microsoft Word files or similar, for example text-only or rich-text-format files. We use SOURCE throughout this chapter, and because NVivo sometimes uses the term "document," we no longer use it for the data files you have created and saved on your computer, network, a memory stick, etc. Instead we use terms that refer to the type of data file we are discussing, such as Microsoft Word files, digital photographs, video files, or Microsoft Excel spreadsheets. When talking generically we refer to the computer files containing your data simply as *data files*, or just *data*, or just *files*.

NVivo provides four areas for storing different types of SOURCES: Internals, Externals, Memos, and Framework Matrices. SOURCES can generally be treated in the same way whichever area they are stored in—for example, all types of SOURCE can be coded, annotated, searched, etc., but SOURCES stored in each area are provided to the NVIVO-PROJECT differently. The areas for storing SOURCES are listed in Table 5.4.

MEMOS are a type of SOURCE and are stored in their own area, but because they are most closely associated with the activity of writing, we discuss them in that section on page 100.

Ways to Provide Data

NVivo offers three ways to provide data to an NVIVO-PROJECT: *importing* files, *linking* files, and directly *creating* SOURCES. You can provide as many data files as you want: there is no limit. And you can do so at any time—all at once at the beginning or some initially and others later.

TABLE 5.4 Areas for storing NVivo sources

Area	Types of Source
Internals	SOURCES imported into NVivo. Unless you leave large multimedia files "not-embedded," importing creates a copy of the original within the NVIVO-PROJECT.
Externals★	Empty SOURCES created within the NVIVO-PROJECT that links to an externally stored file or website. Notes about the external file can be written in the SOURCE inside the NVIVO-PROJECT.
Memos	SOURCES in which to write about any aspect of your project.
Framework Matrices★	Tabular SOURCES displaying CASES as columns and themes as rows in which summaries of linked data can be written.

★At the time of writing the Starter Edition of NVivo 11 for Windows does not include Externals, and NVivo 11 for Mac and the Starter Edition of NVivo for Windows do not include Framework Matrices.

Importing data copies the information in the original files into SOURCES within the NVIVO-PROJECT. After data have been imported, the original files are no longer needed by NVivo. The way data are *imported* and displayed within NVivo depends on the type, and the different versions vary in the types of files that can be imported. More types may be added by the software developers in future updates, so here we list all the types of data files that can be imported irrespective of the NVivo version. Check the QSR International website for up-to-date information on file types that can be imported into the different versions: www.qsrinternational.com/product/product-feature-comparison.

- **Importing text files.** NVivo accepts text files in all common formats—Microsoft Word files, rich text format, text only, and PDF files. NVivo copies text files and creates its own versions within the NVIVO-PROJECT that are then displayed as SOURCES.
- **Importing image files.** Image files in a variety of formats can be imported into an NVIVO-PROJECT. An image SOURCE can optionally be associated with a written log in which the whole image or parts of it can be written about.
- **Importing data from spreadsheet files.** Data files in Microsoft Excel, CSV, or TXT format can be imported into NVivo as dataset SOURCES. These display in the NVIVO-PROJECT as a table, similar to how they look in Microsoft Excel.
- **Importing data from SurveyMonkey or Qualtrics.** To import data directly from SurveyMonkey or Qualtrics, you first link a SurveyMonkey or Qualtrics account to NVivo. The import process extracts the information into SOURCES, NODES, and ATTRIBUTE-VALUES within the NVIVO-PROJECT according to the criteria you specify.
- **Importing bibliographic files.** Collections of references exported from bibliographic software programs such as Endnote, RefWorks, Zotero, and Mendeley can be imported into an NVIVO-PROJECT. The information in the files are extracted and imported as SOURCES, MEMOS, and ATTRIBUTE-VALUES according to the criteria you specify.
- **Importing notes files and emails.** To import data directly from OneNote or Evernote, you either connect to your OneNote or Evernote account using the NVivo add-in, or you export material from OneNote or Evernote and then import it into the NVIVO-PROJECT as a SOURCE. Microsoft Outlook emails can also be imported as SOURCES, along with any email attachments.
- **Importing webpages and social media data.** NCapture is an Internet browser add-on that allows you to capture web content in formats that NVivo can easily import—either as PDF files or special dataset files designed for NVivo.

In addition to importing data, some files can be *linked* to from within the NVIVO-PROJECT:

- **Linking audio and video files.** If you work with large audio or video files, although you *import* them, they actually remain "not-embedded," meaning they are not contained within the NVIVO-PROJECT but are linked to from within it. NVivo accesses the linked files from wherever they are stored on your computer hard drive and displays them in the NVIVO-PROJECT. Once a file is linked, you must not move or edit it outside NVivo, or it can no longer be located by the program or worked with inside the NVIVO-PROJECT.
- **Audio or video files synchronized with their transcripts.** This kind of linking takes place within the NVIVO-PROJECT. The transcripts of audio or video files can be associated with their corresponding media file by inserting timestamps—either manually or by importing a transcript that has timestamps in it that link up with the media file. As you move through either the text or the media SOURCE, the associated transcript follows in sync, highlighting the parts of the transcript that correspond to the portion of the media file being played.

- *Linking to files from External SOURCES.* An empty SOURCE stored in the Externals area can be linked to any file on your computer hard drive or any website.

Finally, SOURCES can be directly created within the NVIVO-PROJECT:

- *Creating empty SOURCES within NVivo.* A new empty SOURCE can be created inside the NVIVO-PROJECT and data typed or pasted in.
- *Creating Framework Matrices.* Tabular SOURCES can be created in the Framework Matrices area that are made up of rows of CASES and columns of NODES. The cells in the table can be linked to coded data and summaries written about each CASE/NODE intersection within the table.

Organizing Data into Sources

There are many possible ways to organize the information in your data files before adding them to the NVIVO-PROJECT. For example, if you are interviewing 10 participants three times each, you could make one Microsoft Word file for the transcript of each interview, leading to 30 SOURCES in all. This would be the most straightforward way to organize the data. Or you could have one Microsoft Word file for each participant and put each participant's three interview transcripts all in one file, leading to 10 SOURCES in all, one per person. The way you organize the data into files before adding them to the NVIVO-PROJECT affects whether or not you can SELECT or CONSTRUCT TOOLS that act on SOURCES to fulfill a particular ANALYTIC TASK. For example, if the purpose is to compare each participant's first interview with their last, and each participant's first, second, and third interview are all in one SOURCE, you could not use SOURCE-level TOOLS for this purpose. However, there will always be other ways to accomplish the same task, albeit less conveniently, and so the organization of the data is never critical, but more a matter of convenience. Nevertheless, to allow the most efficient use of the program, it makes sense to think about your research objectives when organizing data files before you add them to the NVIVO-PROJECT. Once you have finished studying this chapter and have the broad overview of the whole program, it will be possible to make informed decisions about the most efficient way to organize data into SOURCES.

In general you only have one opportunity to organize the data before adding the files to the NVIVO-PROJECT and they become SOURCES. This is the only area of NVivo that is fixed—everything else can be changed easily at will. There is one exception that is discussed in the next section—text SOURCES are editable within NVivo and so can be changed after they have been added to the NVIVO-PROJECT. All other kinds of SOURCES, including PDF SOURCES, cannot be edited or changed within NVivo.

Editing Text Sources

If you later realize after importing text files to the NVIVO-PROJECT that there would have been a more convenient way to organize the data into SOURCES, it is possible to edit the text. Therefore in theory it is possible to reorganize a whole set of SOURCES by cutting and pasting text from one to another. In practice this is not a common solution because it is almost always easier to SELECT or CONSTRUCT alternative TOOLS to fulfill a task in a different way. Editing SOURCES is usually adopted for smaller tasks than reorganizing the data.

Many researchers are uncomfortable with changing or editing the data. But there are many housekeeping as opposed to analytical purposes for SOURCE editing, such as removing inadvertent identifying information from transcripts, correcting transcription errors, or appending new data to a SOURCE such as new online discussion forum data.

Exploring Sources

Once files have been added to an NVIVO-PROJECT, a common first step is to explore the SOURCES. In the most general sense this means looking for what is in the data prior to identifying and conceptualizing data segments, but exploration is also undertaken throughout a project. Exploring is different from interrogating, discussed later, which is asking questions about what has already been done in order to move to the next step.

At the strategy levels *exploring data* has different meanings depending on the methodology. Some methodologies seek clear-cut, descriptive accounts of content, and the resulting ANALYTIC TASKS may include careful reading of the data as well as various counts of its content. For methodologies that are more concerned with the interpretation of lived experience, exploration is an interpretive process of sense making before segmenting or conceptualizing the data. And other methodologies are between these extremes. In Chapter 6 we discuss a variety of ANALYTIC TASKS whose purpose is exploration. In this chapter we are concerned with the mechanisms of exploring SOURCES that will be useful in a variety of ANALYTIC TASKS. NVivo offers the following features for finding, searching, and counting the content of SOURCES:

- **Searching a SOURCE.** A SOURCE that is displayed in the Detail View can be searched for any contiguous sequence of characters, whether a whole word or part of a word. The "hits" are shown in their location within the SOURCE.
- **Searching across SOURCES and auto-coding.** The Text Search Query finds any sequence of characters, whether a whole word, part of a word, a phrase, or a selection of related words in selected SOURCES. The results can be auto-coded and the resulting CODED-REFERENCES can then be accessed and worked on later. Auto-coding is discussed further in the section on conceptualizing data.
- **Counting and visualizing words.** The Word Frequency Query counts the number and percentage of each word in SOURCES and offers a variety of settings and options for visualizing, coding, and outputting the results.

Figure 5.3 illustrates how SOURCES appear in NVivo. We now invite you to go to the companion website to view the *Component Orientation* video for this COMPONENT.

Folders

FOLDERS are storage locations for COMPONENTS that can be acted upon as groups. Each area in the Navigation View has a number of system-defined FOLDERS appearing at the top level, which cannot be deleted or renamed. For example, the Sources area has system folders called Internals, Externals, Memos, and Framework Matrices, and the Classifications Area has system folders called SOURCE Classifications, CASE Classifications, and Relationship Types.

Sub-FOLDERS can be created under most system folders to manage COMPONENTS. For example, you may create sub-FOLDERS under the MEMOS FOLDER to store different types of writing, such as Project Information, Respondent Memos, Analytic Notes, Thesis Chapters, etc. The substructure that you create can be revealed and hidden, and you can rename, copy, move, and delete the sub-FOLDERS you create at any time. In addition, you can move COMPONENTS between FOLDERS of the same type. The sub-FOLDER structure need not be complicated but can instead represent simple descriptive groupings so that you can find COMPONENTS quickly and easily.

Each COMPONENT should only be stored in one FOLDER; otherwise, there will be multiple versions of the same COMPONENT, and then you will have to do everything on all versions to keep everything up to date. SETS & SEARCH-FOLDERS are shortcuts to COMPONENTS rather than duplicates and therefore provide alternative ways of grouping COMPONENTS outside of their FOLDER locations. Therefore this restriction of FOLDERS is unproblematic. We discuss SETS & SEARCH-FOLDERS later.

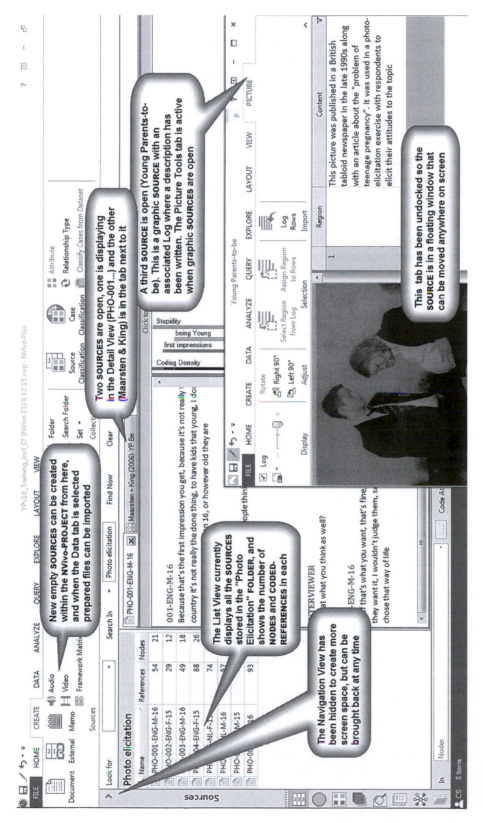

FIGURE 5.3 SOURCES

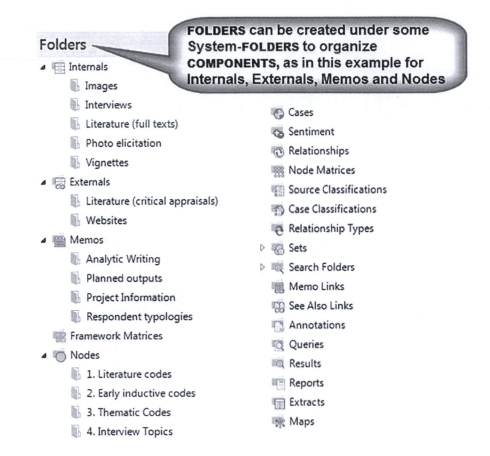

FIGURE 5.4 FOLDERS in the different versions and editions of NVivo

Figure 5.4 illustrates how FOLDERS appear in NVivo.

Cases

CASES are used to represent the units that make up your research project when those units are not equivalent to whole SOURCES. You may not need to use CASES; it depends on the design of your project. Deciding whether you need to use CASES involves identifying the units in your project and the factual characteristics about them that you need to interrogate. There are many different possible units in research projects—for example, respondents, groups, organizations, settings, events, etc.—and we discuss these in Chapter 6. If you are interviewing or observing people, then respondents or participants will likely be a unit. But there may also be other units in your project. For example, if interviewing teachers from several schools in two districts, you may have the additional units of "schools" and "districts." Units are important for two reasons: First, because in order to make comparisons on the level of units, they need to be represented in your NVIVO-PROJECT as SOURCES or CASES. Second, because factual characteristics about units—for example, the gender, age or role of respondents, the type and location of schools, etc.—can only be linked to SOURCES or CASES. This is accomplished using ATTRIBUTE–VALUES, which we discuss in the next section. First, we discuss the different ways of representing units in your NVIVO PROJECT so you can think through whether you need to use CASES.

Sometimes the SOURCES you have in a project are equivalent to the units you need to represent. For example, when doing a literature review and full-text journal articles have been imported into the Internals FOLDER, each SOURCE will represent the unit of an "article." Similarly, in an interview study in which each respondent has been interviewed once, each transcript would likely be imported as a separate SOURCE, so each SOURCE would represent the unit of a "respondent." However, some research designs are more complex, and the SOURCES you work with are not equivalent to the units that you need to represent. Focus group transcripts are one example where it is typical to have one SOURCE per focus group transcript. But if you need to differentiate between the male and female participants within the focus group, you cannot do this on the level of the whole SOURCE because several participants are represented within the SOURCE. Another example is a project in which each respondent provides data from several different data collection methods—perhaps each respondent has filled out a survey and taken part in an interview. In this situation data from each respondent are contained in more than one SOURCE, so an individual SOURCE cannot be used to represent that respondent as a whole unit. In these situations you can use CASES to represent the units.

CASES, then, offer ways of splitting SOURCES when more than one unit is contained within them, as with focus groups. CASES also offer a means of combining whole or parts of SOURCES when data relating to a unit are contained within more than one SOURCE, as when the same respondent has been interviewed more than once. This brings together all the relevant data so that each unit— each CASE—can be worked with independently. The factual characteristics about the CASES can be recorded using ATTRIBUTE-VALUES, which we discuss in the next section.

CASES are a type of NODE in NVivo, meaning that data can be coded to them. This is the way that all the data relating to each unit are brought together. CASES can be created in three ways:

- **Create SOURCES as CASES.** Whole SOURCES can be created as CASES as part of the process of importing SOURCES—if you know at that point that you need them. Alternatively, CASES can be created out of SOURCES within the NVIVO-PROJECT at any time.
- **Create CASES out of parts of SOURCES manually.** Parts of SOURCES can be created as CASES by selecting the relevant parts and coding them to CASES manually.
- **Create CASES out of parts of SOURCES automatically.** SOURCES can be auto-coded to CASES according to formatted structures within them—either paragraphs or heading levels.

The way you create CASES depends on from where you are capturing data that relate to each CASE and the way SOURCES are formatted when transcribed. We discuss auto-coding using formatted structures later in the section "Manual Coding and Auto-Coding," page 88.

Figure 5.5 illustrates how CASES appear in NVivo. We now invite you to go to the companion website to view the *Component Orientation* video for this COMPONENT.

Attribute-Values

SOURCES and CASES can have characteristics called ATTRIBUTE-VALUES assigned to them that relate to the unit that the SOURCE or CASE represents. This might include, for example, the sociodemographics of respondents or file metadata such as the journal an article is published in, the year the article was published, and so on. Using ATTRIBUTE-VALUES you can also assign information to a CASE based on higher-level units of analysis, as discussed earlier where, for example, the respondents' school or district also needs to be compared.

In order to apply ATTRIBUTE-VALUES to SOURCES or CASES, you first create Classifications and Attributes. If the units you are classifying are equivalent to SOURCES, you use SOURCE Classifications, and if the units you are classifying have been created as CASES, you use CASE Classifications.

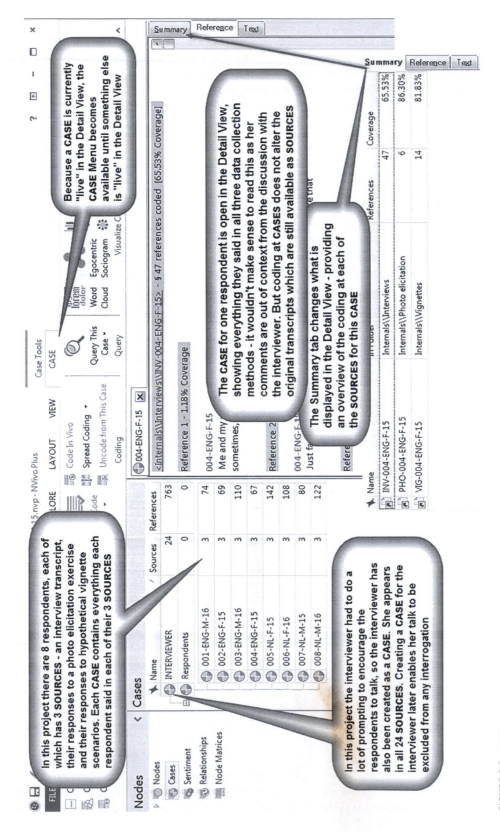

FIGURE 5.5 CASES

Classifications, Attributes, and ATTRIBUTE-VALUES are related to one another hierarchically, meaning that Classifications can have numerous Attributes, and Attributes can have numerous ATTRIBUTE-VALUES. Classifications are named to describe the nature of the entity being classified, for example, "respondents," "settings," "events," "articles," etc. Attributes are named to describe the characteristics of the units being classified. For example, Attributes relating to respondents may include "gender," "age," "occupation," etc. ATTRIBUTE-VALUES are the values of Attributes; for example, "male" and "female" are the values of the Attribute "gender," and "doctor" and "nurse" may be the values of the attribute "occupation."

Classifications are the overarching storage locations under which Attributes and then ATTRIBUTE-VALUES are created. Therefore you must create either a SOURCE or a CASE Classification and respective Attributes in order to apply ATTRIBUTE-VALUES to SOURCES or CASES. However, neither Classifications nor Attributes are COMPONENTS in our way of describing NVivo because you do not act upon them; they are simply ways of organizing the ATTRIBUTE-VALUES—which can be acted upon and therefore are COMPONENTS.

There are no fixed rules about when to use SOURCE Classifications or CASE Classifications, as it depends on where the units you want to classify are represented. However, if you are unsure how to proceed, the following may help get you started:

- SOURCE **Classifications** are often useful for capturing meta-information about documentary-type evidence where the entire SOURCE represents a unit in itself. Examples include SOURCES that are literature files, policy documents, newspaper articles, artifacts, etc. In addition, you may use SOURCE Classifications for interview-type data where each SOURCE contains one transcript, you have only interviewed each respondent once, and there is no need to differentiate what the interviewer said from what the respondent said.

- CASE **Classifications** will be needed when a SOURCE contains more than one unit to which factual information is relevant or where more than one SOURCE combines to represent one unit. Examples include interview data where there is a need to differentiate between when the interviewer and the respondent speaks; focus group discussions where several respondents participate, their sociodemographic characteristics are different, and these need to be recorded; and field notes where observations have been made about different settings, actors, or events. CASE Classifications are also required when data relating to the same case, setting, or event are contained within different sources.

The ATTRIBUTE-VALUES you assign to SOURCES or CASES are displayed in Classification Sheets, tabular displays that show the units being classified (i.e., named SOURCES or CASES) as rows and Attributes as columns, with the relevant ATTRIBUTE-VALUES in the appropriate cells. Applying ATTRIBUTE-VALUES to SOURCES and/or CASES sets up the possibility for grouping and querying on the basis of individual ATTRIBUTE-VALUES or combinations of them. However, note that specific types of coding queries that include ATTRIBUTE-VALUES are only enabled when CASE Classifications have been used, rather than SOURCE Classifications.

Figure 5.6 illustrates how ATTRIBUTE-VALUES appear in NVivo. We now invite you to go to the companion website to view the *Component Orientation* video for this COMPONENT.

Conceptualizing Data

Conceptualizing data is the most general way of describing what occurs in all kinds of qualitative analysis, regardless of the methodology. Five of the 13 COMPONENTS most closely associated with this activity are REFERENCES, NODES, CODED-REFERENCES, SETS & SEARCH-FOLDERS, and QUERY-RESULTS as explained in Table 5.5.

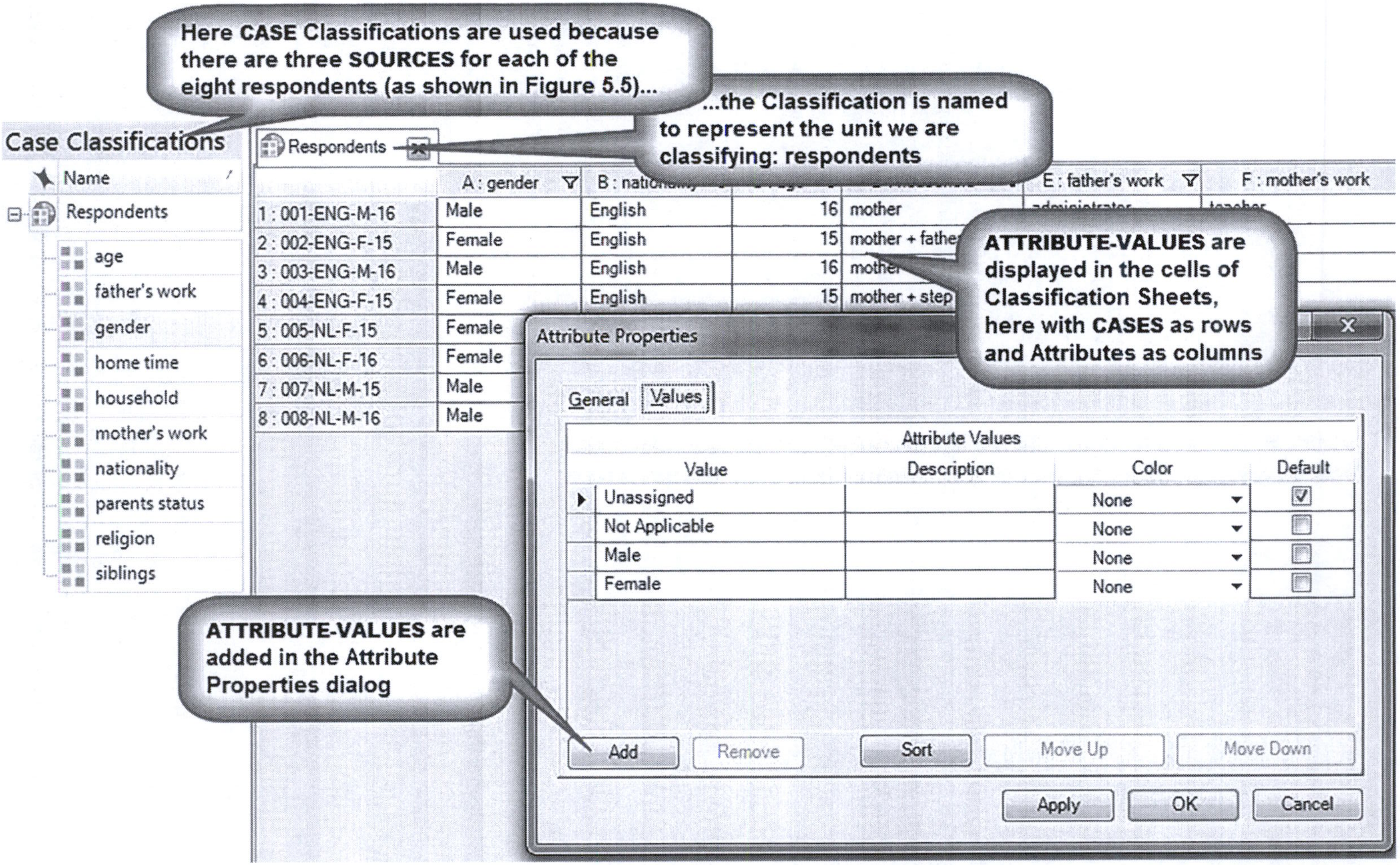

FIGURE 5.6 ATTRIBUTE-VALUES

TABLE 5.5 Components most associated with conceptualizing data

Components	Definition
REFERENCE	A defined segment of data that can be linked to NODES to produce a CODED–REFERENCE, commented upon in an ANNOTATION, and linked to other REFERENCES
NODE	A named concept that can be linked to other COMPONENTS for either analytic or housekeeping purposes
CODED–REFERENCE	A REFERENCE linked to one or more NODES
SETS & SEARCH–FOLDERS	A group of related COMPONENTS
QUERY–RESULT	The saved result of a query

References

A primary activity of many qualitative methodologies is to first explore the data and then identify and mark segments that are considered meaningful. In NVivo defined segments of data are called REFERENCES. REFERENCES can be identified in any type of SOURCE, but what they consist of differs according to the type of data. For example, REFERENCES in text SOURCES consist of stretches of text of any length, but in graphic SOURCES such as photographs or drawings, they consist of rectangular selections of parts of the image. The same applies to the text and embedded graphical parts of PDF documents and to Twitter, Endnote, and Evernote data. In audio and video files, REFERENCES may consist of a number of milliseconds of audio or frames of video. If you have synchronized a written transcript with the media file, REFERENCES can instead be created in the transcript and read when listening to the audio or viewing the video.

References Can Be of Any Size

There are no restrictions on the size of the REFERENCES that you chose to work with. They can be as small as one character of text, or even a single space, or at the other extreme as long as the entire SOURCE, which is useful for several specialized purposes. Almost all REFERENCES fall somewhere between these extremes. For example, when working with text data, REFERENCES may consist of a sentence or a few sentences, a short paragraph or a few paragraphs, but there are no rules: it depends on the nature of the data, the dictates of the methodology, and the purpose of the particular ANALYTIC TASK being undertaken.

The principles that apply to working with REFERENCES are the same whatever the form of the data. The only differences between using text, graphic, audio, or video REFERENCES are how they are presented on the screen, slight differences in the mechanics of operating the software, and the way REFERENCES are outputted once they have been linked to NODES.

References Can Overlap

There are no restrictions on the locations of REFERENCES in a SOURCE, meaning that REFERENCES can overlap one another in any way. One REFERENCE might comprise a large paragraph of text, and another REFERENCE might comprise just one sentence in the middle of the same paragraph. This second REFERENCE is technically completely unrelated to the first, even though the same lines of text appear in both the embedded and the enclosing REFERENCE. The smaller REFERENCE comprises a different and independent unit of meaning that serves a different analytic purpose than the REFERENCE comprising the entire paragraph.

A Reference Can Be Redefined at Any Time

A REFERENCE can be made larger or smaller at any time, in other words, resized to have different amounts of data associated with it. When working with text data, for example, it is common to reread a REFERENCE on screen and decide to extend its range in order to include the additional context in the following two or three sentences. Or you may decide to include the interview question that helps make sense of the response.

Pairs of References Can Be Linked

Any pair of REFERENCES can be linked together. This can be useful in many circumstances, for example, when two REFERENCES that are physically separated in the data comprise a single unit of meaning when linked, such as when the beginning and the end of a single story are recounted at different times in an interview. Linking REFERENCES to one another may also serve the purpose of tracking a process, a contradiction, or other meaningful associations among pairs of REFERENCES. Linking REFERENCES is not an alternative to coding, but instead is a separate task with different purposes.

REFERENCES can also be linked to MEMOS, external files, or webpages using hyperlinks. These sorts of links may serve many purposes. For example, linking a REFERENCE to a MEMO may be useful to connect a segment of data to your observations and insights about it. Linking a REFERENCE to an external file may be useful to illustrate a setting or environment discussed in the data. Linking REFERENCES to webpages may serve to provide easy access to the context about a service, policy, or event discussed in data. In addition, when working with Matrix Frameworks, text within a summary can be linked to the REFERENCE that is being summarized.

References Can Be Annotated

A REFERENCE can be commented upon using an ANNOTATION. This works similarly to how footnotes or comments work in Microsoft Word. We discuss ANNOTATIONS in more detail later, on page 100.

The Status of References

It is important to realize that REFERENCES are not independent objects in their own right. By this we mean two things. First, unlike most other COMPONENTS, there is no central location within NVivo where all REFERENCES are stored together. Second, although REFERENCES can be linked to MEMOS and other REFERENCES and commented upon using ANNOTATIONS, they cannot be lifted out of their SOURCE context unless they are linked to NODES, thus becoming CODED-REFERENCES. Therefore, strictly speaking REFERENCES are not COMPONENTS because they cannot be acted upon unless they have been linked to NODES. However, we think of them as COMPONENTS because the process of identifying meaningful chunks of data and working with them is central to qualitative analysis. Thinking about REFERENCES as if they were COMPONENTS is therefore key to learning to harness NVivo powerfully.

Figure 5.7 illustrates how REFERENCES appear in NVivo. We now invite you to go to the companion website to view the *Component Orientation* video for this COMPONENT.

Nodes

The term NODE in NVivo refers to any named concept that represents what is identified in the data as meaningful in relation to the project objectives. NODES can be linked to other COMPONENTS for various purposes, but before we describe these, we need to discuss codes and concepts and the difference between codes at the strategies levels and NODES at the tactics levels.

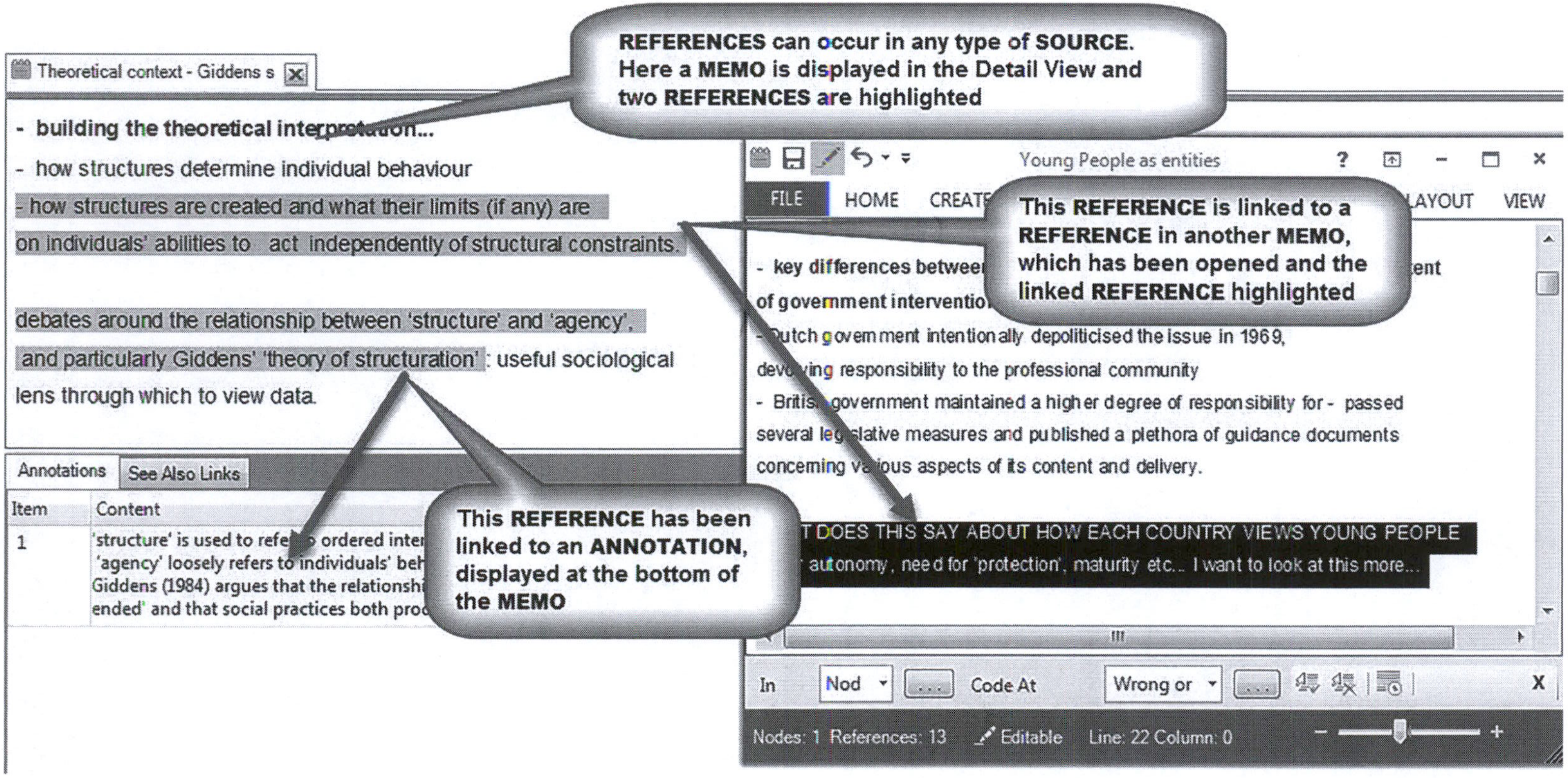

FIGURE 5.7 REFERENCES

Codes and Concepts

We use the term *concept* for the name and meaning of any collection of things (for a fuller discussion see page 37). In qualitative research, concepts are created and named to represent collections of data segments. This is part of the general process of reducing a large volume of unstructured data to a small and digestible number of related concepts that communicate the researcher's account of a whole body of data. The meaning of a concept is not fixed, but is emergent to varying degrees—its meaning evolves as more data are explored and associated with the concept. Most methodologies do not describe qualitative analysis as a basic conceptualizing process in this way, but rather they give different kinds of concepts specific names to communicate their purpose. Saldaña (2015) suggests that in "traditional approaches" to qualitative analysis there are four increasingly general kinds of concepts: *code*, *pattern*, *category*, and *theme*. A code is a word or short phrase that evokes an attribute of an item of data. Coding gives rise to recurring patterns, which are grouped and transformed into categories, and in turn grouped into themes that represent larger "implicit topics" (Saldaña 2015, p. 11–13). Saldaña (2015) notes that coding is definitely not the only way to conduct a qualitative analysis, but it is "one of the most frequently used methods, particularly for those undertaking grounded theory studies" (p. 12). Coding is also the basis for conceptualizing in other methodologies, such as qualitative content analysis. But coding plays a smaller role or comes into play much later in the process in the more interpretive styles of qualitative research such as discourse analysis and the various forms of phenomenology.

This does not even scratch the surface of the range of opinions on codes and coding as the basis of conceptualizing qualitative data. And every methodological text that does prescribe coding defines the nature and purpose of codes specifically for their methods of analysis. For those interested in coding as a method in itself, Saldaña's (2016) *Coding Manual for Qualitative Researchers* provides a resource of 32 distinct coding methods.

Codes at the Strategy Levels Are Different From Nodes at the Tactics Levels

This discussion of codes and coding refers to the strategy levels of the *Five-Level QDA* method. At the strategy levels a "code" refers to something different from one methodology to the next, with different types of codes serving different purposes. For example, in one style of grounded theory there are *open codes*, *axial codes*, and *selective codes* (Corbin & Strauss, 2014), and in another *open codes*, *focused codes*, and *theoretical codes* (Charmaz, 2014).

At the tactics levels, any of these types of code could be represented by several different COM-PONENTS in the software. It is true that one COMPONENT in NVivo—NODE—is most commonly used to represent codes at the strategy levels. But a code at the strategy levels is sometimes better represented by a different tactics-level COMPONENT, such as a MEMO or an ANNOTATION. Conversely, the COMPONENT in NVivo called a NODE can be used for housekeeping purposes unrelated to any conceptualizing activity involving codes and coding. Therefore, NVivo's use of the term NODE helps distinguish a code at the strategy levels and the use of a NODE at the tactics levels, which may be used to represent a code or be used for some other purpose. However, it is common for researchers not to think of a NODE in this way, but rather to assume a code and a NODE are one and the same, or in other words, to assume that NODE is just the name that NVivo uses to mean a code. This is not the case. This incorrect assumption can lead to One-Level QDA thinking, which conflates strategies and tactics into a single process of *what-you-plan-to-do-and-how-you-plan-to-do-it*. Researchers whose methods are not centered around codes and coding can then become concerned that NVivo is an unsuitable program for their projects. This is also not the case because methodologies that are not centered around codes and coding can TRANSLATE their

ANALYTIC TASKS into other COMPONENTS of the software for their purposes and do not have to use NODES in the software at all.

The conclusion is to note that a code is a concept at the strategy levels of a project, and a NODE is a COMPONENT at the tactics levels. Although it is common for a NODE to represent a code, it is most helpful to think of the two as separate and independent.

The Multiple Roles of Nodes at the Tactics Levels

Whereas there is only one kind of NODE in the software at the tactics levels, there are many different purposes for which these NODES are harnessed. Even though NODES are mechanical and always work in the same way, creating NODES must be a thoughtful and cautious process to ensure that they best serve the purpose of the project objectives. But because it is so effortless to create NODES, a common problem is uncontrolled NODE creation and the unfortunate question asked of research consultants: "I've created 300 NODES and coded my data. That was easy. What's next?" In *Five-Level QDA* terms this means the researcher has remained at the tactics levels rather than alternating back and forth between strategies and tactics and TRANSLATING between them. Often there isn't anything next other than recognizing that although a lot has been learned about the data from this uncontrolled coding, the resulting multiplicity of NODES has not been focused on fulfilling the needs of particular ANALYTIC TASKS, and the only practical way forward is either to start again or to engage in significant restructuring, grouping, and merging of codes to mold them into what is required at the strategy levels. To avoid this issue and keep the NODE-creation process intentional, it helps to think about four main purposes of NODES that are harnessed during TRANSLATION:

- *NODES **used for concepts.*** This is a very common use. NODES directly represent concepts in the data, and they are typically linked to REFERENCES to produce CODED-REFERENCES that are examples of the concept.
- *NODES **used for counting.*** NODES can be created specifically to count instances of meaning in data whenever there is a need to quantify. For example, in a video project studying nonverbal interaction, each use of a particular hand gesture could be coded with a NODE for that gesture in order to quantify its frequency. These NODES would be used for different purposes than other NODES used to conceptualize the types or other characteristics of gestures.
- *NODES **used for evaluation.*** A separate set of evaluative NODES can supplement concept NODES. This avoids having a single NODE serve two purposes and thereby reduce the power of later interrogations. If our bullying study is concerned with exploring the impact of bullying on aspects of self-esteem, we might create two kinds of NODES: evaluative NODES named *low, medium,* or *high impact* (to code for the degree of impact) and various self-esteem concept NODES.
- *NODES **used for housekeeping.*** NODES can serve administrative or organizational purposes. For example, at the end of a working day you may link a NODE named *where I am* to the last REFERENCE worked on—this allows you to jump straight there the next morning. Or a NODE named *good quote* might be linked to REFERENCES that are candidates for illustrating a concept in a report.

Nodes Must Be Organized

There is no set way to organize the list of NODES in NVivo. This is good, because everybody develops their own ideas about what it means to organize NODES based on how they like to work and the nature of their projects. The default listing of NODES in the List View is alphabetical, but they can also be sorted in various ways, for example, according to the number of REFERENCES that have so far been linked to them or the number of SOURCES in which they occur. Six increasingly sophisticated ways of bringing organization to NODES are listed next. However, sophisticated doesn't mean better. Each way of organizing NODES has advantages and disadvantages and is appropriate for different purposes.

- *Using prefixes.* The names of certain NODES can begin with a symbol, for example, *#Low*, *#Medium*, and *#High*. This draws attention to the specialized purpose or features of these NODES and causes them to sort together in the List View. Many groups of NODES serving different purposes can have names starting with their own symbol.
- *Using colors.* NODES can be given a color to draw attention to their purpose or particular features they might have or to indicate which team member uses which NODES, yet they can still all sort together alphabetically. The List View can be sorted according to color applied to NODES, and the margin area that displays NODES as they have been applied to CODED-REFERENCES can be filtered according to the color applied to NODES.
- *Using hierarchies.* A hierarchical structure of NODES can be created in the List View, such that NODES appear hanging under one another. NODES that have others hanging under them are called "Parent Nodes." Those underneath are called "Child Nodes." Parent NODES can be aggregated to gather up all the CODED-REFERENCES at the immediate Child NODES. Opening an aggregated Parent NODE retrieves all the CODED-REFERENCES at the Parent NODE and any of the Child NODES immediately underneath.
- *Using SETS & SEARCH-FOLDERS.* NODES can be grouped into shortcut collections called SETS & SEARCH-FOLDERS. These COMPONENTS are described further later.
- *Using relationships.* NODES can be linked together using a special kind of NODE, called Relationships. The nature of the link between the NODES is specified using a Relationship Type, for example, *is associated with, leads to,* or *is a property of.* Relationship NODES are stored in their own FOLDER and the NODES that form part of the Relationship also remain in the NODES List View. Because Relationships are a kind of NODE, REFERENCES can also be linked to them, so the evidence for each Relationship can be coded at and accessed from the Relationship NODE. In addition to linking NODES, Relationships can be used to link other COMPONENTS, for example, linking CASES can be used to record how respondents are related—"Nick *is married to* Sara" or "Christina *works with* Nick." Not all projects require COMPONENTS to be linked in this way, but if yours does, you can create as many Relationship Types as necessary.

Manual Coding and Auto-Coding

Creating NODES and linking them to REFERENCES is generally a manual process accomplished one REFERENCE at a time with a great deal of thought. But there can also be a role for auto-coding in which you instruct NVivo to find a string (for example, part of a word, a whole word, or a phrase) and automatically link the "hits" to a specified NODE. A helpful feature allows you to look for more than one word if you consider them synonyms in the data. In the bullying study you could ask the auto-coder to look for *bull* (to find *bullying, bullied,* etc.), but also *shov* (to find *shoved, shoving,* etc.) and *push* (to find *pushed, pushing,* etc.) Phrases can be used, such as *big bully*, if there is confidence the phrase would always appear exactly in that form.

Auto-coding is not a substitute for manual coding. One reason is that possible transcribing or spelling mistakes make searching for a specific sequence of characters unreliable. A more significant reason is that a particular sequence of characters will rarely identify a concept reliably. Although *bull* will find sentences containing *bullying* and *bullied*, it will also find *the teacher's ebullience made for a happy classroom*—not what we had in mind. Auto-coding is therefore most helpful for special purposes, such as the following examples:

- **Technical terms.** Often not much is learned just because a particular word is used in the data. But if technical or highly specific words do reliably indicate a meaningful response, then auto-coding is a useful timesaver.
- **First cut through data.** The use of certain words may point to an area of the data that merits further consideration. In these situations auto-coding based on this group of words and phrases can be used as a first cut through the data, followed by a second round of manual coding.
- **Earlier examples of a new NODE.** If a new NODE is created partway through a project, a choice has to be made about whether to go back to explore the already coded data for what the NODE represents. Depending on methodology, the new NODE could be ignored in the earlier data, or the earlier data could be entirely reread to find examples of the new NODE. Between these two extremes could be auto-coding the already coded SOURCES for all words considered synonymous with the new concept, with the hope that this locates most of the missed examples.
- **Exploring structure in the data.** In data with repeated structures, for example, multiple speakers in a focus group transcript, each individual's responses can be transcribed with identifiers to allow auto-coding for later interrogation of, for example, responses about certain issues by particular individuals, or just the females, etc. Any repeated structure in the data can be explored and captured with the auto-coder in this way, provided the data have been transcribed consistently. Transcribing data using consistent Heading Levels to indicate repeated structures are particularly powerful for this type of auto-coding.

The Plus Edition of NVivo 11 for Windows has three additional auto-coding features: theme-based auto-coding, auto-coding for sentiment, and auto-coding based on existing coding patterns. These features may be useful when working with very large sets of text data, but they should be used with extreme caution because you have very limited control over what the program identifies as a theme, a sentiment, or a pattern. Although these features may speed up coding, they are likely to capture text that is not interpretively meaningful, and the results always need to be carefully reviewed in order to determine their relevance for the ANALYTIC TASK. In addition, it is important to remember that these automatic tools may fail to capture relevant data. Even the NVivo developers caution you in their Help Menu to use these experimental features with care.

- **Theme-based auto-coding.** This feature in NVivo Plus analyzes SOURCES and suggests commonly occurring "themes." These "themes" are grouped into proposed Parent and Child NODES and sorted according to the frequency with which they are found. You then choose which of the identified "themes" to create as NODES and the amount of surrounding context to code, for example, the sentence or the paragraph. Technically this feature combines Word Frequency and Text Search querying to identify the "themes."
- **Auto-coding for sentiment.** This feature in NVivo Plus uses a predefined sentiment scoring system to categorize words according to whether they are "very negative," "moderately negative," "neutral," "moderately positive," or "very positive." REFERENCES containing expressions of sentiment according to this scale are automatically coded at special sentiment NODES. At the time of writing it is not possible to define or set your own parameters for what counts as an expression of each sentiment.
- **Auto-coding based on existing coding patterns.** This feature in NVivo Plus automatically applies NODES to uncoded SOURCES based on how other SOURCES have already been coded. It compares text passages in the uncoded SOURCES to those in the coded SOURCES, and if the content is similar, it will automatically code them to existing NODES.

Figure 5.8 illustrates how NODES appear in NVivo. We now invite you to go to the companion website to view the *Component Orientation* video for this COMPONENT.

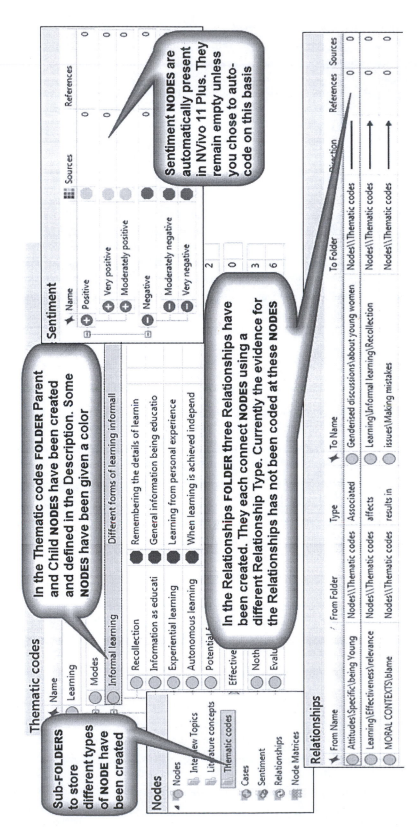

FIGURE 5.8 NODES

Coded-References

A CODED-REFERENCE is a REFERENCE that has been linked to a NODE. The same REFERENCE can be linked to any number of NODES. Just like REFERENCES, CODED-REFERENCES can be of any size, can overlap one another, and can be redefined at any time. CODED-REFERENCES can be created and worked with from CASES and NODES as well as SOURCES. This is because when a CASE or NODE is open in the Detail View, you are looking at and working with the original data, not a copy of it. This is useful in many situations. For example, if you have created a CASE to represent a particular respondent and you have coded all that respondent's data from several different SOURCES at that CASE, it may be that you want to analyze all that data together. You do not have to open up each of the SOURCES one by one, but instead you can open the CASE and work from there. All the options for searching, annotating, and coding can be undertaken from a CASE or a NODE as well as a SOURCE. This is a particular strength of NVivo.

Viewing Coded References

There are unlimited reasons for viewing and reading CODED-REFERENCES. A common reason is to view all CODED-REFERENCES for one NODE in order to read together all the different pieces of evidence for the concept reflected by the NODE. The purpose may be to assess the quality or validity of the coding or to assess the meaning or validity of the evolving concept reflected by the NODE.

There are three ways to view CODED-REFERENCES:

- *View CODED-REFERENCES out of context.* Opening a NODE or CASE retrieves all the CODED-REFERENCES linked to that NODE or CASE, displaying them in a Detail View without their surrounding context. This is useful when there is a need to focus only on the CODED-REFERENCES relating to a particular concept, represented by a NODE, or to a particular unit of analysis, such as a respondent, represented by a CASE.
- *View CODED-REFERENCES in context.* CODED-REFERENCES can be viewed on screen in context as a highlighted segment within a SOURCE, CASE, or NODE with their surrounding data visible above and below. This is useful for quick reviews of the data associated with a NODE or where reading data in context is important.
- *Extract and export.* CODED-REFERENCES can be extracted from their context for review outside of NVivo, for example, in a Microsoft Word, HTML, or PDF file. This is useful for reading and reflecting on a larger number of CODED-REFERENCES associated with a NODE, or perhaps a group of NODES. In addition to text, all graphical, audio, and video CODED-REFERENCES appear in outputted files that are saved in HTML format.

Figure 5.9 illustrates how CODED-REFERENCES appear in NVivo.

Retrieving Coded-References

A set of CODED-REFERENCES is often the final outcome of interrogating activities, meaning the many kinds of follow-up work on what has already been done. For example, the purpose of interrogation is often to seek a focused set of CODED-REFERENCES based on some combination of the NODES linked to REFERENCES. This provides a snapshot of your current thinking about a concept, or finds evidence for a concept, or helps understand the substance of a concept. Other interrogations of CODED-REFERENCES serve different purposes. For example, we mentioned earlier the "housekeeping" use of a NODE named *good quote* to code REFERENCES for potential inclusion in a report. The CODED-REFERENCES can be interrogated at any time for all examples of REFERENCES coded both to, say, *verbal bullying* and to *good quote*, and a list of the CODED-REFERENCES that qualify would be found.

Interrogating the NVIVO-PROJECT to produce CODED-REFERENCES can involve two general kinds of activities. The first is finding or getting a focused set of CODED-REFERENCES that meet a coding criterion, which is generally referred to as *retrieval*. The second is *counting* CODED-REFERENCES in various ways.

Simple and Complex Retrieval

NVivo retrievals can be either simple or complex. The simplest possible criterion by which CODED-REFERENCES can be retrieved is to get all the CODED-REFERENCES that have been linked to a single NODE. This software operation is performed extremely frequently in order to read and review the REFERENCES currently linked to a NODE. Once retrieved, the CODED-REFERENCES can be viewed in the ways described earlier. Figure 5.9 illustrates simple retrieval of all CODED-REFERENCES for one NODE.

Complex retrievals also produce a set of CODED-REFERENCES that meet a coding criterion, but they go beyond retrieving REFERENCES linked to a single NODE. Complex retrievals therefore play a major role in fulfilling the purposes of more sophisticated ANALYTIC TASKS. NVivo allows CODED-REFERENCES to be retrieved based on their coding to more than one NODE. This works by combining two or more NODES into a formula, referred to as a *query*, using operators. NVivo has three types of queries that allow complex retrievals of CODED-REFERENCES. These are in addition to the Text Search and Word Frequency queries discussed earlier, page 76, and the Group query and Coding Comparison query, both discussed later, pages 96 and 110.

- *Coding Query.* This query retrieves CODED-REFERENCES according to patterns in coding across or within SOURCES, CASES, or NODES.
- *Matrix Coding Query.* This query is a qualitative cross-tabulation that compares the occurrence of NODES, CASES, SOURCES, or ATTRIBUTE-VALUES in relation to one another and displays the results in a table.
- *Compound Query.* A Compound query combines a Text Search and Coding Query. For example, you can search for a word or phrase, but only in CODED-REFERENCES already linked to a particular NODE.

Six operators allow a wide variety of interrogations to be performed using queries. Operators fall into two types:

- *Boolean operators.* These are the straightforward logical operators, *OR, AND,* and *NOT.* The *OR* operator is the most expansive, retrieving all CODED-REFERENCES linked to *either* one NODE *or* another NODE *or* both. *AND* is the most restrictive, even though it sounds expansive. This operator retrieves CODED-REFERENCES linked to *both* one NODE *and also* another NODE. *NOT* excludes CODED-REFERENCES linked to a NODE.
- *Proximity operators.* These operators retrieve CODED-REFERENCES based on the proximity of one CODED-REFERENCE to another. There are three kinds of proximity: first, where CODED-REFERENCES are *NEAR* to one another (within a specified distance); second, where CODED-REFERENCES linked to one node *PRECEDE* CODED-REFERENCES linked to another NODE (again within a specified distance); third, where a CODED-REFERENCE linked to one NODE *SURROUNDS* a CODED-REFERENCE linked to a second NODE.

Queries can be scoped to SOURCES, FOLDERS, CASES, SETS & SEARCH-FOLDERS, and ATTRIBUTE-VALUES. The ability to retrieve CODED-REFERENCES based on both coding criteria and scoping greatly increases the range of analytic possibilities. A demonstration of the Query Wizard is included in the *Component Orientation* video for CODED-REFERENCES.

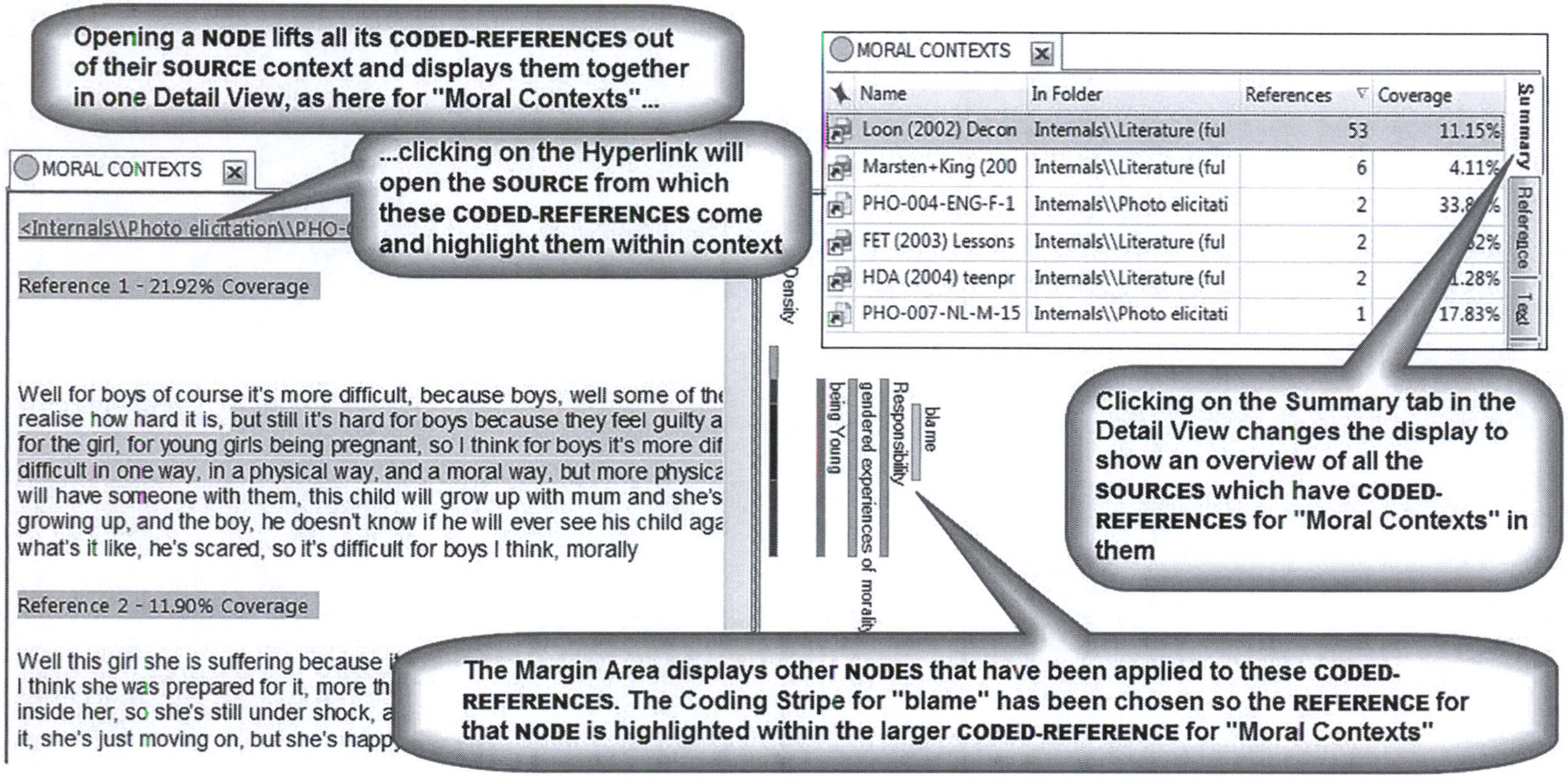

Name	In Folder	References ▽	Coverage
	MORAL CONTEXTS ☒	53	11.15%
Loon (2002) Decon	Internals\Literature (ful	6	4.11%
Marsten+King (200	Internals\Literature (ful	2	33.8%
PHO-004-ENG-F-1	Internals\Photo elicitati	2	.2%
FET (2003) Lessons	Internals\Literature (ful	2	
HDA (2004) teenpr	Internals\Literature (ful	2	.28%
PHO-007-NL-M-15	Internals\Photo elicitati	1	17.83%

Clicking on the Summary tab in the Detail View changes the display to show an overview of all the SOURCES which have CODED-REFERENCES for "Moral Contexts" in them

blame
Responsibility
gendered experiences of morality
being Young

The Margin Area displays other NODES that have been applied to these CODED-REFERENCES. The Coding Stripe for "blame" has been chosen so the REFERENCE for that NODE is highlighted within the larger CODED-REFERENCE for "Moral Contexts"

Opening a NODE lifts all its CODED-REFERENCES out of their SOURCE context and displays them together in one Detail View, as here for "Moral Contexts" ...

...clicking on the Hyperlink will open the SOURCE from which these CODED-REFERENCES come and highlight them within context

Density

	MORAL CONTEXTS ☒

<Internals\Photo elicitation\PHO-0

Reference 1 – 21.92% Coverage

Well for boys of course it's more difficult, because boys, well some of the
realise how hard it is, but still it's hard for boys because they feel guilty a
for the girl, for young girls being pregnant, so I think for boys it's more dif
difficult in one way, in a physical way, and a moral way, but more physica
will have someone with them, this child will grow up with mum and she's
growing up, and the boy, he doesn't know if he will ever see his child aga
what's it like, he's scared, so it's difficult for boys I think, morally

Reference 2 – 11.90% Coverage

Well this girl she is suffering because
I think she was prepared for it, more th
inside her, so she's still under shock, a
it, she's just moving on, but she's happ

FIGURE 5.9   CODED–REFERENCES

Sometimes a query is run once and then the task is complete. But sometimes a query will be useful again, for example, to later retrieve data meeting these criteria after additional coding has been undertaken. In this case the query can be saved for future use. Saved queries are listed in the Queries FOLDER and can be named, defined, edited, and rerun at any time.

Counting

Counting things is a major part of many projects and is valued by many qualitative researchers, but it is of less value or even contentious to others. For some methodologies the *frequency* with which certain words are used may be an indicator of meaning, or the *amount* of data associated with a code may indicate the salience or validity of a concept. For example, the count of the number of CODED–REFERENCES linked to each NODE might be used to identify NODES with fewer than, say, three CODED–REFERENCES in order to assess the salience of these infrequently expressed concepts. Conversely, this count may be used to identify and investigate all NODES linked to a single REFERENCE in order to seek out potentially discrepant cases, if this analytic activity is prescribed by the methodology. However, for other methodologies it is the *content* of the retrieved data that tells the researcher what is important rather than the *frequency* or *amount* of data having significance.

- *Counts of COMPONENTS.* Most COMPONENTS (but not FOLDERS, ATTRIBUTE–VALUES, and REFERENCES) have their own List View with the total number of items always displayed. These lists have columns displaying the counts of the COMPONENT's various characteristics. For example, the Node List has one column displaying the number of REFERENCES linked to each NODE and another column displaying the number of SOURCES in which each NODE appears.
- *Counts of CODED–REFERENCES.* Wherever a NODE is opened, all the CODED–REFERENCES linked to it are displayed. This view can be altered to show a Summary of the CODED–REFERENCES rather than the CODED–REFERENCES themselves. This Summary counts the number of CODED–REFERENCES at the NODE in each SOURCE and gives a percentage of 'coverage'—the proportion of the total SOURCE coded at that NODE.
- *Counts of QUERY–RESULTS.* All QUERY–RESULTS can be visualized in the Summary View, as described earlier, to provide basic frequency information. But Matrix Coding Queries always display the QUERY–RESULTS initially in a table that counts the CODED–REFERENCES, satisfying the intersection between each row and each column. The basis upon which the frequency is presented in each cell can be altered in several ways. For example, you can choose to count the number of words coded for text data at each intersection, the duration of CODED–REFERENCES for audio or video data in each intersection, or the number of SOURCES or CASES coded at each intersection. In addition, row and column percentages can be shown. Regardless of the frequency information provided in each cell of a Matrix Coding QUERY–RESULT, double-clicking on a cell always opens a Detail View displaying the CODED–REFERENCES that underlie the intersection.

Figure 5.10 illustrates a Coding Query, which is one way of generating complex retrievals of CODED–REFERENCES. We now invite you to go to the companion website to view the *Component Orientation* video for all aspects of this COMPONENT.

Query-Results

A QUERY–RESULT is the saved result of a query. The results of all queries except Word Frequency Queries can be saved as QUERY–RESULTS. The choices for how to save QUERY–RESULTS depend on the type of query. For example, QUERY–RESULTS from Coding Queries and Compound Queries can be

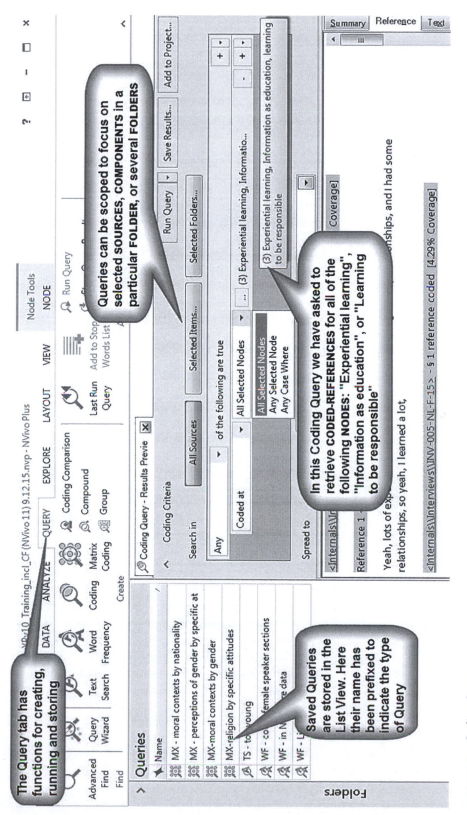

FIGURE 5.10 Coding Query

created as a new NODE, merged into an existing NODE, created as a new SET, added to an existing SET, or created as a new NODE hierarchy. In contrast, the QUERY-RESULTS of Text Search Queries can either be saved as a new NODE or be merged into an existing NODE.

The default location for saving QUERY-RESULTS is the Results FOLDER, but QUERY-RESULTS can also be saved in other FOLDER locations according to their type. For example, Matrix Coding QUERY-RESULTS can be saved in the Node Matrices FOLDER and the results of other queries in any FOLDER in the Nodes area. The location of QUERY-RESULTS affects what can subsequently be done with them. QUERY-RESULTS that remain in the Results FOLDER cannot be changed because they are saved snapshots of the results at the time the query was run. However, QUERY-RESULTS saved in other FOLDERS can be changed. For example, the size of the CODED-REFERENCES stored at these QUERY-RESULTS can be expanded to include more surrounding context, or CODED-REFERENCES can be removed. However, if new items that satisfy the criteria of a QUERY are added, already saved QUERY-RESULTS will not be updated. Therefore it is useful to save QUERIES so that you can rerun them easily to gain up-to-date results at any point.

When you run a query, you do not have to save the QUERY-RESULTS. The default option is to display results in the Detail View. This is useful when you need to check something out but are not yet ready to rely on the result, perhaps because you are still coding. Depending on the type of query, there are different options for how to view the results. For example, a Text Search query can be viewed in Summary View (listing all the SOURCES in which the searched-for words or phrases occur and the frequency of "hits"), in Reference View (showing each hit in its surrounding source context), in Text or PDF View (a combination of Summary and Reference View, showing each hit in each source separately), or in Word Tree View (displaying hits as a tree with branches showing the surrounding context).

Figure 5.11 illustrates how QUERY-RESULTS appear in NVivo. We now invite you to go to the companion website to view the *Component Orientation* video for this COMPONENT.

Sets *& Search-Folders*

SETS & SEARCH-FOLDERS are dynamic shortcuts to COMPONENTS, meaning that their members remain in FOLDERS but can additionally be accessed via SETS & SEARCH-FOLDERS. SOURCES, CASES, NODES, QUERY-RESULTS, MEMOS, and other SETS & SEARCH-FOLDERS can be added to a SET or SEARCH-FOLDER. Any one of these COMPONENTS can belong to any number of SETS & SEARCH-FOLDERS. We group SETS & SEARCH-FOLDERS as one COMPONENT because the actions that can be taken on them are the same; the only difference is how they are created.

SETS are shortcut groupings to any collection of COMPONENTS that you group together for an analytic purpose. There are many reasons for creating SETS manually. For example, you may create a SET for each research question and add the COMPONENTS that contribute to answering each question into its SET. Or you may create a SET called "codes I'm not sure about yet" and put all the NODES that need rethinking or refining into that SET to remind you to go back and consider them in more detail later. Or you may use SETS to gather the COMPONENTS you will use to write up each chapter or your thesis, or the different articles or other outputs you intend to write. There are unending purposes for creating SETS manually. In addition, you can create and populate a SET as one of the outcomes of running a Coding, Compound, or Group Query, to gather together all the COMPONENTS that satisfy that query.

SEARCH-FOLDERS are created using NVivo's Advanced Find feature to find COMPONENTS that meet one or more search criteria. There are a range of different criteria for finding COMPONENTS. You can choose from a set of predefined criteria or specify multiple criteria of your choice. Just like SETS, there are many reasons for creating SEARCH-FOLDERS. A common reason is to group

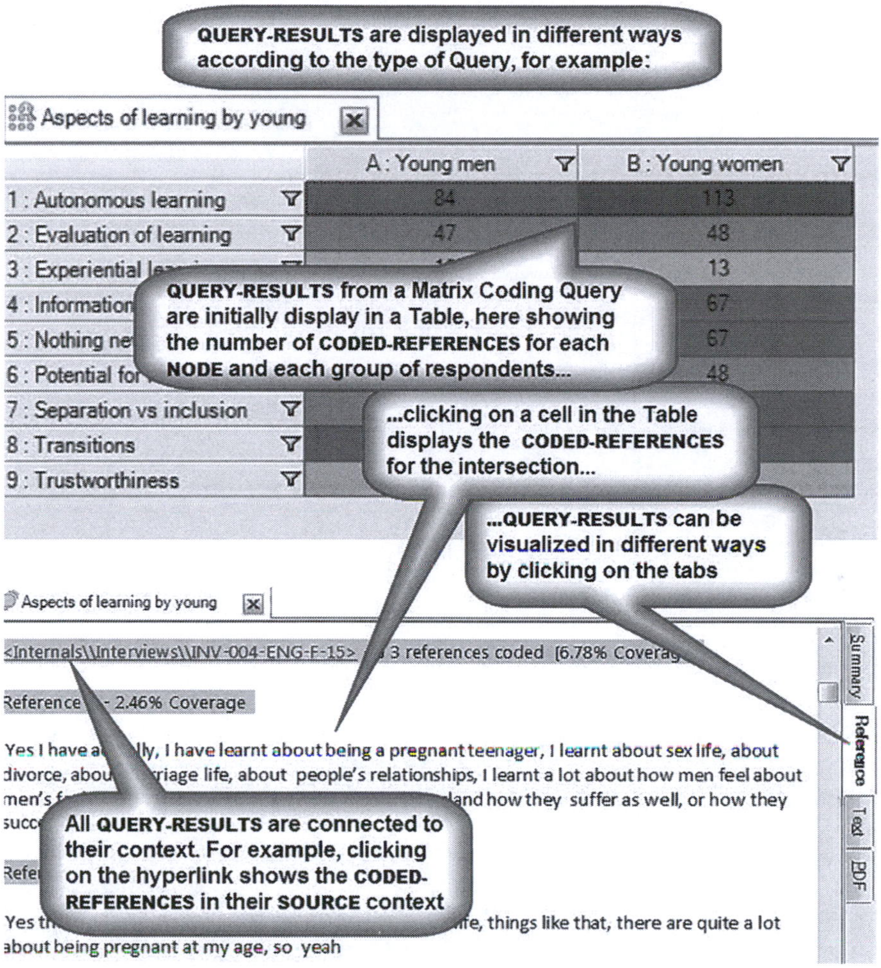

FIGURE 5.11   QUERY–RESULTS

SOURCES or CASES based on the ATTRIBUTE-VALUES applied to them—for example, journal articles published in a particular year or in a particular journal, or male focus group respondents living in New York City.

SETS & SEARCH-FOLDERS are powerful analytic entities for two reasons: First, because their creation and use do not affect the structures in place elsewhere in the NVIVO-PROJECT, meaning the FOLDERS that COMPONENTS are stored in. Second, because queries can be scoped to SETS & SEARCH-FOLDERS, meaning they provide ways of isolating subsets of data for interrogation purposes. Therefore SETS & SEARCH-FOLDERS are a flexible additional layer of organization that allow you to think about, focus on, query, and visualize groups of COMPONENTS. In qualitative analysis we need the flexibility to have an idea, run with it, and if it turns out to be a good idea, continue with it. But if the idea proves fruitless, we need to be able to drop it without damaging any other lines of inquiry. This is exactly what SETS & SEARCH-FOLDERS offer.

Figure 5.12 illustrates how SETS & SEARCH-FOLDERS appear in NVivo. We now invite you to go to the companion website to view the *Component Orientation* video for all aspects of this COMPONENT.

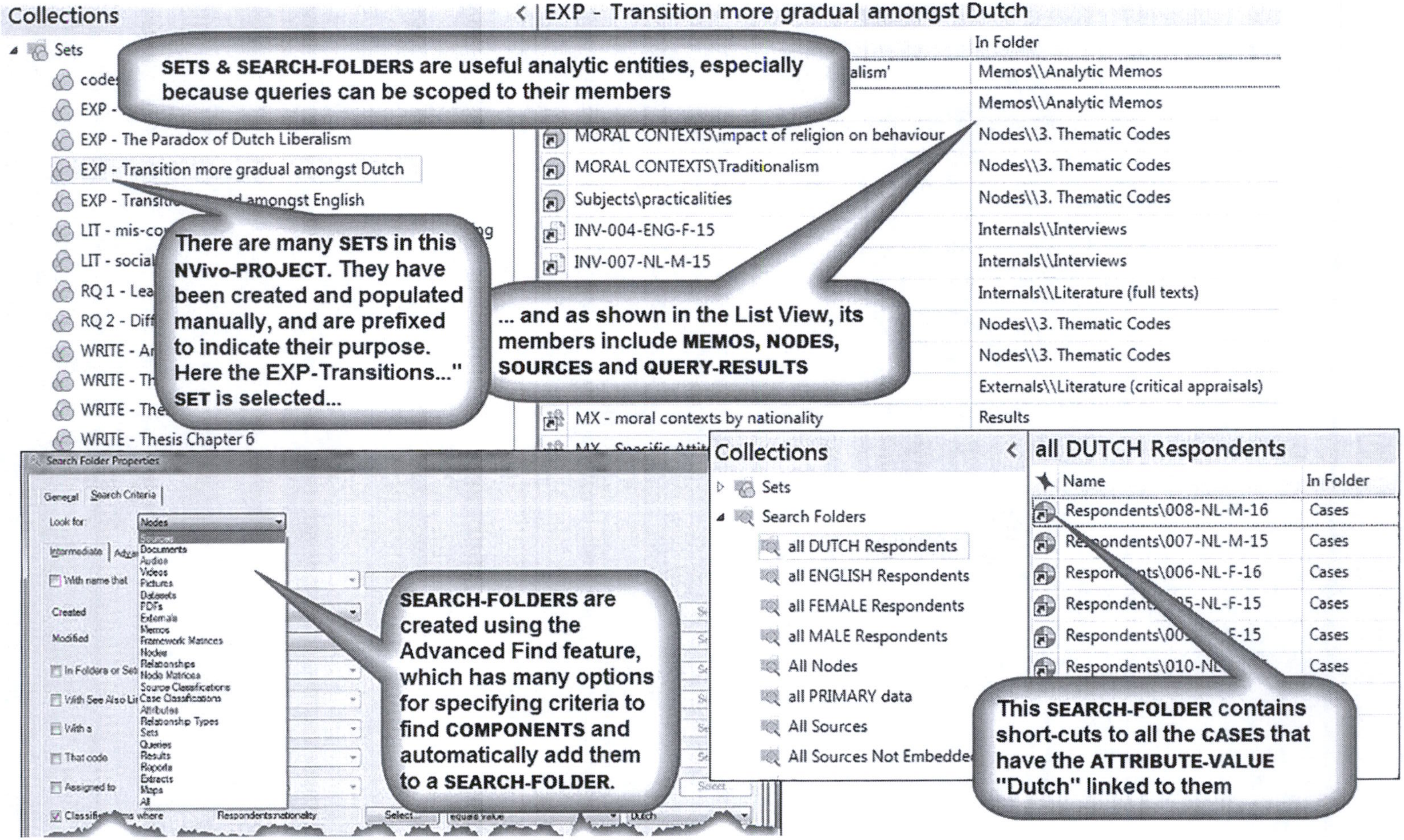

FIGURE 5.12 SETS & SEARCH-FOLDERS

TABLE 5.6 Components most associated with writing

Components	Definition
ANNOTATION	A comment linked to a REFERENCE
MEMO	A type of SOURCE in which you can write about anything.

Writing

Writing is central to qualitative research. NVivo makes it easy to capture all thoughts and insights in their appropriate context as they occur. Two of the 13 COMPONENTS most closely associated with this activity are ANNOTATIONS and MEMOS, displayed in Table 5.6.

All analytic activities in a qualitative project lead to the central activity of writing. Writing is best done at every step, not just at the end, in order to capture every thought, insight, interpretation, or new question about what is going on in the data analysis. Every methodology has its own recommendations about what, how, and when to write. Our philosophy is to think like an economist, from a purely cost–benefit point of view, and capture every stray thought that might bear on the data analysis. The greatest "cost" in qualitative analysis—meaning effort and time expended—is engaging your mind in making sense of a segment of data. What did the person mean by that statement? What does that image convey, and what does it hide? How does this unit of meaning support or contrast with the meaning of other parts of the data? Which ways of looking at this segment of data are most helpful for answering the research question? These significant mental acts bring to bear the researcher's entire lifetime of accumulated sense-making experience onto a single segment of data, what artificial intelligence cannot (currently) do as well. At the moment of sense making, valuable thoughts emerge that may contribute to the progress of the qualitative data analysis, and they should be captured then and there. The cost of writing down a thought already experienced is quite small, but the benefit of capturing it as soon as it is experienced is truly great—weeks later the thought will not be easily remembered, especially if subtle, and certainly not its location in the data. Real-time writing capitalizes on the significant mental investment we make in the sense-making process.

In addition to all this analytic writing, other kinds of writing are needed—writing about the methods you are using and the processes you are going through, summarizing or appraising previous literature about your topic, describing a respondent or case or situation, or keeping notes about discussions with supervisors or team members.

NVivo offers great flexibility in capturing all these kinds of writing in different spaces. For example, in addition to ANNOTATIONS and MEMOS, every COMPONENT has a Description field where a definition can be written. And as discussed earlier, text SOURCES can be edited, and Externals and Framework Matrices are special types of SOURCES for writing about data. The following two sections discuss ANNOTATIONS and MEMOS as writing spaces.

Annotations

ANNOTATIONS are not independent writing spaces, but an inseparable comment about a REFERENCE. Technically speaking, an ANNOTATION is not an independent COMPONENT. Although they are listed in their own folder in the Navigation View, ANNOTATIONS cannot be retrieved or outputted separately from the REFERENCES they are linked to.

Any REFERENCE can be selected from within any SOURCE, CASE, or NODE and be written about in an ANNOTATION, irrespective of whether that REFERENCE has also been linked to a NODE. REFERENCES that have ANNOTATIONS are highlighted in blue in the SOURCE and whenever else the REFERENCE is viewed, for example, in any Detail View. When generating an output file to view and work with

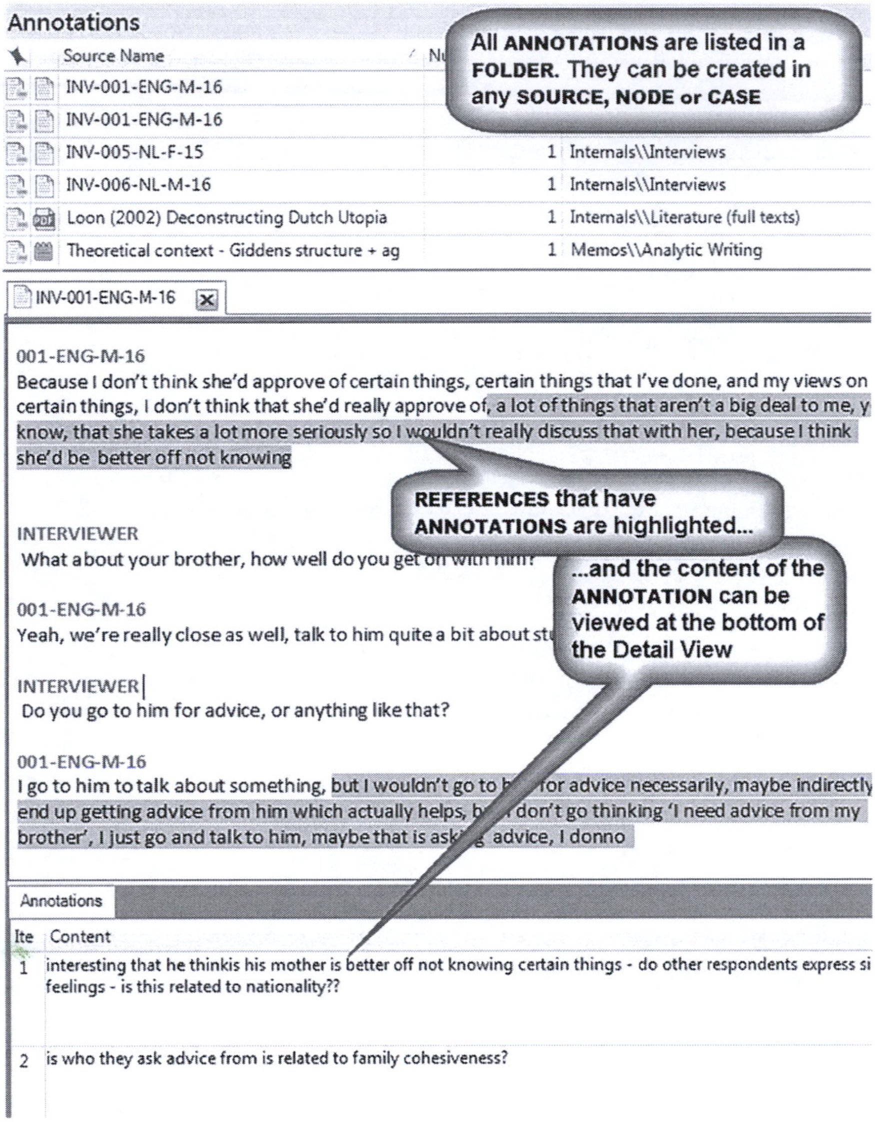

FIGURE 5.13 ANNOTATIONS

outside of NVivo, you have the option of including ANNOTATIONS as endnotes. However, in order to see REFERENCES and their ANNOTATIONS out of their data context, the REFERENCES must also be coded. It is therefore useful to create a housekeeping NODE to which all REFERENCES that have ANNOTATIONS are linked. This enables all REFERENCES and their ANNOTATIONS from anywhere in the NVIVO–PROJECT to be viewed together in one Detail View and outputted together.

Figure 5.13 illustrates how ANNOTATIONS appear in NVivo. We now invite you to go to the companion website to view the *Component Orientation* video for all aspects of this COMPONENT.

Memos

Most textbooks use the term *memo* to refer to all the kinds of writing we have been discussing. But NVivo uses this term for just one of the writing spaces in the program. To avoid confusion and to clearly distinguish strategies from tactics, we do not use the term *memo* at all at the strategy levels; instead we use *writing* with an appropriate adjective—*analytic writing*, *process writing*, and so on. At the tactics levels we use the term MEMO to refer to the NVivo writing space.

In contrast to ANNOTATIONS, MEMOS are independent pieces of writing, separate from the COMPONENTS you may be writing about. Think of them as a set of independent Microsoft Word files, except that they are named spaces inside the NVIVO-PROJECT. In fact, MEMOS are a type of SOURCE, stored in the Internals FOLDER. This means their content can be treated in the same way as the content of any other SOURCE. For example, their content can be coded, searched, and queried. A MEMO can contain text, images, or embedded tables, and each MEMO can be linked to one other SOURCE, NODE, CASE, or REFERENCE. Although MEMOS are SOURCES, we think of them as separate COMPONENTS, as their role in a research project is different from other types of SOURCES.

Each memo can be linked to one other SOURCE, NODE, CASE, or REFERENCE. This is one way in which your writing can be integrated with the data you are writing about.

Figure 5.14 illustrates how MEMOS appear in NVivo. We now invite you to go to the companion website to view the *Component Orientation* video for this COMPONENT.

Visualizing

Visualizing means working visually with COMPONENTS by displaying them graphically. The two COMPONENTS most closely associated with this activity are MAPS and CHARTS, displayed in Table 5.7.

Maps

NVivo's MAPS can be used for many kinds of visual interrogation. MAPS can be used as a working tool, integrated with the rest of the NVIVO-PROJECT, as well as an after-the-fact drawing feature to represent part of a completed project in graphical form. Any number of separate MAPS can be saved to display parts of the project in different ways. There are three types of MAPS in NVivo:

- **Mind MAPS.** These MAPS provide a space for brainstorming and visualizing ideas. COMPONENTS cannot be displayed or worked with in Mind MAPS, but the objects created within them can be turned into NODES. In this way Mind MAPS can function as spaces to graphically create a coding scheme, rather than doing so in the NODES List View.
- **Concept MAPS.** These MAPS are similar to Mind MAPS, but certain COMPONENTS can be visualized within them—SOURCES, NODES, CASES, RELATIONSHIPS, SETS, QUERY-RESULTS, and ATTRIBUTE-VALUES (but not REFERENCES, CODED-REFERENCES, OR ANNOTATIONS). Connections can be created between the abstract ideas represented by Shapes and the components visualized in a Concept MAP. At the time of writing Concept MAPS are only available in the Pro and Plus editions of NVivo 11 for Windows—not the Starter edition or NVivo 11 for Mac.
- **Project MAPS.** These MAPS are integrated with the rest of the NVIVO-PROJECT as they display COMPONENTS and visualize their associations with other COMPONENTS. For example, a Project MAP can be created to show which SOURCES are coded at a particular NODE, which COMPONENTS

TABLE 5.7 Components most associated with visualizing

Components	Definition
MAP	Graphical windows to display and work visually with COMPONENTS
CHART	Graphical displays showing the CODED-REFERENCES and the association of COMPONENTS to one another

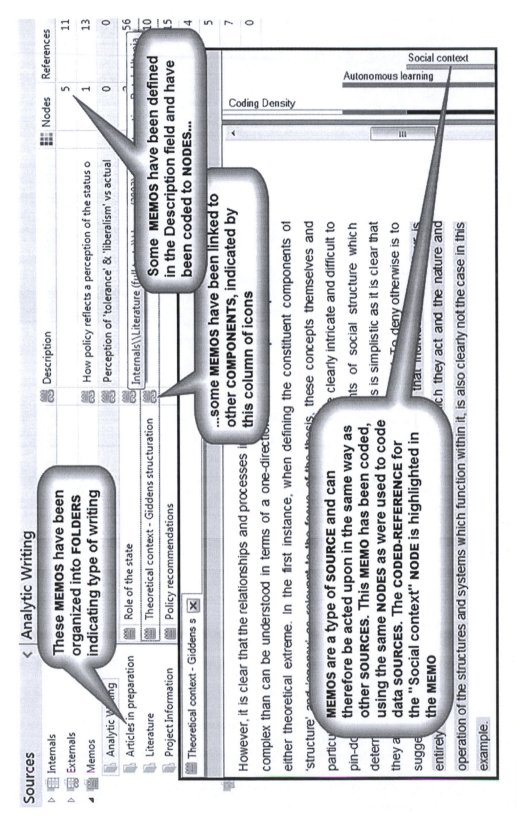

FIGURE 5.14   MEMOS

are members of a particular SET AND SEARCH-FOLDER, or which ATTRIBUTE-VALUES are associated with which CASES. In this way project MAPS can be used as interrogation tools, offering a visual way to interrogate patterns and relationships in data. At the time of writing Project MAPS are only available in the Pro and Plus editions of NVivo 11 for Windows—not the Starter edition or NVivo 11 for Mac.

One use of Concept and Project MAPS is to display NODES and link them to represent new or evolving ways of thinking about the related concepts in a project. NODES are displayed in these MAPS as individual circles that can be physically placed to represent their interrelationships. An advantage of working with NODES in these MAPS is that the associated CODED-REFERENCES for any NODE can always be accessed from within the MAP and browsed to in context. This allows you to remain close to the data while working conceptually with the NODES. There are many uses of MAPS of NODES, including:

- Displaying a typology of NODES to communicate the results of a content analysis
- Building a model of a social process
- Displaying an existing theory to visually contrast and link to NODES that represent emerging concepts identified in the data
- Developing an ongoing, freeform, organic concept model to represent an emerging set of findings as they become apparent
- Constructing a hierarchy of related concepts that can be turned into NODES for coding

To facilitate this visual working style, COMPONENTS can be connected to one another in Concept and Project MAPS. These connections can be labeled to represent the nature of the relationship between the connected COMPONENTS, but connecting COMPONENTS in MAPS does not affect any other aspect of the NVIVO-PROJECT. For example, connecting NODES in MAPS is different from using Relationship NODES, because the connections made in MAPS are only present in the MAP in which they were created. In contrast, Relationship NODES connect COMPONENTS together across the NVIVO-PROJECT.

Figure 5.15 illustrates how MAPS appear in NVivo. We now invite you to go to the companion website to view the *Component Orientation* video for this COMPONENT.

Charts

Charts are graphic displays that provide an additional way of visualizing COMPONENTS and the associations between them. Not all of these visualizations are called *charts* in NVivo, but for simplicity we refer to all of them as CHARTS because they are all ways of displaying, or charting, elements of the NVIVO-PROJECT. The different versions and editions of NVivo 11 vary in terms of the types of CHARTS that are available. We list all CHARTS here, but the version you are using may not include all CHARTS—check the QSR website for up-to-date information on which CHARTS are available in the version you are using.

- **Charts.** These are graphs that display information about SOURCES, CASES, NODES, and ATTRIBUTE-VALUES. Many different types can be generated—Bar Charts, Pie Charts, Bubble Charts, Heat Maps, and Radar Charts. The type depends on what information you are visualizing. Some CHARTS visualize aspects of your coding—for example, information about a particular SOURCE, how a particular NODE has been used to code SOURCES, or the association between NODES and ATTRIBUTE-VALUES. Other CHARTS visualize information about SOURCES or CASES—for example, which SOURCES have which ATTRIBUTE-VALUES linked to them or which combinations of ATTRIBUTE-VALUES have been applied to which CASES.

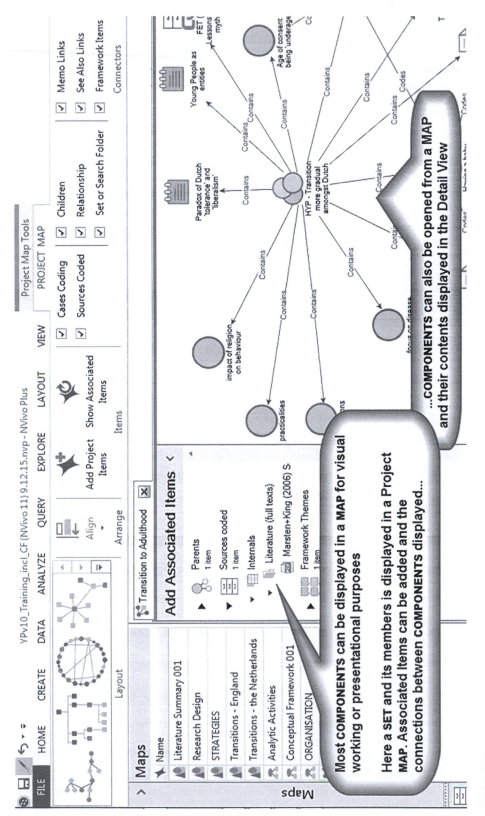

FIGURE 5.15 MAPS

- *Hierarchy Charts.* These CHARTS visualize patterns in coding hierarchically. They can be displayed in two visualizations: Tree Maps and Sunbursts. Tree Maps display a set of nested rectangles of different sizes to visualize the amount of coding for NODES or SOURCES, or the number of CASES or sources that ATTRIBUTE-VALUES are linked to. Sunbursts are radial Tree Maps, meaning the levels in the hierarchy are displayed as rings rather than rectangles, with the top level of the hierarchy occupying the innermost ring.
- *Cluster Analysis.* These CHARTS are diagrams that group SOURCES or NODES that share similar words or ATTRIBUTE-VALUES or are coded similarly by a particular NODE. They can be used to visualize similarities and differences in your NVIVO-PROJECT. A Cluster Analysis chart can be visualized in five different ways: as a 2D cluster map, a 3D cluster map, a Horizontal Dendrogram, a Vertical Dendrogram, or a Circle Graph.
- *Comparison Diagram.* These CHARTS show the COMPONENTS that two SOURCES, NODES, or CASES have in common. For example, you could visualize the NODES that two interview transcripts have in common by creating a Comparison Diagram of two SOURCES. Or you could visualize all the CASES that were coded to two particular NODES.
- *Explore Diagram.* These CHARTS focus on an individual SOURCE or NODE and show all the other COMPONENTS that are connected to them. For example, an Explore Diagram on a NODE would show all the SOURCES, CASES, and MEMOS that the NODE is linked to.
- *Sociograms.* These CHARTS are designed to facilitate social network analysis, a methodological approach that focuses on the links between people or other social entities. There are two types of Sociograms. An Egocentric Sociogram displays how one CASE is connected to other CASES in your NVIVO-PROJECT. A Network Sociogram visualizes the connections between a group of CASES.
- *Word Clouds.* These CHARTS provide one way of visualizing the results of a Word Frequency query. They display the 100 most frequently occurring words in varying font sizes—the larger the font size, the more frequently the word has been found. QUERY-RESULTS of Word Frequency queries can also be visualized as Tree Maps and Cluster Analysis diagrams.
- *Word Trees.* These CHARTS are one way of visualizing the results of a Text Search Query. They display the searched-for word as a tree, with branches representing the contexts within which the word occurs. The size of the font of the words in the branches indicates the frequency with which those words appear in close proximity to the searched-for word.

Figure 5.16 illustrates how CHARTS appear in NVivo. We now invite you to go to the companion website to view the *Component Orientation* video for this COMPONENT.

The NVIVO-PROJECT as a Whole

This section covers various tasks and housekeeping features not related to specific COMPONENTS of the program: *interrogating, outputting, keeping up to date,* and *backing up and moving projects.*

Interrogating

Interrogate means to *ask questions about something.* At the strategy levels of deciding how best to answer a research question, the entire analysis can be thought of as an interrogation of the data, with no limit to the range, uniqueness, and subtlety of interrogation activities. NVivo offers three broad kinds of software operations that support interrogation activities: *retrieving* groups of CODED-REFERENCES based on what they are linked to, *counting* things, and *displaying* COMPONENTS graphically in MAPS and CHARTS. These have been discussed individually in the context of the various COMPONENTS that they operate on.

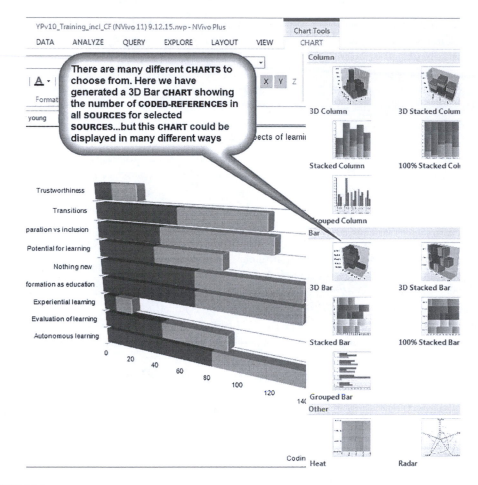

FIGURE 5.16 CHARTS

Outputting

NVivo is well designed for working primarily on screen and navigating around its interconnected COMPONENTS. However, there are times when outputting information is very useful. For example, it is common when engaged in a challenging ANALYTIC TASK to need to think deeply about all the CODED–REFERENCES for a NODE or all the CODED–REFERENCES that have two NODES in common. Sometimes there is no substitute for printing them out and doing the deep thinking with paper and pencil at a pleasant coffee shop before returning to navigate around the NVivo screen.

Outputs can be *displayed on screen* in a separate window, sent directly to a *printer*, saved as a *file*, or saved as a file and immediately *opened* in the appropriate program.

- **Content of Detail Views.** The content of any Detail View can be outputted. The file type that these outputs can be saved in depends on the content being exported. Outputs of CODED–REFERENCES from a Detail View can include or exclude ANNOTATIONS and other related content, such as the Description, links to REFERENCES and MEMOS, and paragraph numbers, depending on the purpose.
- **Coded SOURCES, NODES, and CASES.** A graphical output reproduces the text or graphics of any SOURCE, NODE, or CASE with the margin area displaying any NODES, just as it appears within NVivo.

- *MAPS and CHARTS.* Any MAP or CHART can be outputted to a printer or saved as a graphical file outside of NVivo.
- **List Views and Tables.** Any List View or Table can be exported from NVivo to be viewed and worked on in another program. This includes any list of COMPONENTS displayed in a List View and the tabular results of Word Frequency and Matrix Coding queries.
- **Classification Sheets.** Classification Sheets that display the ATTRIBUTE-VALUES assigned to SOURCES or NODES can be exported from NVivo to be viewed and worked on in another program. Classification Sheets can also be imported from other programs.

Keeping Up to Date

NVivo releases major new versions every few years. These new versions maintain the same underlying philosophy and functionality of NVivo, so fortunately it has not been necessary to relearn how to use NVivo powerfully with each new version. Some users always buy the latest version to take advantage of new or more efficient features. Others continue with the current version they are happy with. One reason researchers delay upgrading is to ensure that all team members are using the same version. If one team member upgrades to Version 11 and others do not, it is not possible to merge everybody's work.

Minor updates to correct bugs or add minor improvements come out every few weeks or months. Whenever you open the program NVivo checks to see if updates are available and invites you to update if this is the case. You can also update manually by going to the File menu, then to Help, and then choosing Check for Software Updates.

Backing Up and Moving Projects

NVivo has features for *saving* your current work, for *backing up* an NVIVO-PROJECT as a safeguard of your work or as an archive, and for moving an NVIVO-PROJECT to another computer.

Saving Your Current Work

All work done in an NVIVO-PROJECT is saved by NVivo wherever you choose to save the project file. Saving your work therefore only requires pressing the Save button. There are no separate project files to save or to be concerned with. As there is no automatic backup, we press the Save button very regularly, sometimes every few minutes in the midst of valuable work.

Backing Up a Project

Backing up an NVIVO-PROJECT means saving a copy of it for safekeeping while you continue on with the working version. This can be done at any time using the Copy Project feature and saving the NVIVO-PROJECT with another name. You can then continue work in the current version and always be able to open and look back at a previous version. Some researchers save these archive versions of their NVIVO-PROJECT regularly, which also creates an audit trail to help with the write-up of the methods of the project. Adding the date as part of the NVIVO-PROJECT name in these archive versions allows easy selection of an earlier version that you may be interested in reviewing.

Moving Projects

Moving a project to another computer is straightforward. Just close NVivo, copy the project file, save it on another computer, and then open it in NVivo on the new computer. This will work fine as long as both computers have the same version of NVivo installed.

If the NVIVO-PROJECT you are moving has not-embedded files, such as large video files, which are read by NVivo rather than being contained within the project file (as discussed on page 74), or if you have linked to external files or websites, you will also have to ensure that these files are available on the other computer for NVivo to link to.

Importing Pre–Version 11 Projects

NVIVO-PROJECTS originally conducted in earlier versions of NVivo can be opened. The NVIVO-PROJECT is converted and saved as a Version 11 project. Converting leaves the original older NVIVO-PROJECT in its original version to go back to, but once converted, the new Version 11 NVIVO-PROJECT cannot be imported back and used in earlier versions.

We now invite you to go to the companion website to view the *Component Orientation* video *The* NVIVO-PROJECT *as a whole.*

Working in Teams Using NVivo

Using NVivo in a team situation involves considering both the human aspect of *who does what* from a research perspective and the technical aspect of *merging each team member's contributions.* We discussed the human aspects of team working in Chapter 4. Here we describe the technicalities of the merge process when working with standalone versions of NVivo (the Pro and Plus editions of NVivo for Windows, or NVivo for Mac). If you are working with NVivo for Teams, you do not need to merge, as different team members can work on the same NVIVO-PROJECT at the same time.

The Starter, Pro, and Plus editions of NVivo for Windows and NVivo for Mac are not multiuser programs, so each team member works independently on their own copy of the NVIVO-PROJECT. As discussed in Chapter 4 there are different ways of distributing the analytic work among team members. However work is assigned, periodically each team member submits their NVIVO-PROJECT for merging and stops work while all the NVIVO-PROJECTS are merged. A copy of the newly merged NVIVO-PROJECT containing everyone's work is then distributed back to each team member for their next round of work. Management of a team project therefore involves some kind of "merge cycle," either ad hoc or on a routine schedule, for collecting all the NVIVO-PROJECTS, merging them, and redistributing the merged NVIVO-PROJECT.

Merging involves importing one NVIVO-PROJECT into another. This is smooth and effortless from a technical point of view, involving little more than clicking a button. But if the merge cycle procedures are not thought through, the resulting merged NVIVO-PROJECT can unintentionally include or exclude or duplicate some items and waste a great deal of time in sorting it out. Long experience with team projects has led us to adopt a "foolproof method." It requires no thinking—the same procedures are followed every time, leaving all the thinking time for the more important research activities. Arguments can be made that this foolproof approach is unnecessarily rigid, and some teams prefer to cut corners. We prefer not to.

Every team project is different in the details of implementing the foolproof method, but all follow the same general principles. We begin with the principles and then outline the procedures.

Everyone on the Same Cycle

Even if one team member has done no work between the last merge cycle and the current one, the foolproof method has them submit their NVIVO-PROJECT for merging and not continue working until they receive the merged NVIVO-PROJECT. In theory missing a merge cycle if you have done no work since the last one should not be a problem, but the possibility for human error is great—in real life people just forget things that they have done.

What Happens When You Merge

The process starts with the "master" NVIVO-PROJECT open, and one or more NVIVO-PROJECTS are imported into it. When importing one NVIVO-PROJECT into another, you have three choices concerning what to import and two choices for what to do with *duplicate items*, meaning those COMPONENTS that exist in both NVIVO-PROJECTS.

- *Import all items (including content).* This option will import an entire NVIVO-PROJECT, meaning everything from one NVIVO-PROJECT is merged into the open NVIVO-PROJECT.
- *Import selected items (excluding content).* This option allows you to select what to import into the open NVIVO-PROJECT, but only the structure is imported, meaning that the items you choose are represented in the open NVIVO-PROJECT, but their content is not. For example, if you choose to import CASES, they will be listed in the open NVIVO-PROJECT, but no data will be linked to them
- *Import selected items (including content).* This option allows you to select what to import into the open NVIVO-PROJECT and will bring all the content you choose. For example, if you choose to import NODES and their coding, the NODES will not only be created but the CODED-REFERENCES linked to them will also be imported—as long as the relevant SOURCES are already present in the NVIVO-PROJECT or are also imported at the same time.
- *Merge duplicate items.* This option will merge items of the same type that have exactly the same name and are stored in the same FOLDER. There are additional criteria for when duplicate items will be merged, specific to item type, too numerous to list here, but these can be found in the Help Menu.
- *Create new item.* This option will create a new item even if it already exists in the open NVIVO-PROJECT. Duplicate items can then be merged manually after import.

Principles of the Foolproof Method

The foolproof method is intended to avoid errors by accomplishing the merge with the least amount of thinking, variation, or choices. The following general principles are always followed.

- *User system.* Each user is registered with a user name in each NVIVO-PROJECT. All COMPONENTS added or modified are then tagged with their user name, and in the merged NVIVO-PROJECT it is possible to see who created or modified any COMPONENTS.
- *The merge manager.* The foolproof method requires centralized management by a "merge manager" who becomes the team expert in the process. The right personality helps—detail oriented, control oriented, and proficient with keeping track of incoming NVIVO-PROJECT files. The right person will automatically think to develop a naming convention for each team member's NVIVO-PROJECT and will create a log of when it arrives and when it is sent back out.
- *All NVIVO-PROJECTs contain all SOURCES.* If some team members add their own SOURCES to their NVIVO-PROJECT (perhaps just the ones they work on) and others have a different selection of SOURCES, the potential for ending up with duplicate SOURCES and coding in the merged NVIVO-PROJECT is great. The safest procedure is that only the merge manager is permitted to add new SOURCES to an NVIVO-PROJECT immediately after each merge. This can be inconvenient and sometimes requires everyone stopping work for a merge only in order to add new SOURCES, but this is essential to eliminating human error. When this corner is cut, the potential for human error is great.
- *No editing SOURCES.* If SOURCES are edited from within NVivo by one team member, those SOURCES will become different from other team members' copies of the SOURCES, and those SOURCES will be duplicated upon import, with part of the coding in one SOURCE and part in the new

duplicate. All this can be avoided by disallowing team members from editing their SOURCES from within the NVIVO-PROJECT.

Procedures of the Foolproof Method

The following three steps are an ideal that is always followed overall, but each step is necessarily adapted to each situation. Although these steps may be accomplished somewhat differently, the adaptations should never violate any of the principles described earlier.

- Step 1: The next merge is announced. Each team member saves their work, creates a copy of their NVIVO-PROJECT, and sends it to the merge manager.
- Step 2: The merge manager opens each submitted NVIVO-PROJECT to confirm that each one contains all SOURCES. Then she imports the NVIVO-PROJECT one by one.
- Step 3: The merge manager adds any new SOURCES to the merged NVIVO-PROJECT and then makes a copy to send to each team member for the next round of work.

Inter-rater Reliability

There is no general agreement on what it means to calculate the inter-rater reliability of qualitative coding. The Pro and Plus editions of NVivo 11 for Windows and NVivo 11 for Mac include the Coding Comparison Query. This allows the comparison of coding done by two team members or two groups of team members. The SOURCES and NODES to be compared can be selected, and the QUERY-RESULT then displays the results in a table, showing statistics of agreement and disagreement in coding between team members for the chosen SOURCES and NODES. You can choose to calculate the percentage agreement, use the kappa coefficient statistical measure, or both. Details about how NVivo calculates these measures can be found in the Help Menu.

We now invite you to go to the companion website to view this *Component Orientation* video.

References

Charmaz, K. (2014). *Constructing grounded theory* (2nd ed.). Thousand Oaks, CA: Sage Publications.
Corbin, J., & Strauss, A. (2014). *Basics of qualitative research: Techniques and procedures for developing grounded theory* (4th ed.). Thousand Oaks, CA: Sage Publications.
Saldaña, J. (2015). *Thinking qualitatively: Methods of mind.* Thousand Oaks, CA: Sage Publications.
Saldaña, J. (2016). *The coding manual for qualitative researchers* (3rd ed.). London: Sage Publications.

6

MASTERING THE PROCESS OF TRANSLATION

This chapter provides practical instruction in the five steps of TRANSLATION. In Chapter 2 we described TRANSLATION very generally as the *transformation* of strategies into tactics, similar to translating from one language to another. This is true but not sufficiently detailed to actually know what to do. In Chapter 3 we described the process in more detail as *matching* the units of an ANALYTIC TASK to a COMPONENT of the software. This is also true but still not sufficiently detailed. TRANSLATION in practical terms means *representing* the UNITS of an ANALYTIC TASK by the most appropriate of all the possible COMPONENTS to which they could be matched, and this requires taking account of the purpose of the task and knowing the actions that can be taken on COMPONENTS.

This is a good moment to remind you that we are not inventing something new and complicated, but only describing what expert users of NVivo have come to do automatically and unconsciously so that you can begin to do it too. Initially we need to spell out the steps in detail, but once this detailed process is understood and used just a few times, it will become simple and automatic, and you will be able to draw productive analogies from our case illustrations to your own project and begin harnessing NVivo powerfully. You may choose to continue using the ANALYTIC PLANNING WORKSHEETS in your own projects, as many of our students do, or you may not feel it is necessary to do so. But for learning purposes it is an important TOOL.

We begin by explaining why TRANSLATION is a heuristic process. We then describe how to write ANALYTIC TASKS at an appropriate level of detail, and we introduce the ANALYTIC PLANNING WORKSHEET for planning, managing, and documenting *Five-Level QDA* projects. We then provide instruction in each of the five steps of TRANSLATION: *identifying units, describing purposes, identifying possible components, choosing appropriate components,* and *finalizing* SELECTED- or CONSTRUCTED-TOOLS. By necessity we present the steps of TRANSLATION in sequence. In practice, after some experience with the process, the steps become less separate and discrete than our presentation suggests. Each step includes examples and is illustrated with a running sample ANALYTIC TASK, with its ANALYTIC PLANNING WORKSHEET gradually being filled until it is complete at the end of Step 5. This instruction in each step of TRANSLATION will be sufficient if you already use NVivo and have some experience with qualitative research. If you are new to either NVivo or qualitative research, additional and more elaborated illustrations are provided in appendices. These appendices will be especially useful when you are ready to conduct each step in your own project. The instruction and the various tables provided in each step are also a preparation for the video demonstrations of TRANSLATION on the companion website. These videos are described in more detail in Chapter 7.

Translation as a Heuristic Process

In Part I we highlighted the difference between the emergent nature of qualitative analysis and the cut-and-dried nature of computer software. TRANSLATION falls somewhere in the middle and involves a different kind of thinking or mind-set. When working at the strategy levels we are thinking with an emergent mind-set—once a task is completed, the outcome suggests or leads to the next task without it being anticipated in detail in advance. At the tactics levels of operating the software, we are thinking with a step-by-step or algorithmic mind-set in which each operation, such as pressing a button or accessing a menu, has a predetermined and reliable outcome. Between the two, at the level of TRANSLATION, we are thinking in a third way with a heuristic mind-set, because TRANSLATION is more of an art than a science. One way of describing expertise in the *Five-Level QDA* method is the ability to naturally move among these three mind-sets without thinking too much about it. Figure 6.1 illustrates this.

A heuristic is like a rule of thumb, a practical or commonsense approach to solving a problem based on experience with similar problems. A heuristic has guidelines rather than a precise set of rules. That well describes the TRANSLATION process. A heuristic mind-set is a different way of thinking from the emergent mind-set at the strategy levels. At the strategy levels we allow the data in our projects to determine the emergence of each new step of strategy, rather than take examples of other projects as a heuristic for making analytic choices of our own. A heuristic mind-set is also a different way of thinking from the algorithmic mind-set we adopt when learning and operating the software, which is a rules-based domain, with each action having a predetermined outcome. We will return to this issue of heuristic thinking as we point out how and why our examples of TRANSLATION are only examples and guidelines, not hard-and-fast rules. We call these *learning heuristics*, rules of thumb appropriate when starting out with the *Five-Level QDA* method. As your

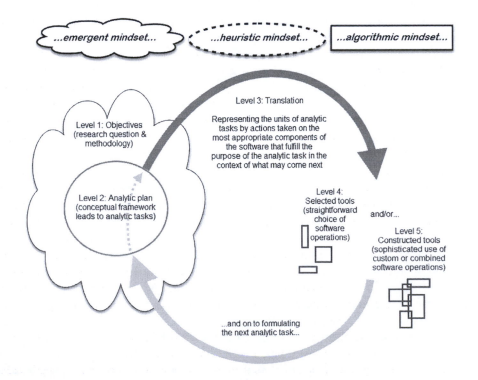

FIGURE 6.1 Emergent, heuristic, and algorithmic mind-sets

experience and expertise in TRANSLATION develop, your own rules of thumb for your own kind of data analysis will evolve accordingly.

Writing Analytic Tasks

Without an appropriately written ANALYTIC TASK, there is nothing to TRANSLATE. ANALYTIC TASKS are the smallest items of analytic activity. This is not a precise definition, and there is no neat and tidy procedure for deciding the best level of detail for writing an ANALYTIC TASK. In Chapter 2 when discussing the gourmet meal, we suggested that the best approach for deciding the appropriate level of detail for a task was to consider *what you plan to do next*, so that the outcome of the task most easily led on to the next task. For example, *chop salad ingredients evenly* was most helpful in leading on to the next task, *cut up fish*. Identifying a much broader task, such as *prep all the ingredients*, was too large a scale for suggesting a specific next step. Conversely, a task such as *open refrigerator door* was too detailed, requiring the next task to be something equally detailed, such as *get salad ingredients out of the fridge*, an absurdly unhelpful sequence of small-scale steps.

In the *Five-Level QDA* method the goal is to write ANALYTIC TASKS that readily reveal their UNITS and purpose in order to identify the appropriate software COMPONENTS to harness. Many researchers intimately know their strategies and what they want to do next in their project. But they initially find it difficult to write these intentions as ANALYTIC TASKS that are precise and specific, but not too specific, for the purposes of TRANSLATION.

As an example, consider the common task of familiarizing yourself with your data before beginning detailed analysis. In our workshops it is common for participants to express this as *find out what's going on in the data* or *explore the data with regard to content and meaning*. These are worthy tasks, but for the purposes of TRANSLATION they are too general—equivalent to the cooking task *prep all the ingredients*. In workshops we help participants rewrite these at a more detailed level by asking questions about the project, for example, what kind of data are being used, why is this something that needs to be achieved, and what has already been done and is intended to be done next? These are good questions to ask yourself. Depending on the answers, we would rewrite their ANALYTIC TASKS to be more specific, but not too specific. In the context of an interview project, the task *find out what's going on in the data* might be rewritten more specifically as *read interview transcripts to identify potential concepts for coding*. This naturally leads to the next ANALYTIC TASK, which might be *organize and set up initial coding scheme*. But it is not so detailed as, for example, *read the first interview*, which is on a similar level of fine detail as *open refrigerator door*. At this fine level of detail, way too many individual tasks would have to be written for no benefit.

Appendix 1 illustrates 14 examples of ANALYTIC TASKS from very different research contexts written at the appropriate level of detail for TRANSLATION. One of these tasks—*compare teachers' reactions to different kinds of bullying*—will serve as the running sample ANALYTIC TASK throughout this chapter. For each illustrative ANALYTIC TASK in Appendix 1, three columns display a version of the task that is too general (e.g., *find out what's going on in the data*), a version that is unnecessarily detailed (e.g., *read the first interview*), and a version at an appropriate level of detail for TRANSLATION (e.g., *read interview transcripts to identify potential concepts for coding*). When you are ready to write your own ANALYTIC TASKS, this appendix will be a helpful resource. The examples are grouped by five major kinds of analytic activity that occur in a qualitative analysis, as described by Silver and Lewins (2014):

- *Integrating.* Combining parts into a whole by bringing together the elements that make up a research project and thinking about how they relate to one another.
- *Organizing.* Creating structures related to objectives in order to reflect on meaningful aspects of the data in relation to project objectives.

- *Exploring.* Examining the content and structure of the data in order to consider the inherent nature of data.
- *Reflecting.* Considering carefully and deeply about what is going on in the project in order to record analytic insights and the process.
- *Interrogating.* Asking questions about data in order to follow up the work we have done so far.

Thinking in terms of these five analytic activities is helpful when developing an analytic plan and writing ANALYTIC TASKS at Level 2 of the *Five-Level QDA* method. As the strategy levels of qualitative research are not the subject of this book, we do not discuss analytic activities further, but we use them as a logical way of grouping our examples of ANALYTIC TASKS in the appendices. Appendix 2 provides a deeper look at the Silver and Lewins (2014) framework of five analytic activities.

The Analytic Planning Worksheet

The ANALYTIC PLANNING WORKSHEET is a display of the *Five-Level QDA* process in a standard format. It is primarily a learning TOOL for mastering the five steps of TRANSLATION as quickly and smoothly as possible. But it is also a working TOOL for managing and documenting a qualitative analysis. Having a standard format is useful for demonstrating the integrity and quality of a project (Tracy, 2010); for providing an audit trail through the different phases of a project (Lincoln & Guba, 1985); and for offering an opportunity to review the details of earlier steps of analysis, which are easily forgotten in the iterative and emergent unfolding of data analysis. Many researchers find it a helpful way to source progress on a project, and students use the worksheets to communicate the progress of a thesis or dissertation to their academic advisors. All the video demonstrations of ANALYTIC TASKS on the companion website are accompanied by completed ANALYTIC PLANNING WORKSHEETS, which can be printed or downloaded and are referred to in the videos. A template of the worksheet can also be printed or downloaded.

The Format of the Analytic Planning Worksheet

Each ANALYTIC PLANNING WORKSHEET displays a small number of ANALYTIC TASKS that, taken together, are a coherent set of related tasks that we call a *phase* of the analysis. A whole project will therefore have a succession of ANALYTIC PLANNING WORKSHEETS, one for each phase.

The format of the ANALYTIC PLANNING WORKSHEET follows the five levels of the *Five-Level QDA* method. The top two sections for Levels 1 and 2 serve as a reminder of the objectives, methodology, and current iteration of the analytic plan, which are best kept in mind as the details of the current ANALYTIC TASKS are thought out and entered into the worksheet. This is of particular value to researchers who are obliged to be away from their projects from time to time and need to efficiently reorient themselves on returning to the research. Also included in the top sections are the context of the current phase, consisting of a summary of what has been accomplished so far, the name of the current phase, and what is anticipated to happen next. Filling out these top sections is not a formality or bureaucratic exercise, but helps ensure the current analytic activity is congruent with the current iteration of the objectives, methodology, and analytic plan, which are updated as necessary in each successive ANALYTIC PLANNING WORKSHEET. These iterations of the project strategies in the top sections of the worksheet therefore also provide a record of their emergence through the life of the project. The lower sections of the worksheet source the process of TRANSLATION, recording of the name of each ANALYTIC TASK, the steps of TRANSLATION, and the resulting SELECTED- and CONSTRUCTED-TOOLS that are used to fulfill each ANALYTIC TASK. Figure 6.2 displays an illustrated template of the ANALYTIC PLANNING WORKSHEET.

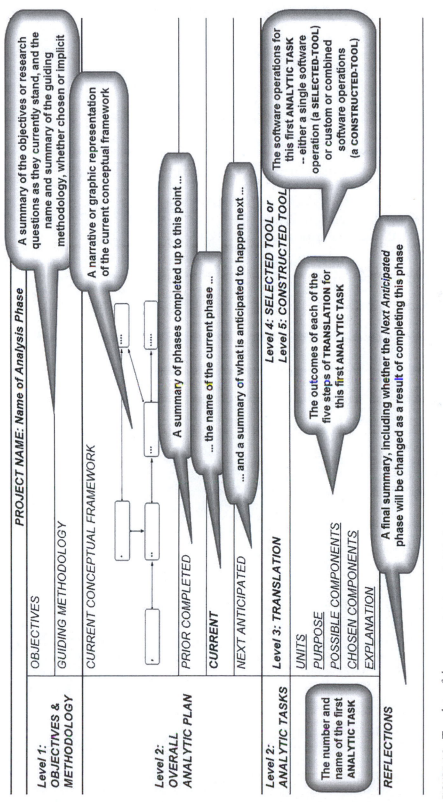

FIGURE 6.2 Template of the ANALYTIC PLANNING WORKSHEET

Analytic Planning Worksheet for the Sample Analytic Task

Our sample analytic task is part of an imagined research project on bullying in schools, a topic of continuing research interest. Researchers have found that teachers' and pupils' definitions of bullying are different (Naylor, Cowie, Cossin, Bettencourt, & Lemme, 2006) and that teachers adopt a range of strategies to react to cases of reported bullying (Rigby, 2014). This imagined interview-based thematic-analysis study aims to understand teachers' reactions to different kinds of bullying in two contrasting schools in order to inform the design of a new evidence-based bullying intervention program.

Figure 6.3 displays the top section of the ANALYTIC PLANNING WORKSHEET for this project. The analytic plan is illustrated with a graphical conceptual framework, broken into planned phases. Our preference is for graphical conceptual frameworks—other researchers prefer lists, tables, or a short narrative in this section of the worksheet. This particular ANALYTIC PLANNING WORKSHEET is for the phase of analysis named *Explore teacher reactions to bullying*. The prior completed phase is indicated in the diagram, but the subsequent phase is tentative and will surely evolve. In a real-world project this diagram would therefore be updated in each iteration of the worksheet.

The Five Steps of Translation

Figure 6.4 displays the sequence of five steps of TRANSLATION. The first step is to *identify the units* in the ANALYTIC TASK. Units are the building blocks of any analysis. Identifying the units means listing the major entities that are *contained* within the ANALYTIC TASK. *Entities* refers broadly to *the kinds of things being analyzed* or *what is being looked for* in accomplishing the task. The second step is to *describe the purpose* of the ANALYTIC TASK—why the task is being done. The third step is to *identify possible* COMPONENTS that could represent the units. The fourth step is to *choose appropriate* COMPONENTS to accomplish the ANALYTIC TASK by considering its context, which includes what has been achieved previously and what is anticipated to come next. The final step is to finalize the software operations by SELECTING or CONSTRUCTING TOOLS. A TOOL is a combination of a COMPONENT and an action appropriate for a specific ANALYTIC TASK in its context. Whether there are more SELECTED–TOOLS or more CONSTRUCTED–TOOLS in a project does not indicate a more or less sophisticated analysis or more or less skill in harnessing NVivo. The choice depends solely on the specifics of each ANALYTIC TASK and its context. The remainder of this chapter consists of discussions and illustrations of each of these five steps.

Step 1: Identifying Units

In Chapter 3 we introduced the central idea of units in research for describing the things that are being analyzed (see page 45). We discussed how the primary objective of a project would be reflected in a major unit, and there would generally be additional or secondary units either at the outset or that emerge as the analysis proceeds. We also indicated that it is not always standard practice in qualitative research to explicitly identify and name the units of analysis. One reason is because many styles of qualitative analysis are *grounded*, meaning that units emerge as the data are analyzed.

For purposes of the *Five-Level QDA* method it is important to specify units, as these are what are TRANSLATED into SELECTED– and CONSTRUCTED–TOOLS. ANALYTIC TASKS must be written at a level of detail that is not too general but not too specific. This ensures that their units "jump out." If they do not jump out, the ANALYTIC TASK is rewritten until they do. To avoid ambiguity, we use regular type when referring to the concept of units generally, but we use SMALL CAPS when discussing the UNITS we identify in individual ANALYTIC TASKS for the specific purpose of TRANSLATION.

One stumbling block to internalizing the meaning of a unit is its ambiguity. *Unit* means something different at two different levels, so it helps to think of two separate terms: a *unit* and an *instance of a unit*. *School* is a unit, the name of a collection of things. "Santa Barbara High School"

THE ROLE OF TEACHERS IN MITIGATING BULLYING BEHAVIORS IN SCHOOLS
Analysis Phase: Explore teacher reactions to bullying

Level 1: OBJECTIVES & METHODOLOGY

OBJECTIVES
Exploratory study to understand the role of teachers in resolving entrenched bullying behaviors in order to inform the design of interventions

GUIDING METHODOLOGY
Semi-structured interview study with 20 teachers from two schools with differing levels of reported bullying, using thematic analysis to explore teacher reactions to different kinds of bullying in order to inform evidence-based intervention

CURRENT CONCEPTUAL FRAMEWORK

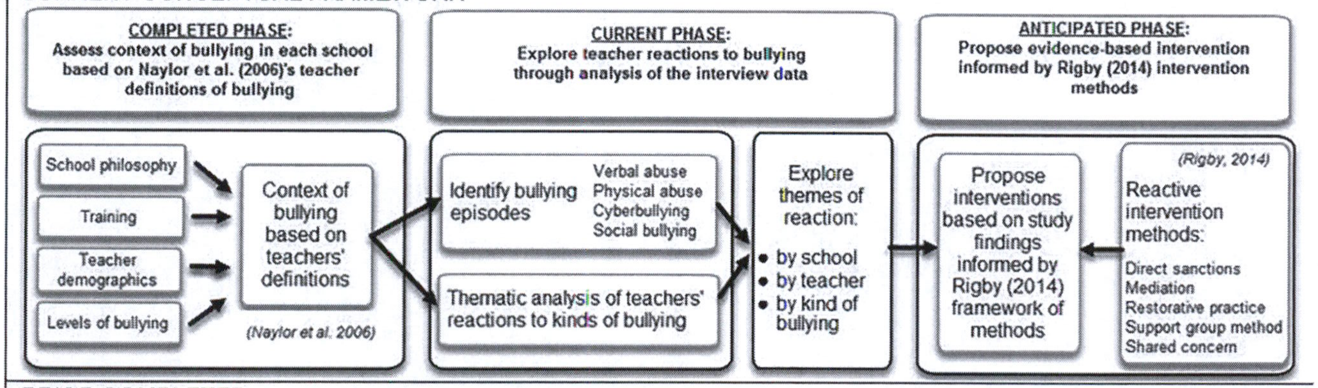

Level 2: OVERALL ANALYTIC PLAN

COMPLETED PHASE:
Assess context of bullying in each school based on Naylor et al. (2006)'s teacher definitions of bullying

- School philosophy
- Training
- Teacher demographics
- Levels of bullying

→ Context of bullying based on teachers' definitions

(Naylor et al. 2006)

CURRENT PHASE:
Explore teacher reactions to bullying through analysis of the interview data

- Identify bullying episodes
  - Verbal abuse
  - Physical abuse
  - Cyberbullying
  - Social bullying
- Thematic analysis of teachers' reactions to kinds of bullying

→ Explore themes of reaction:
- by school
- by teacher
- by kind of bullying

ANTICIPATED PHASE:
Propose evidence-based intervention informed by Rigby (2014) intervention methods

→ Propose interventions based on study findings informed by Rigby (2014) framework of methods

→ Reactive intervention methods:
- Direct sanctions
- Mediation
- Restorative practice
- Support group method
- Shared concern

(Rigby, 2014)

Level 2: ANALYTIC TASKS

PRIOR COMPLETED
Coding to capture different reactions to each kind of bullying

CURRENT
Identify patterns of teacher reactions by comparing different reactions to different kinds of bullying

NEXT ANTICIPATED
Determine whether patterns of most problematic or most productive reactions of teachers may inform mitigation of bullying behaviors

Level 3: TRANSLATION

Level 4: SELECTED TOOL or
Level 5: CONSTRUCTED TOOL

FIGURE 6.3   ANALYTIC PLANNING WORKSHEET for sample analytic task

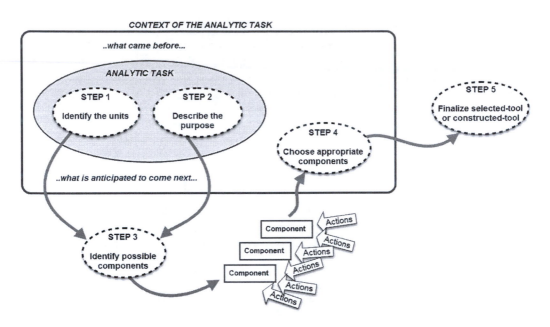

FIGURE 6.4 The steps of TRANSLATION

and "Gillingham Comprehensive School" are both schools, but they are instances of the unit rather than the unit itself. Unit may have the connotation for us as a single thing, rather than a group of things. But in research "unit" refers to a collection of things of one kind and "instance" refers to a particular example of the collection.

Think about each ANALYTIC TASK in terms of three types of units: *units of analysis*, which are the major entities that are the subject of the analysis; *units of data*, which indicate the form of the data that you have collected; and *units of meaning*, which are the parts of your data or the analytic entities you create that have meaning in your analysis. Other writers identify other types of units for different purposes (e.g., di Gregorio & Davidson, 2008, discuss their use of units of observation), but for our purposes units of analysis, data, and meaning have proved most helpful. These three types of units are distinct when ANALYTIC TASKS are straightforward, but they overlap in more sophisticated ANALYTIC TASKS.

Looking for these three types of units in your ANALYTIC TASKS helps you ask the right questions, which brings the idea of a unit alive so that the UNITS of your precisely written ANALYTIC TASKS jump out at you. Once a UNIT has been identified, it is entered into the ANALYTIC PLANNING WORKSHEET. The type of unit does not directly affect the following steps of TRANSLATION, but we enter the types into the ANALYTIC PLANNING WORKSHEET just as an aid in thinking through the following steps.

Units of Analysis

Units of analysis indicate the entities in a project that are the subject of the analysis. These could be anything—individuals, groups of individuals, organizations, parts of organizations, events, settings, programs, sources, artifacts, countries, places, etc. There is often one major unit of analysis and several additional units, but there is no ideal number of units of analysis to aspire to: it depends on the kind and complexity of the research questions.

In the bullying project we may be comparing episodes of bullying within two different schools, so there would be two units of analysis: *schools* and *episodes of bullying*. If we were also investigating teachers' responses to episodes of bullying, then we would additionally have *teachers* as a unit of analysis. These units let us know what the subject of the analysis is. But if instead we were investigating students' lived experiences of being bullied within one particular school, there would be one unit of analysis: *students*. If we were evaluating the effectiveness of programs designed to minimize bullying within schools located in a particular district of a large city, there would be four units of analysis: *programs*, *schools*, and two sets of individuals—*students* and *teachers*. If the focus of analysis changes as the project advances, additional units may be identified.

Units of Data

The data for this project also come in units. One factor in identifying units of data is the complexity of the data collection procedures. If data collection is straightforward, then the source of material may be the only unit of data. For example, if the bullying project involved in-depth interviews with individual teachers and also focus group discussions with many teachers, it would be typical to transcribe each interview and each focus group into its own Microsoft Word file. If the intention is to consider the data from the individual interviews and the focus groups as equivalent and to analyze all the data in the same way, then for TRANSLATION purposes *transcript* would be the single unit of data, and each interview and each focus group would be an instance of this one unit. But if the intention is to first analyze the focus group data and later use the conclusions to inform the analysis of the individual interviews, then there would be two different units of data: *interview* and *focus group*. Identifying units therefore involves both the form in which the data have been collected or prepared and the purpose to which they will be put. These principles apply in the same way to all kinds of data, for example, survey data containing qualitative responses, collections of images, video data, social media content, and so on.

Some projects are more sophisticated and involve more units of data. In the bullying project an additional objective may be to compare the responses of each person in the focus groups, perhaps because each respondent has been selected to represent a stakeholder group, such as an academic department. If the focus groups have been transcribed with a marker of some kind in the text to indicate who said what, then there are three units of data: *interview* and *focus group* for the first objective, and *focus group respondent* for the second. In this case *focus group respondent* is also a unit of analysis—it is an "entity" in the project that is being analyzed. But this does not mean *focus group respondent* is two different units. Thinking separately about units of data and units of analysis is only helpful in identifying *focus group respondent* as a unit in the context of two different purposes. Once a unit is identified, it is not important whether it is a unit of data or a unit of analysis or both.

Units of Meaning

It is helpful to think of two kinds of units of meaning. The first are the meaningful concepts created for the analysis. As we discussed in Chapter 2 (page 37), we use "concept" as the general term for all the different kinds of meaningful entities created in the analytic process. These are variously referred to in different methodologies and research traditions as codes, labels, topics, content areas, categories, themes, properties, dimensions, etc.

The second kind of unit of meaning are the segments of data that are meaningful because they are instances of concepts and are therefore conceptualized in some manner. For example, data segments could be tagged with a code name or interpreted in analytical writing. A unit of meaning of textual data could be a single word, a phrase, a sentence, a paragraph, many paragraphs, or a whole source. Some methodologies prescribe "line-by-line coding," although this is somewhat ambiguous with electronic data, as the number of words on a "line" depends on how wide the margin is set. In still images a unit of meaning may be based on the whole image, a selected portion of an image, or a series of images. In video recordings a unit of meaning may be the whole video, a scene, a clip, or series of clips. In Twitter data a unit of meaning may be each individual tweet, all the tweets posted using a particular hashtag, all the tweets posted in response to another tweet, or all tweets posted on a topic in a particular time frame.

These units of meaning may appear to be similar to units of data. The difference is in their purpose. Units of data are identified based on how the data are organized. Segments of data are identified as units of meaning because they are instances of meaningful concepts. Yet both different units may be based on the same data, with one embedded in the other. For example, a *transcript* of a source may be identified as a UNIT in an ANALYTIC TASK, and a *survey response* that appears in that source may be identified as a UNIT in a different ANALYTIC TASK. The *transcript* UNIT was identified when thinking about the ANALYTIC TASK in terms of units of data, and the *survey response* UNIT was identified when thinking about a different ANALYTIC TASK in terms of units of meaning. Types of units are helpful as an aid in identifying UNITS.

Appendix 3 provides numerous examples of the three types of units.

The Rule of Thumb of Two Units

At the levels of strategy—objectives, methodology, and analytic plan—a research project with fewer units suggests a more straightforward study, and a project with many units suggests greater complexity or a more sophisticated analysis. This does not follow for UNITS of ANALYTIC TASKS. The strategy levels deal with the analysis as a whole, the big picture; in contrast, the ANALYTIC TASK is the smallest item of analytic activity. For an individual ANALYTIC TASK, more than two UNITS is not a sign of sophistication, but only complicates the process of TRANSLATION. That is why when learning and initially practicing TRANSLATION, the rule of thumb is that no more than two UNITS should be identified for each ANALYTIC TASK.

If more than two UNITS are identified, there are two possibilities to consider. First, the ANALYTIC TASK may be too large. By rewriting the ANALYTIC TASK, it is usually possible to divide it more conveniently into two smaller tasks. Second, there may be good reason for the ANALYTIC TASK to have more than two UNITS—that is why the rule of thumb is only a heuristic, not a firm rule that must not be broken. Our sample ANALYTIC TASK—*compare teachers' reactions to different kinds of bullying*—is a good example. As discussed in Appendix 1, this ANALYTIC TASK has three UNITS—*teacher, reactions,* and *kinds of bullying*—but is not amenable to being split into two separate tasks. Reducing the task to two units requires thinking about whether any pair of these three UNITS is really a single UNIT for the purposes of TRANSLATION. For example, is *teacher* a unit of analysis in the study that is independent of the teachers' *reactions* to different kinds of bullying, or are they a single unit? Similarly, are *reactions* to bullying and concepts about *kinds of bullying* best represented as a single unit of meaning—*reactions to different kinds of bullying*—or will subsequent ANALYTIC TASKS have different purposes and require two UNITS of meaning—*reactions* and *different kinds of bullying*? How do we know all this from the ANALYTIC TASK as written? We don't. We know it from the analytic plan, which is conveniently displayed in the ANALYTIC PLANNING WORKSHEET for reference as the analysis proceeds. Figure 6.5 displays the first iteration of the worksheet, which indicates that in this example three units are called for—*teachers, reactions,* and *kinds of bullying*—based on the purpose of the task, which is the subject of the next section. We added the type of each unit to the worksheet in Figure 6.5 as a reminder of how we were thinking about the task, but this is optional as the type of unit is not used for TRANSLATION.

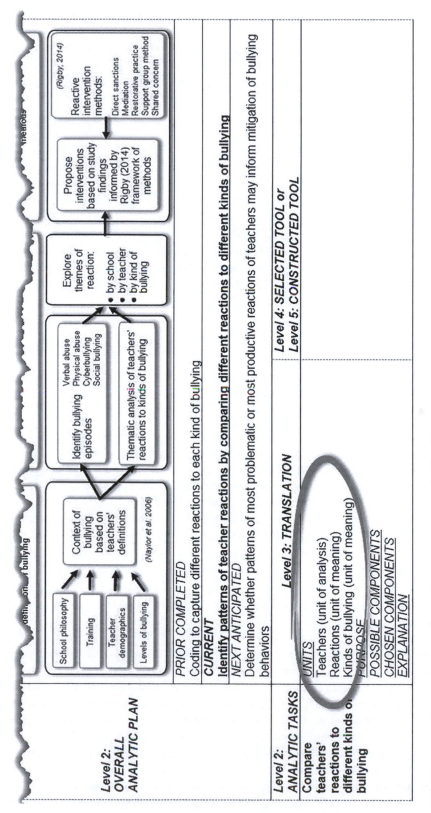

FIGURE 6.5 ANALYTIC PLANNING WORKSHEET for sample analytic task: Identifying units

For further illustration of identifying UNITS, Appendix 4 identifies and discusses the UNITS of our 14 example ANALYTIC TASKS. Appendix 4 will be a helpful resource when you are ready to identify the UNITS of your own ANALYTIC TASKS. Some of the examples follow the rule of thumb that an ANALYTIC TASK contains only one or two UNITS, and some do not. Some of these examples also demonstrate why the purpose of an ANALYTIC TASK must be known to properly identify its UNITS for TRANSLATION.

Step 2: Describing Purposes

Qualitative analysis is, to varying degrees, emergent, and it is common to feel unsure what to do next. Asking yourself *why* you need to accomplish an ANALYTIC TASK prevents you from acting without a focus or a reason. This question of *why* at the most detailed level of an ANALYTIC TASK mirrors the broadest question at the highest level of strategy: *Why* am I undertaking this research project? When that essential question is answered, the result is a clear, coherent research question that guides the entire project. When the *why* question is answered at the detailed level of an ANALYTIC TASK, the result is a clear purpose that is intimately involved in choosing the appropriate COMPONENTS from the identified list of possibilities for fulfilling the task. This will be discussed further in "Step 4, Choosing Appropriate Components."

As in every step of TRANSLATION, there is a rule of thumb for describing purposes: an ANALYTIC TASK written at the most helpful level of detail tends to have a single purpose so that its outcome leads easily to identifying the next task. But as with all heuristics, this is not always the case.

The Difference Between a Purpose and an Action

One stumbling block to identifying the purposes of ANALYTIC TASKS is that it is easy to confuse a *purpose* with an *action*. Whereas a purpose is the reason *why* an ANALYTIC TASK is planned, an action is *how* it will be accomplished. We always include the purpose—the *why*—when writing ANALYTIC TASKS, but we only include the action—the *how*—when it is a help in the TRANSLATION process. Whether or not you include the action is influenced by the guiding methodology for the project, as well as the context of the task—what has come before and what is anticipated to come next. Deciding whether to include the action when writing an ANALYTIC TASK quickly becomes second nature after going through the TRANSLATION process a few times, but this initially requires some thought.

Consider again the ANALYTIC TASK from Appendix 1—*read interview transcripts to identify potential concepts for coding.* At first glance this has two purposes: to read the transcripts and to identify the potential concepts. But thinking of a purpose as *why* and an action as *how* makes clear that there is actually only one purpose: *to identify the concepts.* This is the *why* of the task—its purpose—and it is accomplished by the *how* of the task—the action of reading. This task therefore has a single purpose, which is the rule of thumb.

It may have been appropriate to include the action in the task—*read interview transcripts*—perhaps because the guiding methodology emphasizes that the researcher read the transcripts in their entirety before identifying any concepts. A different methodology with completely different objectives and methods for analyzing texts might emphasize identifying concepts in a different way, perhaps in a granular manner at the detailed level of each small segment of data or at a high level based on the frequency of occurrence of key words. In these situations the ANALYTIC TASK might be better written as *identify potential concepts for coding*, which expresses the purpose but leaves open the action to fulfill the purpose. In the TRANSLATION process various possibilities for acting on COMPONENTS would then be identified in the software, some that involve close reading, but perhaps others that would not involve close reading, such as auto-coding or Word Cloud operations.

Other examples of ANALYTIC TASKS in which it is helpful to include an action as well as a purpose are included in Appendix 5, which discusses the purposes of all 14 ANALYTIC TASKS introduced in Appendix 1.

The Rule of Thumb of One Purpose

A single purpose for an ANALYTIC TASK simplifies the process of TRANSLATION. This is because the TRANSLATION process takes account of what is anticipated to come next, and this is more complicated for a task with more than one purpose. A single purpose is therefore a helpful learning heuristic.

But often it is more productive to have two purposes than to split an ANALYTIC TASK in two. Consider this ANALYTIC TASK that has been written in sufficient detail to ensure there is a single purpose: *review codes and the coding scheme. Review* is a shorthand way of describing the purpose—*assess the codes that have been created in order to check they are of value within the coding scheme.* This single-purpose task easily leads to what we intend to do next—if we decide a NODE is not useful for some reason, we would do something about it. For example, we may rename it to more precisely reflect its characteristics, or we may merge it with another NODE that we realized represents the same concept, and so on. This following ANALYTIC TASK would be *refine codes and the coding scheme.* Although each ANALYTIC TASK indeed conforms to the learning heuristic of one purpose, in practice it would be difficult to *review codes and the coding scheme* and not at the same time *refine codes and the coding scheme* as needed, because this is an iterative process—refining one NODE influences the review of the next NODE. Reviewing all the codes (the first task) and then going back and refining them all (the second task) does not make sense. In this case it would be more appropriate to write an ANALYTIC TASK with two purposes as they go hand in hand, for example, *review and refine codes and the coding scheme.* This is the way we have presented this ANALYTIC TASK in Appendices 1, 4, and 5.

Regarding our sample ANALYTIC TASK, *compare teachers' reactions to different kinds of bullying,* we noted in Step 1 when identifying UNITS that we don't know from the wording of the task alone whether to identify two UNITS—*teachers* and *reactions to kinds of bullying*—or three—*teachers, reactions,* and *kinds of bullying.* The purpose of the task lets us know. If the purpose is *to investigate how individual teachers react to different kinds of bullying,* the focus is on the kinds of bullying and two UNITS are most helpful. If the purpose is *to investigate whether individual teachers display similar or different reactions to different kinds of bullying,* then the reactions and kinds of bullying must be differentiated and three UNITS are called for—*teachers, reactions,* and *kinds of bullying.* The second purpose is the one assumed in our sample ANALYTIC TASK, as displayed in Figure 6.6, the second iteration of the ANALYTIC PLANNING WORKSHEET.

For further illustration, Appendix 5 discusses the purposes of each of the 14 example ANALYTIC TASKS. Appendix 5 will be a helpful resource when you are ready to identify the purposes of your own ANALYTIC TASKS. Some of the examples follow the one-purpose rule of thumb, and some do not.

Step 3: Identifying Possible Components

In Chapter 3 we introduced the idea of TRANSLATION as a simple *matching* of a unit of an ANALYTIC TASK to a COMPONENT of the software, but in practice TRANSLATION means something richer: *representing* the UNITS of an ANALYTIC TASK by the most appropriate of all the possible COMPONENTS to which they could be matched. This requires taking account of the context of the task and knowing the actions that can be taken on the COMPONENTS. For purposes of exposition and to provide a learning heuristic, we divide the process into two parts: first, *identifying* all the possible COMPONENTS that could be used to fulfil an ANALYTIC TASK (Step 3); and second, *choosing* the most appropriate

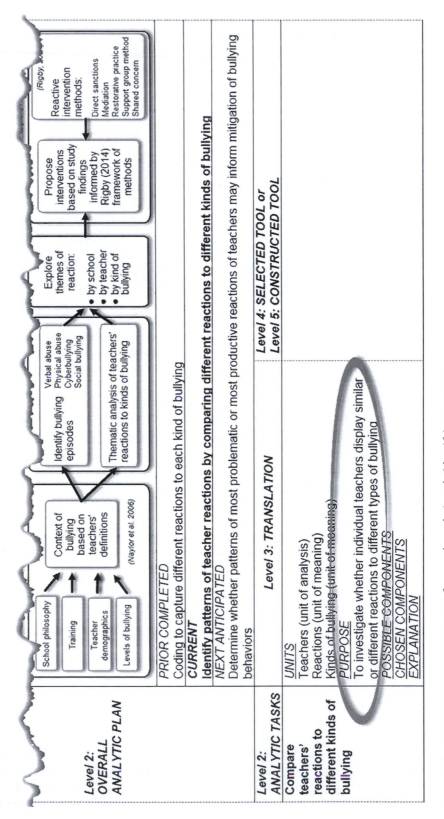

FIGURE 6.6 ANALYTIC PLANNING WORKSHEET for sample analytic task: Identifying purposes

COMPONENTS from among these possibilities (Step 4). When learning the process it is helpful to think about these two steps as distinct. After a small amount of experience, our students come to think of these steps in the manner of experienced users of NVivo—as a single thought process—and it is likely you will too. But for learning purposes we begin by identifying the possible COMPONENTS that could be used to fulfil an ANALYTIC TASK.

In Chapter 3 (page 49) we compared the TRANSLATION of ANALYTIC TASKS to the translation of languages. In language translation a simple word-by-word rendition of one language into another is called the *formal equivalence* of the words in each language. This may be adequate for asking directions or translating technical terms that don't involve shades of meaning. But a formal word-by-word translation is not sufficient for translating idioms or subtleties from one language to another. This requires *dynamic equivalence* between the original and the translated text. This means finding appropriate words in the second language that ensure that the original and the translated versions have roughly the same effect on their respective readers, something not accomplished by a mechanical word-by-word translation.

The distinction between *formal equivalence* and *dynamic equivalence* in language translation is the basis for our rule of thumb for identifying possible COMPONENTS. We first look for *formal equivalence*. This means a clear and obvious match between a UNIT and a COMPONENT that is suggested by the affordances of the software, meaning the way the software is designed and presented on the screen with this equivalence in mind. We then consider any *dynamically equivalent* COMPONENTS, meaning those that are not as obvious a match to a UNIT. This ensures that we take advantage of the full flexibility of NVivo and not limit ourselves to *formally equivalent* COMPONENTS that might not be the best candidate in a particular context.

The distinction between *formally equivalent* and *dynamically equivalent* COMPONENTS is a helpful learning heuristic, but it is not necessary to think too deeply about whether an equivalence between a UNIT and a COMPONENT is formal or dynamic. Knowing about this distinction is enough to prompt us to first identify the obvious matches suggested by the program's affordances and then identify out-of-the-box matches that may prove more productive. As experience grows and you become more familiar with using the various COMPONENTS, the distinction will fade. In the meantime, we use the terms *formal equivalence* and *dynamic equivalence* when necessary in the remainder of this section to draw attention to the different thinking processes.

We now return to the sample ANALYTIC TASK—*compare teachers' reactions to different kinds of bullying*. Table 6.1 summarizes all the possible COMPONENTS that could represent the UNITS of the task—*teachers*, which is a unit of analysis, and *reactions* and *kinds of bullying*, which are both units of meaning. Following Table 6.1 we discuss the rationale for identifying each possible COMPONENT, and we then display the updated ANALYTIC PLANNING WORKSHEET with the possible COMPONENTS entered.

Possible Components for the First Unit

In this sample ANALYTIC TASK we are thinking of *teachers* as a UNIT of analysis independent of their reactions to different kinds of bullying (see Appendix 4). We therefore need to identify COMPONENTS that could be used to represent *teachers* independent of any other UNIT in the study.

Source

A SOURCE can be used to represent a teacher when the entirety of each teacher's contributions to the study is contained within one SOURCE. This would likely be the situation in an interview-based study in which each teacher had been interviewed once. The whole of each interview would have been transcribed into a separate Microsoft Word file and added to the NVIVO-PROJECT as a separate

TABLE 6.1 Summary of possible components for "teachers," "reactions," and "kinds of bullying"

Component	"Teachers"	"Reactions"	"Kinds of bullying"
SOURCE	possible component		
FOLDER			
CASE	possible component		
ATTRIBUTE–VALUE	possible component		
REFERENCE			
NODE		possible component	possible component
CODED–REFERENCE		possible component	possible component
QUERY–RESULT		possible component	possible component
SET AND SEARCH FOLDER	possible component	possible component	possible component
ANNOTATION		possible component	possible component
MEMO	possible component	possible component	possible component
MAP	possible component	possible component	possible component
CHART	possible component	possible component	possible component

SOURCE. There would thus be a *formal equivalence* between the UNIT of a teacher and the COMPONENT of a SOURCE.

Case

A CASE can be used to represent a teacher when there is more than one SOURCE per teacher. This may be the situation in a longitudinal project if each teacher had been interviewed on three separate occasions. In the NVIVO-PROJECT we would therefore have three SOURCES per teacher, so each SOURCE is not *formally equivalent* to the UNIT of teacher. A CASE can also be used to represent a teacher when several teachers' contributions to the study are contained within a single SOURCE. This may be the situation in a focus group study when several teachers come together to discuss bullying in a moderated discussion. The focus group discussion would be added to the NVIVO-PROJECT as one SOURCE. There would also not be a *formal equivalence* between the UNIT of a teacher and each SOURCE, because the SOURCE includes the voices of multiple teachers. In either of these situations we need to seek a *dynamic equivalence* between the UNIT and a COMPONENT. We could use CASES for this purpose, one per teacher, at which we would either code each teacher's three SOURCES or all her contributions to the focus group discussion. We would then have created one COMPONENT, a CASE to represent each UNIT, the teacher.

Attribute-Value

An ATTRIBUTE-VALUE can be used to represent a teacher when there is more than one SOURCE or CASE per teacher. This may be the situation in a longitudinal project if the responses expressed in different interviews at different points of time may be important. Rather than combining the three separate SOURCES into one CASE, it may be more appropriate to have a separate CASE for each teacher at each data collection phase in order to be able to identify differences in their opinions, experiences, or characteristics between each data collection phase. We need to seek a *dynamic equivalence* between the UNIT and the COMPONENT. We could use ATTRIBUTE-VALUES for this purpose, one for each teacher, which would be linked to each of her three CASES or SOURCES.

Set & Search-Folder

A SET & SEARCH-FOLDER can be used to represent a teacher when there is more than one SOURCE per teacher. This may be the situation in a longitudinal project if each teacher had been interviewed on three separate occasions. In the NVIVO-PROJECT we would therefore have three SOURCES per teacher, so each SOURCE is not *formally equivalent* to the UNIT of teacher. We therefore need to seek a *dynamic equivalence* between the UNIT and a COMPONENT. We could use SETS & SEARCH-FOLDERS for this purpose, one per teacher, into which we would add each teacher's three SOURCES. We would then have created one COMPONENT, a SET & SEARCH-FOLDER, to represent each UNIT, the teacher.

Memo

A MEMO can be used to represent the UNIT *teachers* when it is appropriate for all the researcher's insights about an individual teacher to be written up in one space. This is a natural use for a MEMO, and this *formal equivalence* may be appropriate in many types of study—for example, an analytic plan may call for summarizing teachers' reactions by writing analytic interpretations about each teacher separately.

This use of MEMOS is independent of data collection strategies. *Teachers* may also be represented by other COMPONENTS for other purposes. There is no reason that a UNIT cannot be represented in multiple ways for different purposes.

Map

MAPS can be used to display and work with COMPONENTS visually and can therefore be used as a *dynamic equivalent* for any UNIT. In the example of *teachers* with three interviews each, a Concept or Project MAP can be created to display all three SOURCES, and a variety of tasks can be undertaken in this visual display if it is determined in Step 4 that this is more appropriate than other ways of working—see Chapter 5 for information about the three different types of MAPS.

Chart

CHARTS can also be used to display COMPONENTS in the NVIVO-PROJECT, but only to display the COMPONENTS and not to continue work on them. CHARTS can therefore be used as a *dynamic equivalence* for any UNIT that is already represented by another COMPONENT in the NVIVO-PROJECT.

Possible Components for the Second Unit

Reviewing the ANALYTIC PLANNING WORKSHEET for our sample ANALYTIC TASK, we know that teachers' *reactions* and *kinds of bullying* are considered separate UNITS of meaning, rather than a single UNIT of *reactions to kinds of bullying*, based on the purpose of the task (page 124). Because both UNITS are of the same type, the thought process involved in identifying possible COMPONENTS is the same. In this section we only discuss the UNIT *reactions* to avoid unnecessary duplication.

Node

A NODE representing a concept or a unit of meaning is the most obvious *formal equivalence*. A NODE can be used to represent a teacher's *reaction* when it is anticipated that several instances of each kind of reaction will be identified across different SOURCES and there is a need to gather them all together, or retrieve them. This would likely be the situation if several different teachers had been interviewed, had been observed, or had taken part in focus group discussions. A NODE would be created and named for each reaction and linked to REFERENCES where those concepts were explicitly stated or implied by teachers, for example, *disapproval* and *censure*.

Coded-Reference

If NODES were used to represent teachers' *reactions*, then linking the NODES to REFERENCES produces CODED-REFERENCES that are instances of each *reaction*. For some purposes these CODED-REFERENCES that represent the instances of reactions in the data may be acted upon independently.

Query-Result

When a query retrieves CODED-REFERENCES from two or more NODES, the saved QUERY-RESULT represents the resulting concept. For example, if it was necessary to think about just some of the *active reactions* together, but not all of them, we could run a Coding Query to combine the NODES *short-term exclusion* and *permanent exclusion* and save the QUERY-RESULT. This is particularly useful in longitudinal projects, for example, if there is a need to compare teachers' *reactions* at the end of each wave of data collection.

Set & Search-Folder

A SET & SEARCH-FOLDER could be used to represent different types of *reactions* if NODES had first been used to represent teachers' *reactions*. For example a SET & SEARCH-FOLDER named *passive reactions* could contain the NODES *disapproval, censure,* or *regret,* and another SET & SEARCH-FOLDER called *active reactions* could contain the NODES *physical restraint* and *exclusion*. SETS & SEARCH-FOLDERS may therefore represent higher-level concepts in order to work separately with all passive reactions and all active reactions.

In addition, SETS & SEARCH-FOLDERS could be used to represent teachers' *reactions* if the concept being represented is at the next higher level of abstraction. For example, various NODES may represent different teacher *reactions* to three kinds of bullying—*physical, verbal,* and *cyber* bullying. These three groups of *reaction* NODES can be grouped into three SETS of the same names. This is one level of abstraction higher than the individual *reaction* NODES. If the purpose of an ANALYTIC TASK is to retrieve data only related to face-to-face bullying (i.e., physical or verbal but not cyber bullying), then a SEARCH-FOLDER could be created to be *formally equivalent* to the concept *face-to-face bullying*. The two relevant SETS—*physical bullying* and *verbal bullying*—can be combined to create a SEARCH-FOLDER that can be used to retrieve all CODED-REFERENCES from the NODES in the two face-to-face bullying SETS.

Annotation

An ANNOTATION can be used as a *dynamic equivalence* for a *reaction* if it was decided to familiarize oneself with the data by closely reading through interview transcripts before coding REFERENCES at NODES. In this situation ANNOTATIONS are natural spaces for writing insights about a specific reaction.

The ANNOTATION will always be available wherever the REFERENCE is viewed, whether onscreen or in printed or exported form.

Memo

A MEMO can be used to represent a teacher's *reaction* when all the researcher's insights about each reaction need to be written up in a separate space. This is a natural use for a MEMO, and this *formal equivalence* may be appropriate in many types of study—for example, an analytic plan may call for summarizing teachers' *reactions* by writing analytic notes about each reaction separately and then analyzing these summaries rather than the original data.

Map

As described earlier, a MAP can be used as a *dynamic equivalent* for any UNIT. Any of the COMPONENTS discussed previously to represent teachers' *reactions* can be displayed in a MAP, and tasks can be undertaken in this visual display if it is determined in Step 4 that this is more appropriate than other ways of working.

Chart

CHARTS can also be used to display COMPONENTS in the NVIVO-PROJECT, but only to display the COMPONENTS and not to continue work on them. CHARTS can therefore be used as a *dynamic equivalence* for any UNIT that is already represented by another COMPONENT in the NVIVO-PROJECT.

In summary, NVivo is flexible when harnessed powerfully. There is no fixed one-to-one relationship between a particular UNIT and a particular COMPONENT. The same UNIT of an ANALYTIC TASK can often be represented by several different COMPONENTS, and conversely, the same COMPONENT can represent different UNITS in the same NVIVO-PROJECT. Additionally, the use of COMPONENTS can change as an analysis proceeds. For example, one UNIT may be represented by more than one COMPONENT if it is required for different ANALYTIC TASKS at different stages of a project. Identifying COMPONENTS is therefore not done once and set in stone, but is an emergent process that parallels the emergent process at the strategy levels.

Additional Possible Components When Purposes Require Writing or Visualizing

In addition to UNITS, purposes can play a role in identifying COMPONENTS. This is the case when the UNITS of an ANALYTIC TASK do not call for COMPONENTS that involve writing or visualizing, yet the purpose of the task does require writing or visualizing. For example, five of the 14 ANALYTIC TASKS in Appendix 5 have writing or visualizing purposes that stand alone from the UNITS of the task identified in Appendix 4. For these five ANALYTIC TASKS, the purpose suggests additional needed COMPONENTS for *explaining, summarizing* or *interpreting*:

- Compare theoretical and emerging concepts and *explain* their similarities and differences.
- Review field notes to *summarize* athletes' body language with same- and opposite-gender coaches.
- Create and *explain* relationships between concepts.
- *Summarize* differences in verbal and nonverbal interaction between doctors and patients.
- *Interpret* media representations of local politicians in relation to attitudes expressed by focus group respondents.

When identifying possible COMPONENTS we therefore ask ourselves a final question: *Does the purpose of the* ANALYTIC TASK *call for additional possible* COMPONENTS *to support writing or visualizing?* For example, these actions of *explaining, summarizing,* or *interpreting* indicate a need to either write about or graphically represent what is seen while undertaking the task. Therefore ANNOTATIONS, MEMOS, MAPS, and CHARTS are additional possible COMPONENTS for these tasks—as *formal equivalents* to their purposes. In the case of our sample ANALYTIC TASK, these COMPONENTS have already been identified. However, for some ANALYTIC TASKS these COMPONENTS may not have been identified from the UNITS and therefore it is always important to consider whether the purpose of the task calls for additional COMPONENTS to support writing or visualizing.

Figure 6.7 displays all the possible COMPONENTS that we have identified in the third iteration of the ANALYTIC PLANNING WORKSHEET.

Step 4: Choosing Appropriate Components

Step 4 involves choosing the appropriate COMPONENTS to fulfill an ANALYTIC TASK. This means evaluating the possible COMPONENTS identified in Step 3 in terms of the *actions* that can be taken on those COMPONENTS and the *context* of the task. The context of an ANALYTIC TASK consists of three elements: its purpose, what has been accomplished previously, and what is anticipated to happen next.

We illustrate Steps 4 and 5 differently from Steps 1, 2, and 3, so we begin by discussing the differences. We then describe all the actions that can be taken on COMPONENTS in NVivo and illustrate the process of choosing appropriate COMPONENTS.

Illustrations for Steps 4 and 5

In the first three steps of TRANSLATION we provided a variety of illustrations in the chapter text as well as further examples for each of the 14 ANALYTIC TASKS in the appendices. Our purpose was to facilitate this way of thinking through multiple examples that offer models to be adapted and transferred to your own project. Steps 4 and 5, however, are different. These last two steps describe in detail a way of thinking about the completion of the TRANSLATION process using our straightforward sample ANALYTIC TASK. How this thinking is applied in different contexts is extremely varied because every project is so different and there are many possible contexts for each ANALYTIC TASK. For this reason we cannot provide a range of written illustrations wide enough to serve as models to be adapted for Steps 4 and 5, and therefore there is no appendix of additional examples for these steps of TRANSLATION. Instead, Steps 4 and 5 are preparation for the video demonstrations in Part III that illustrate TRANSLATION of a selection of ANALYTIC TASKS in real-world projects. Chapter 7 provides more detail about the videos and how to learn from the case illustrations.

Steps 4 and 5 are the heart of the practical instruction in TRANSLATION. Table 6.2 reviews the sequence of this practical instruction.

Actions That Can Be Taken on Components

You already have an understanding of NVivo's 13 COMPONENTS from Chapter 5 and the accompanying *Component Orientation* videos. The definitions of each COMPONENT are found in Table 5.2 (page 68). But you also need to know what actions can be taken on COMPONENTS. Some actions can be taken on all COMPONENTS, which we call *common actions*. These are listed in Table 6.3. Other actions are specific to particular COMPONENTS. These *component-specific actions* are listed in Table 6.4. We only list actions that are relevant for analytic purposes. We do not list every possible routine or housekeeping action, such as *open* a window, *close* a window, *save, print, output, delete,* etc. These two

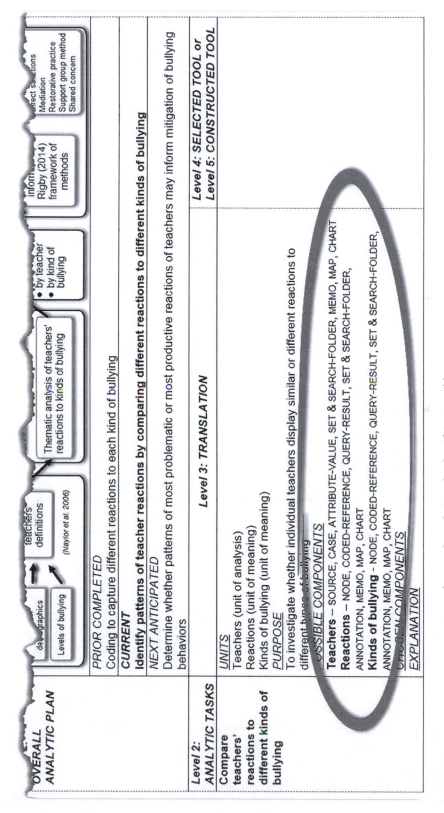

FIGURE 6.7   ANALYTIC PLANNING WORKSHEET for sample analytic task: Identifying possible components

TABLE 6.2 The sequence of practical instruction in NVivo's components

Chapter 5 and accompanying *Component Orientation* videos	Chapter 5 and accompanying videos are organized by COMPONENT and focus on the mechanics of each COMPONENT—how they are designed and how they work. These resources can be used at any time to remind yourself how a particular COMPONENT functions.
Chapter 6 Steps 3, 4, and 5	Steps 1 and 2 prepare the groundwork for TRANSLATION, identifying UNITS and purposes in ANALYTIC TASKS. Steps 3, 4, and 5 focus on the COMPONENTS. Step 3—*identifying possible components*—is presented in a similar manner to Steps 1 and 2, with a comprehensive review of all the commonly used COMPONENTS.
	Steps 4 and 5 do not attempt to provide a comprehensive range of examples, but instead focus on the detailed thinking process in one straightforward example of TRANSLATION. The learning objective is to understand the process. The video demonstrations in Part III provide a range of examples of this thinking process in real-world projects that you can adapt to your own work.
Chapters 8 and 9 and accompanying *Case Illustration* videos	Chapters 8 and 9 provide two fully documented real-world case illustrations. The accompanying video demonstrations include examples of real-world TRANSLATION of ANALYTIC TASKS as they occurred in each project.
Harnessing Components videos	The final set of *Harnessing Components* videos are the culmination of the instruction. They are organized by COMPONENT and demonstrate contrasting ways to harness COMPONENTS in different contexts.

TABLE 6.3 Analytic actions that can be taken on all components

Common Actions	
Create new	Create a new COMPONENT at any time. There is never a need to think in advance of all the COMPONENTS that need to be created before beginning work.
Rename	Rename COMPONENTS at any time. COMPONENTS are given names when they are created. We can change the name of any COMPONENT at any time.
Search	Search for any string of characters in the name or the content of COMPONENTS, or find COMPONENTS based on specified characteristics. A listing is produced of all the items that meet the search criteria.
Write	Write a definition in the Description field of any COMPONENT, write an ANNOTATION on a REFERENCE, write in a MEMO, or use the program's *edit mode* to write in a SOURCE.
Sort	Sort lists of COMPONENTS in various ways in the List View and other tables, for example, by column headers.
Visualize in maps and charts	Display and work with COMPONENTS visually. Some actions on COMPONENTS in MAPS are put into effect throughout the NVIVO-PROJECT, for example, renaming a COMPONENT. Other actions are only put into effect within the MAP in which they are taken, such as linking components with connectors. CHARTS display components and their associations.

tables of analytic actions are referred to in the coming sections and in all the video demonstrations on the companion website.

Note that *any* analytic action can be taken at *any* time in NVivo. For example, the action *import* SOURCES is not restricted to the beginning of a project; additional SOURCES can be added or imported at any time as the project proceeds.

TABLE 6.4 Component-specific analytic actions

Component	Component-specific analytic actions
SOURCE	**Import** into the NVIVO–PROJECT **Edit** to change the content (text sources only) **Group** into FOLDERS, OR SETS & SEARCH–FOLDERS **Link** to MEMOS, REFERENCES, CASES, or NODES **Interrogate** SOURCES
FOLDER	**Add or remove** members **Interrogate** FOLDERS
ATTRIBUTE–VALUE	**Link to** SOURCES or CASES **Interrogate** ATTRIBUTE-VALUES
CASE	**Group** into FOLDERS, HIERARCHIES, or SETS & SEARCH–FOLDERS **Link** to REFERENCES, other CASES, NODES, MEMOS, or ATTRIBUTE–VALUES **Interrogate** CASES
REFERENCE	**Link** to NODES, other REFERENCES, SOURCES, or MEMOS **Resize** to include more or less data
NODE	**Group** into FOLDERS, HIERARCHIES, or SETS & SEARCH–FOLDERS **Link** to REFERENCES, CASES, other NODES, or MEMOS **Aggregate** coding from Child NODES **Interrogate** NODES
CODED–REFERENCE	**Retrieve** groups of REFERENCES based on how they are coded **Link** to other REFERENCES, other NODES, SOURCES, or MEMOS **Interrogate** CODED–REFERENCES
QUERY–RESULT	**Group** into FOLDERS or SETS & SEARCH–FOLDERS **Convert** into a NODE **Interrogate** QUERY–RESULTS
SET AND SEARCH–FOLDERS	**Add or remove** members **Combine** into a new SETS & SEARCH–FOLDERS **Interrogate** SETS & SEARCH–FOLDERS
ANNOTATION	*An ANNOTATION is a space in which to write about a REFERENCE. Other than the action of writing in them, ANNOTATIONS cannot be acted on independently.*
MEMO	**Import** into the NVIVO–PROJECT **Edit** to change the content **Group** into FOLDERS or SETS & SEARCH–FOLDERS **Link** to SOURCES, REFERENCES, CASES, and NODES **Interrogate** MEMOS
MAP	*A MAP is a display of other COMPONENTS. Actions are taken on the COMPONENTS displayed within a MAP, not on the MAP itself.*
CHART	*A CHART is a display of other COMPONENTS. Actions are taken on the COMPONENTS displayed within a CHART, not on the CHART itself.*

The Context of Analytic Tasks

Qualitative analysis is iterative—we continually reconsider what we are currently doing in light of what has already been done so that the individual parts of an analysis develop together as a whole. The rule of thumb for Step 4 is that the choice of appropriate COMPONENTS for an ANALYTIC TASK is informed by the three elements of its context: what has been accomplished previously, the purpose of the task, and what is anticipated to happen next. This is a guide, not a step-by-step procedure, and in each situation the role of these elements of context will vary. A learning heuristic is to consider each of the following points in turn when choosing appropriate COMPONENTS:

- Review objectives and analytic plan
- Consider previous ANALYTIC TASK
- Evaluate previous ANALYTIC TASK in terms of current purpose
- Choose COMPONENTS in terms of anticipated next task

Review Objectives and Analytic Plan

In qualitative research the analytic plan evolves as the project progresses. In some methodologies even the objectives may change based on the progress of the analysis. It is therefore important to first review the current iteration of the analytic plan, especially if there has been a gap in time since last working on the project.

The objectives and current analytic plan for our sample ANALYTIC TASK are found in the upper part of its ANALYTIC PLANNING WORKSHEET in Figure 6.3 (page 117). In summary, this project is an interview-based study of teachers in two schools with differing levels of bullying, using thematic analysis to understand the role of teachers in resolving entrenched bullying. Figure 6.3 also indicates that the current analysis phase will *explore teacher reactions to bullying*, and the graphical conceptual framework presents the current plan for accomplishing this. The prior completed task and next anticipated task are noted. This review of the worksheet has brought us back up to date on the overall context for the ANALYTIC TASK we are now working on—*compare teachers' reactions to different kinds of bullying*.

Consider Previous Analytic Task

The ANALYTIC PLANNING WORKSHEET for this phase, displayed in Figure 6.3, shows us that the prior completed task involved coding to capture different reactions to each kind of bullying. A review of that prior worksheet would show us that in addition to one unit of analysis—*teachers*—we had identified two separate units of meaning—*teachers' reactions* and *kinds of bullying*. This led to creating two hierarchies of NODES. One hierarchy represented the different kinds of bullying we had identified in the literature—*verbal abuse, physical abuse, cyber bullying*, etc., and another hierarchy represented each type of reaction we found in the interview data—*disapproval, censure, sympathy*, etc.

Each teacher's interview transcript had been added to the NVIVO-PROJECT as a separate SOURCE. Each teacher was interviewed only once, and the interviewer had asked short questions and used simple prompts to encourage them to elaborate. So the vast majority of text within each SOURCE consisted of the teacher speaking, and therefore each teacher could be represented by a single SOURCE. The focus of the thematic analysis was to identify themes by interpreting what was implied as well as what was explicit in the teachers' responses. Therefore the coding had been accomplished by reading through each SOURCE and applying NODES to REFERENCES one by one, without the use of any auto-coding procedure. There is therefore no reason to consider an alternative COMPONENT for representing *teachers* from the possible COMPONENTS we had considered in Step 3.

Reviewing the prior ANALYTIC TASK in this way reminds us of the available building blocks of analysis that have already been created. These building blocks serve as the context for designing the activities in the current task.

Evaluate Previous Task in Terms of Current Purpose

The building blocks made available by the previous ANALYTIC TASK must now be evaluated in terms of the purpose of the current ANALYTIC TASK. The purpose had been entered into the ANALYTIC PLANNING WORKSHEET in Step 2, displayed in Figure 6.6 (page. 124). The purpose is *to investigate whether individual teachers display similar or different reactions to different types of bullying.* This requires a fine-grained set of comparisons that distinguish and compare each type of reaction to each kind of bullying. The issue is whether the building blocks from the prior ANALYTIC TASK will serve this purpose.

We already have each *teacher* represented as a SOURCE from the previous task, so we can continue to use SOURCES to represent this UNIT for the current ANALYTIC TASK.

Regarding the COMPONENTS to represent the *similar or different reactions to different kinds of bullying*, we must now consider if the choices made in the prior ANALYTIC TASK are consistent with the purposes of the current task. In the prior task we had settled on two separate UNITS of meaning—*reactions* and *kinds of bullying*—and coded accordingly. These separate hierarchies of NODES from the prior task provide enough differentiation to support the fine-grained comparisons we intend to perform in the current task because the two elements we want to compare—*reactions* and *kinds of bullying*—have been captured independently from one another. In this straightforward example, there is therefore no reason to consider alternative COMPONENTS—from the numerous possible COMPONENTS we had identified in Step 3—for representing *reactions* and *kinds of bullying*. We can proceed with the comparisons by using the building blocks created in the prior task.

Looking Ahead

This straightforward progress of the analysis is not always the case. It is common to discover that the prior ANALYTIC TASK has been fulfilled in a way that does not make the current task so straightforward. In the final part of Step 5 we will consider the complications that would arise if we had made different choices in the prior task.

Choose Components in Terms of Anticipated Next Task

In order to make the most appropriate decisions about SELECTING or CONSTRUCTING a TOOL, we must also consider what we anticipate doing next. This is the third element of the context of an ANALYTIC TASK.

Thinking ahead reduces the likelihood that we will need to backtrack later. We already know that we made a good choice in the prior task by coding at a sufficient level of detail, creating hierarchies of NODES for two UNITS of meaning—*reactions* and *kinds of bullying*—rather than a single hierarchy of NODES for the single UNIT *reactions to different kinds of bullying*. This choice permitted us to move ahead easily with the current task of comparing teachers' reactions to different kinds of bullying, as we have separate hierarchies of NODES for each UNIT. From the ANALYTIC PLANNING WORKSHEET we also know the purpose of the current task and the actions available to take on the COMPONENTS representing our UNITS. We have almost everything we need to choose how to finalize SELECTED- or CONSTRUCTED TOOLS in order to fulfill this ANALYTIC TASK in the software.

One more thing to consider: what is anticipated to come next. Because qualitative analysis is emergent, anticipating what may come next is not always possible. Therefore it is tempting to think: *What happens next depends on the outcome of the current investigations of similar and different reactions. That is the point at which I will decide what happens next.* But when TRANSLATING ANALYTIC

TASKS, we should always attempt to anticipate the next task more specifically because this focuses our current actions and helps ensure that we make the most appropriate choices. This is not the same as predetermining the next task, but rather choosing the best current action in the context of our best current anticipation of what may come next. This is part of the iterative process of qualitative analysis.

We have an overall analytic plan at strategy Level 2 in the ANALYTIC PLANNING WORKSHEET. This area of the worksheet is designed to facilitate thinking in an emergent manner about what happens next. Figure 6.8 displays schematically these areas of the worksheet. In the central area of the worksheet, at Level 2, we see the general purpose of the current phase that emerged from prior analytic activity: *identify patterns of teacher reactions by comparing different reactions to different kinds of bullying*. The first ANALYTIC TASK in this current phase begins to fulfill this general purpose: *compare teachers' reactions to different kinds of bullying*. Figure 6.8 also indicates the next anticipated phase. This suggests a possible way forward by next considering the extremes of teacher reactions and their impact—the most problematic and the most productive reactions of teachers—perhaps based on prior research. The next anticipated phase indicated in Figure 6.8 is therefore to *determine whether patterns of most problematic or most productive reactions of teachers may inform mitigation of bullying behaviors*. This possible way forward for the next phase is entered to the ANALYTIC PLANNING WORKSHEET because it needs to be considered in the current phase. We do this by thinking through how to integrate this possible way forward while fulfilling the current task, and we come up with a question to ask ourselves as we conduct the analysis: *Do the patterns of teacher reactions that we discover in the current phase help determine whether the most problematic and the most helpful teacher reactions emerge as a helpful way of informing ways to mitigate bullying?* This will be an assessment of the patterns we discover in the current task, and is therefore consistent with our TRANSLATION plans so far. But a new thought also comes to mind. Because we selected two schools with contrasting reports of entrenched bullying, we may find that distinguishing schools, not just teachers, may be helpful in identifying patterns of problematic and helpful teacher reactions. We now realize that we have neglected to consider *school* as a UNIT—it just slipped through the net until this point. However, we know that every teacher teaches at one school or the other. A school is therefore a group of teachers, and so the *school* as a UNIT is simply a higher-level organization of *teachers* as a UNIT. We therefore have confidence that if we decide to go ahead with this new ANALYTIC TASK, we can take account of the new UNIT in Step 5 when we finalize the SELECTED- or CONSTRUCTED-TOOLS for that task.

Considering what is anticipated next is part of the iterative process of making choices about the present task in light of anticipated future tasks. This ensures that our current actions do not preclude anticipated tasks, and also informs our thinking about the current task. Considering what is anticipated next is therefore not the same as predetermining the next task. In our example, we have been alerted to the possibility that patterns of bullying at the school level may be considered in the next task, and so we will be sensitive to this possibility when analyzing reactions at the teacher level in the current task. This may seem obvious in retrospect, but the best insights are often simple rather than complex and often do feel obvious. In this case the insight came from linking the idea of considering the most problematic and most helpful reactions—which may not have been part of the original research design—to the selection of schools with widely varying bullying reports.

In conclusion, if we do not think through what is anticipated next—the third element of the context of an ANALYTIC TASK—we may miss analytic opportunities. Having had this insight, we want to make sure it is not lost, which can easily happen with so many things to think about as the analysis progresses. We therefore note the insight in the *Reflections* box of the ANALYTIC PLANNING

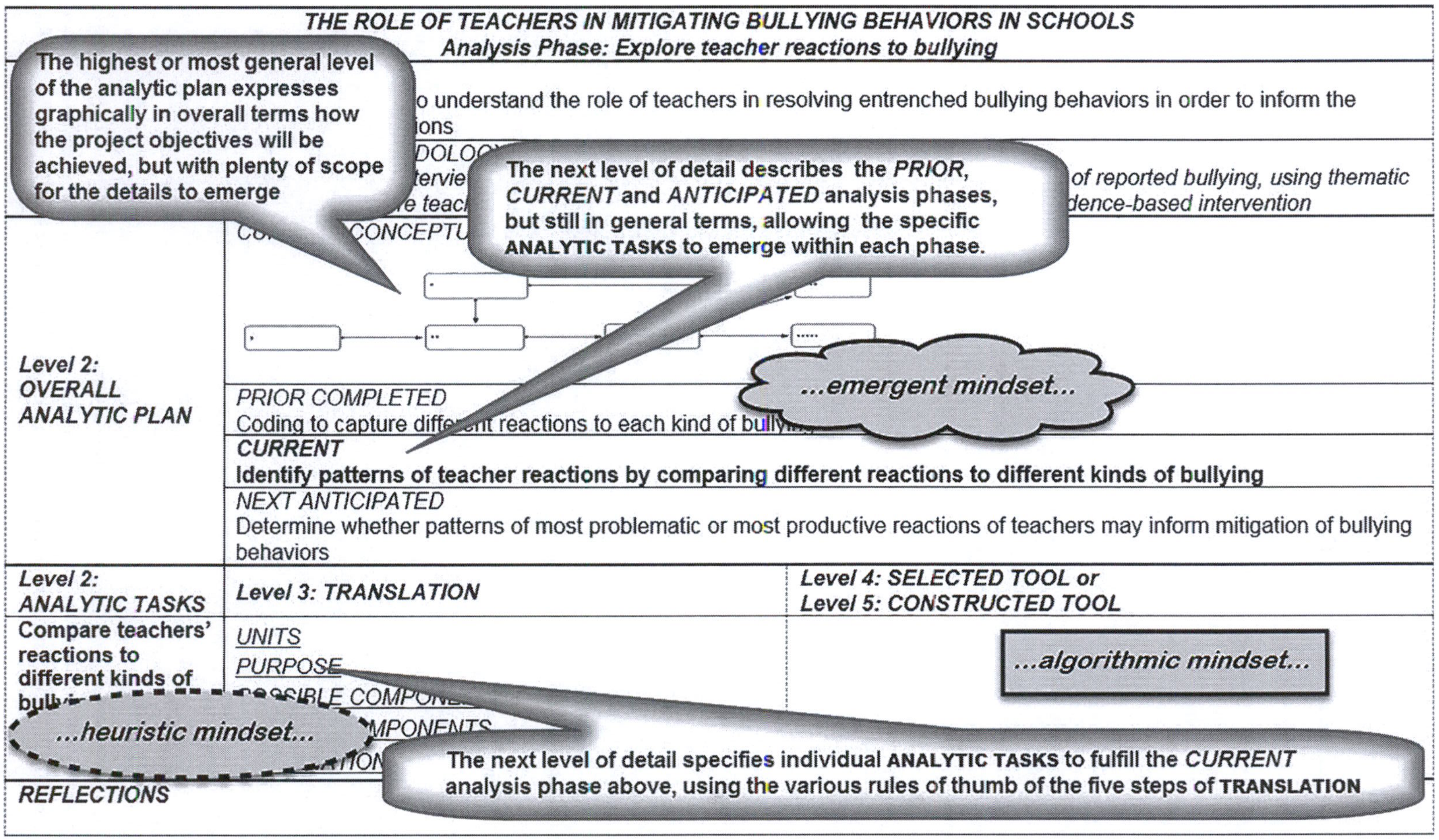
THE ROLE OF TEACHERS IN MITIGATING BULLYING BEHAVIORS IN SCHOOLS
Analysis Phase: Explore teacher reactions to bullying
The highest or most general level of the analytic plan expresses graphically in overall terms how the project objectives will be achieved, but with plenty of scope for the details to emerge
o understand the role of teachers in resolving entrenched bullying behaviors in order to inform the
ions
The next level of detail describes the PRIOR, CURRENT and ANTICIPATED analysis phases, but still in general terms, allowing the specific ANALYTIC TASKS to emerge within each phase.
of reported bullying, using thematic
dence-based intervention
CONCEPTU
Level 2: OVERALL ANALYTIC PLAN
...emergent mindset...
PRIOR COMPLETED
Coding to capture diff
nt reactions to each kind of bu
CURRENT
Identify patterns of teacher reactions by comparing different reactions to different kinds of bullying
NEXT ANTICIPATED
Determine whether patterns of most problematic or most productive reactions of teachers may inform mitigation of bullying behaviors
Level 2: ANALYTIC TASKS
Level 3: TRANSLATION
Level 4: SELECTED TOOL or
Level 5: CONSTRUCTED TOOL
Compare teachers' reactions to different kinds of
UNITS
PURPOSE
...algorithmic mindset...
...heuristic mindset...
The next level of detail specifies individual ANALYTIC TASKS to fulfill the CURRENT analysis phase above, using the various rules of thumb of the five steps of TRANSLATION
REFLECTIONS

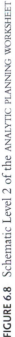

FIGURE 6.8 Schematic Level 2 of the ANALYTIC PLANNING WORKSHEET

WORKSHEET. Figure 6.9 displays these reflections, as well as our final choice of appropriate COMPO-NENTS, in the fourth iteration of the ANALYTIC PLANNING WORKSHEET.

Step 5: Finalizing Selected- or Constructed-Tools

The final step of TRANSLATION is finalizing SELECTED- or CONSTRUCTED-TOOLS that act on the chosen COMPONENTS, thereby fulfilling an ANALYTIC TASK. We use the term TOOL to mean an action taken on a COMPONENT. Figure 2.1 (page 27) displays the two kinds of TOOLS as Levels 4 and 5 of the *Five-Level QDA* method. This section therefore marks the end of our elaboration of the method.

We begin by distinguishing SELECTED- and CONSTRUCTED-TOOLS, and then we provide an example for each of the circumstances that calls for either one. We end each section with a more thoroughly worked example of the sample ANALYTIC TASK in the bullying study.

The Distinction Between Selected- and Constructed-Tools

The distinction between SELECTED- and CONSTRUCTED-TOOLS is only a learning heuristic. It is easy to provide a formal distinction—a SELECTED-TOOL is a *straightforward choice of individual software operations*, and a CONSTRUCTED-TOOL is a *sophisticated use of software by combining operations or using them in a custom way*. But with growing experience the distinction between the two fades. The evolving way in which humans experience the passage of time is a helpful analogy. Babies and children experience time passing very slowly because each perception is a new experience; there are so many new perceptions that each day feels like an eternity. As we get older perceptions and experiences accumulate and are repeated. They start to clump together so that they are experienced as larger events. We therefore perceive fewer of them each day, and the day feels like it passes more quickly. By the time we are elderly we have seen almost everything already, and experiences are connected and clumped into much larger events. The days and weeks and years fly by with far fewer (but larger) individual events perceived each day.

In a similar way, when starting out with the *Five-Level QDA* method we stick to the rules of thumb whenever possible—a couple of UNITS and a single purpose per ANALYTIC TASK—because this simplifies the process. We use many SELECTED-TOOLS and just a few CONSTRUCTED-TOOLS where a SELECTED-TOOL is not available. As experience grows we gradually leave the rules of thumb behind and find ourselves not thinking too much about whether we are using a SELECTED- or CONSTRUCTED-TOOL. More and more of the SELECTED-TOOLS we are using will start to clump into larger CONSTRUCTED-TOOLS. For the expert NVivo user, the entire project becomes an amorphous, giant CONSTRUCTED-TOOL.

We do not write this to encourage you to hurry past the stage of identifying many SELECTED-TOOLS—that would be counterproductive. We mention this because you may wonder why a particular example of an action taken on a COMPONENT in the following sections or in the videos is considered a SELECTED-TOOL rather than a part of a larger CONSTRUCTED-TOOL. The answer is that it helps you learn the process. As you gain experience it is of no concern whether you are thinking in terms of SELECTED-TOOLS or CONSTRUCTED-TOOLS to fulfill your ANALYTIC TASKS. A project with mainly SELECTED-TOOLS most certainly does not imply less sophistication or complexity than a project with mainly CONSTRUCTED-TOOLS, and vice versa.

Next we describe the circumstances for finalizing either a SELECTED- or a CONSTRUCTED-TOOL. We provide an example of each circumstance and how it is documented and explained in its ANALYTIC PLANNING WORKSHEET, and then we describe the thinking process in greater detail for the sample ANALYTIC TASK in the bullying study. Your ANALYTIC TASKS will certainly be very different from all

	...bullying behaviors	
Level 2: ANALYTIC TASKS	**Level 3: TRANSLATION**	**Level 4: SELECTED TOOL or Level 5: CONSTRUCTED TOOL**
Compare teachers' reactions to different kinds of bullying	_UNITS_ Teachers (unit of analysis) Reactions (unit of meaning) Kinds of bullying (unit of meaning) _PURPOSE_ To investigate whether individual teachers display similar or different reactions to different types of bullying _POSSIBLE COMPONENTS_ **Teachers** – SOURCE, CASE, ATTRIBUTE-VALUE, SET & SEARCH-FOLDER, MEMO, MAP, CHART **Reactions** – NODE, CODED-REFERENCE, QUERY-RESULT, SET & SEARCH-FOLDER, ANNOTATION, MEMO, MAP, CHART **Kinds of bullying** - NODE, CODED-REFERENCE, QUERY-RESULT, SET & SEARCH-FOLDER, ANNOTATION, MEMO, MAP, CHART _CHOSEN COMPONENTS_ Teachers = SOURCE Reactions = NODE (resulting in CODED-REFERENCES) Kinds of bullying = NODE (resulting in CODED-REFERENCES) _EXPLANATION_	

REFLECTIONS Remember to bear in mind which school the teachers come from when looking at patterns of reactions – this may help in the next step for deciding whether the most problematic or most productive sets of teacher reactions are related to their schools.

FIGURE 6.9   ANALYTIC PLANNING WORKSHEET for sample analytic task: Choosing appropriate components

these examples, but once the process is learned, it can be applied to your own tasks, in conjunction with the following:

- The list of COMPONENTS (Table 5.2, page 68)
- The actions that can be taken on COMPONENTS (Tables 6.3 and 6.4, pages 132–133)
- The video demonstrations of the TRANSLATION of real-world ANALYTIC TASKS from a wide variety of research projects (described in Chapter 7)

When to Use a Selected-Tool

The rule of thumb for using a SELECTED-TOOL—a *straightforward choice of individual software operations*—is to do so in one of two circumstances. The first circumstance is a chain of one-to-one relationships between UNITS, COMPONENTS, actions, and purposes. The second circumstance is when an affordance of the program can fulfill the purpose of the ANALYTIC TASK.

Using a Selected-Tool When There Is a Chain of One-to-One Relationships

Recognizing a chain of one-to-one relationships means looking for three straightforward conditions:

- An ANALYTIC TASK has only one or two UNITS.
- There is a *formal equivalence* between each UNIT and a COMPONENT.
- A single action on each COMPONENT accomplishes the purpose of the task.

A straightforward ANALYTIC TASK from the 14 example tasks is *read interview transcripts to identify potential concepts for coding*. We determined (in Appendix 4) that this task has two UNITS and (in Appendix 5) that it has one purpose. After identifying possible COMPONENTS for this task and reviewing the analytic actions that can be taken on them (displayed in Tables 6.3 and 6.4, pages 132–133), we choose two COMPONENTS for this task: SOURCES and MEMOS (Figure 6.10). We determine that the task can be fulfilled with a single action: *writing* in each SOURCE MEMO. The ANALYTIC TASK therefore can be fulfilled using a SELECTED-TOOL. The details are described succinctly in the ANALYTIC PLANNING WORKSHEET in Figure 6.10. This completed worksheet includes not only the UNITS, purpose, and COMPONENTS chosen, but also an explanation of how the COMPONENTS will be harnessed and the actions we plan to take in NVivo. This is how ANALYTIC PLANNING WORKSHEETS will appear on the companion website to accompany the video demonstrations of TRANSLATION.

Using a Selected-Tool With an Affordance of the Program

The second circumstance that calls for a SELECTED-TOOL is when an affordance of the program has been specifically designed for the purpose of the ANALYTIC TASK. An affordance is an existing combination of actions and COMPONENTS presented on the screen as a single feature. For example, another straightforward ANALYTIC TASK from the 14 example tasks is *search newspaper articles for the use of evocative terms*. We determine that this task also has two UNITS and one purpose (displayed in Appendices 4 and 5), and as shown in the ANALYTIC PLANNING WORKSHEETS in Figure 6.11, we choose two COMPONENTS for this task: SOURCES and MEMOS. The next step is to review the analytic actions that can be taken on these COMPONENTS (displayed in Tables 6.3 and 6.4, pages 132–133). We determine that the task can be fulfilled with a single action on each component: *interrogating* SOURCES and *writing* in MEMOS. We then determine that NVivo's Word Frequency query (page 76) will serve to interrogate the SOURCES in a manner that permits us to identify the evocative terms while we write

Level 2: ANALYTIC TASKS	Level 3: TRANSLATION	Level 4: SELECTED TOOL or Level 5: CONSTRUCTED TOOL
Read interview transcripts to identify potential concepts for coding	_UNITS_ Interview transcripts (unit of data) Potential concepts (unit of meaning) _PURPOSE_ To identify concepts that may be potential candidates for coding interview transcripts _POSSIBLE COMPONENTS_ _(Not included for this illustration)_ _CHOSEN COMPONENTS_ Interview transcripts = SOURCE Potential concepts = MEMO _EXPLANATION_ This task is exploratory and the next anticipated task is to test the identified concepts in a first round of coding. For testing it will help to know which transcripts produced the potential concepts. We will therefore record them in the MEMO of the SOURCE that inspired them. We can output all the MEMOS for all SOURCES	Selected tool: Open and read a SOURCE, write and output MEMOS: • Open a SOURCE • Create a MEMO linked to the SOURCE and open it in an undocked Detail View • Read the transcript and write potential concepts in the MEMO • Output the MEMOS for all SOURCES

FIGURE 6.10 First example of a SELECTED-TOOL

Level 2: ANALYTIC TASKS	Level 3: TRANSLATION	Level 4: SELECTED TOOL or Level 5: CONSTRUCTED TOOL
Search newspaper articles for the use of evocative terms	*UNITS* Newspaper articles (unit of data) Evocative terms (unit of meaning) *PURPOSE* To find terms within newspaper articles that can be considered evocative *POSSIBLE COMPONENTS* *(Not included for this illustration)* *CHOSEN COMPONENTS* Newspaper articles = SOURCE Evocative terms = MEMO *EXPLANATION* The initial search for evocative words can be fulfilled by the Word Frequency query which can sort all words used in selected SOURCES by length and indicate relative frequency and thus their salience. Evocative words tend to be longer, so the list can be scanned from the longest words and the relatively frequently used evocative terms can easily be typed into an open MEMO.	Selected tool: Run a Word Frequency query on newspaper article SOURCES and record relatively frequently used evocative terms in a MEMO • Create a MEMO in and undock it • Run a Word Frequency query on only newspaper article SOURCES and sort the list by longest first • Scan the list (or the Word Cloud visualization tab) for relatively frequently used evocative terms and type into MEMO

FIGURE 6.11   Second example of a SELECTED–TOOL

in a MEMO either a simple list of the terms we identify or perhaps our first reflections on them. Figure 6.11 displays the details of this SELECTED-TOOL in the ANALYTIC PLANNING WORKSHEET in a similar manner to the previous example, including the explanation and the actions to be taken in NVivo.

Selected-Tool for the Sample Analytic Task

We now return to the sample ANALYTIC TASK to describe in more detail the thinking process for finalizing a SELECTED-TOOL. The purpose of the task is *to investigate whether individual teachers display similar or different reactions to different kinds of bullying*, which was the reason that *reactions* and *kinds of bullying* were differentiated as separate UNITS in Step 1. Including *teachers* as a unit of analysis, the ANALYTIC TASK therefore has three UNITS and one purpose. This is more than the rule of thumb, but in the earlier discussion in Step 1 we decided this was the best way to go, and we anticipate fulfilling the task with a SELECTED-TOOL. (Having three units and one purpose also allows us to explore other implications of this choice later in the chapter.)

We next review the analytic actions displayed in Tables 6.3 and 6.4 (pages 132–133) and decide to consider how to use NVivo for *interrogating* SOURCES and *interrogating* NODES. This requires thinking through the purpose of the task in more detail and then evaluating options for interrogating.

To investigate similar or different *reactions* to different *kinds of bullying*—which is the strategy—we need to find CODED-REFERENCES coded to each *reaction* NODE for each *kind of bullying* NODE—which comprise the tactics. The outcome will be a group of CODED-REFERENCES for each combination of *reaction* NODE, such as *disapproval*, and *kind of bullying* NODE, such as *verbal abuse*. The next strategy is to read the CODED-REFERENCES for each pair of combined NODES to investigate the similarities and differences both within and between the groups of CODED-REFERENCES. This sequence of activities puts into effect a journey around the circular path of *Five-Level QDA* strategies and tactics, as illustrated in Figure 3.9 (page 56). We can't say more about how we will go about investigating the similarities and differences, because this is an emergent activity at the strategy levels, and we don't know in advance where the similarities or differences may lie. But we can say more about the cut-and-dried tactics, because this will be a definite procedure determined by the design of the software.

We have decided to fulfill the purpose of this ANALYTIC TASK by seeking out *intersecting* CODED-REFERENCES. In NVivo, intersecting CODED-REFERENCES are pairs of CODED-REFERENCES in which one REFERENCE is coded to one NODE, and an overlapping REFERENCE is coded to another NODE. The two NODES are therefore found in the same area of the coded data, so they may have some relationship to one another, somewhat similar to a correlation. The intersection, or overlap between, the CODED-REFERENCES can be of any degree. Just one word or even one character that is common to both REFERENCES constitutes an intersection, all the way up to a complete intersection, meaning we have a single REFERENCE coded to two NODES. NVivo retrieves the overlapping data that are common to both CODED-REFERENCES. If we can retrieve all intersecting CODED-REFERENCES for each combination of the *reaction* NODES and the *types of bullying* NODES, this will provide the material for conducting our similarities and differences investigation.

We now consider the two capabilities of NVivo that allow working with intersecting CODED-REFERENCES: the Coding Query and the Matrix Coding Query. If you are new to NVivo, the following discussions are only intended to illustrate a thinking process, not to provide comprehensive instruction in operating NVivo. Each of the capabilities discussed here is demonstrated in the *Harnessing Components* videos on the companion website, but in this section it is the thinking process that is most important. If we used the Coding Query (pages 92 and 95), we could retrieve intersecting CODED-REFERENCES between one pair of NODES at a time, such as *disapproval* and *verbal abuse*, then *disapproval* and *physical abuse*, then *disapproval and cyber bullying*, and so on, until one by one we had retrieved each possible combination of a *reaction* NODE and *kind of bullying* NODE. The Coding Query is very useful for many tasks because of additional capabilities that are not relevant to the task at hand. But as our current task has so many combinations of *reactions* and *kinds of bullying*, the process of working with each pair of NODES one at a time would be both cumbersome and problematic for visualizing patterns of intersection.

However, the Matrix Coding Query (page 92) allows the retrieval of intersecting CODED-REFERENCES for each pair of NODES in two chosen groups. One group of NODES can be chosen for the rows of the table, for example, the *reaction* NODES, and another group of NODES for the columns, for example, the *types of bullying* NODES. Each cell of the table shows the number of intersecting CODED-REFERENCES for the NODE in the row and the NODE in the column. The intersecting CODED-REFERENCES can be directly accessed and viewed from the cells of the table. This will serve the purposes of our ANALYTIC TASK. And this is all the material we need to travel around the circular path of *Five-Level QDA* strategies and tactics and begin to investigate the similarities and differences both within and between these groups of CODED-REFERENCES. Following this analytic activity at the strategy levels of the project, the next ANALYTIC TASK will emerge to be translated in turn into SELECTED- or CONSTRUCTED-TOOLS.

Figure 6.12 displays this fifth iteration of the ANALYTIC PLANNING WORKSHEET—using a SELECTED-TOOL. As we have described the thinking process in detail, the worksheet does not include a summary explanation in the TRANSLATION column.

When to Use Constructed-Tools

The rule of thumb for using a CONSTRUCTED-TOOL—a *sophisticated use of the software by combining software operations or using them in a custom way*—is to do so in one of two circumstances. The first circumstance is when a "larger" ANALYTIC TASK has more UNITS or purposes than the rules of thumb suggest, but the task is better fulfilled by combining multiple TOOLS into a single larger CONSTRUCTED-TOOL rather than artificially splitting the ANALYTIC TASK into two separate tasks. The second circumstance is when a custom way of combining actions and COMPONENTS is needed to fulfill a task.

Using Constructed-Tools for "Larger" Analytic Tasks

One reason to use a CONSTRUCTED-TOOL is to avoid artificially breaking an ANALYTIC TASK into multiple tasks that each follows the rules of thumb, just to make the TRANSLATION process more simple. Soon, with more experience, translating "larger" ANALYTIC TASKS will become as straightforward as TRANSLATING "smaller" tasks, so splitting tasks that are better fulfilled as a whole is not the habit we want to develop.

One ANALYTIC TASK from the 14 example tasks is *watch videos of math lessons to identify types of interaction between students and teachers*. We identify one purpose for the task in Appendix 5—*to identify how students and teachers interact during math lessons*. In Appendix 4 we identify four UNITS to fulfill this purpose: *videos of math lessons, types of interaction, students*, and *teachers*. We discuss these multiple UNITS at length in Appendix 4. In summary, one approach would be to consider students and teachers as instances of a single UNIT, *participants*, leading to two separate tasks, each conforming to the rule of thumb. The first task would be to identify *types of interaction* without regard to *students* and *teachers*, and the second would require going back to identify each type of interaction in relation to *students* and *teachers*. Splitting the task in this way would simplify TRANSLATION into two SELECTED-TOOLS, but at a cost. The two-step process would be cumbersome and also implies this easy separation of *types of interaction* from the people who are interacting. We conclude that the best way forward is not to split the task but to consider both dimensions—*types of interaction* and *who is interacting*—in the same task.

Identify patterns of teacher reactions to different reactions to different kinds of bullying

Level 2: ANALYTIC TASKS	Level 3: TRANSLATION	Level 4: SELECTED TOOL or Level 5: CONSTRUCTED TOOL
	NEXT ANTICIPATED Determine whether patterns of most problematic or most productive reactions of teachers may inform mitigation of bullying behaviors	
Compare teachers' reactions to different kinds of bullying	*UNITS* Teachers (unit of analysis) Reactions (unit of meaning) Kinds of bullying (unit of meaning) *PURPOSE* To investigate whether individual teachers display similar or different reactions to different types of bullying *POSSIBLE COMPONENTS* *(Not included for this illustration)* *CHOSEN COMPONENTS* Teachers = SOURCE Reactions = NODE (resulting in CODED-REFERENCES) Kinds of bullying = NODE (resulting in CODED-REFERENCES) *EXPLANATION* *(Full explanation in the chapter text)*	Selected tool: Use the Code Matrix Query to investigate intersections between the *reactions* NODES and the *kinds of bullying* NODES. • Select all the *reaction* NODES for the rows of the matrix table • Select all the *kinds of bullying* NODES for the columns of the matrix table

FIGURE 6.12   ANALYTIC PLANNING WORKSHEET for sample analytic task: SELECTED-TOOL

We assume that in a prior ANALYTIC TASK we identified every student–teacher interaction in the video DOCUMENTS of math classes and coded each REFERENCE with two CASES: one for the name of the teacher (there is therefore a hierarchy of teacher CASES) and one for the name of the student (there is therefore a hierarchy of student CASES).

We decide to fulfill the current ANALYTIC TASK in an iterative manner. We first watch and interpret each CODED-REFERENCE in the video SOURCES, coding each student–teacher interaction to a NODE that represents the style of interaction. We then generate a Framework Matrix SOURCE of all the teacher CASES by the style of interaction NODES, which will allow re-viewing the CODED-REFERENCES from within the Framework Matrix SOURCE without going back and forth among the video SOURCES. Similarities and differences in the manner in which each teacher interacts are interpreted and written in the Framework Matrix SOURCE at each intersection between a teacher and a style of interaction. The process would be repeated for each style of interaction, with varying amounts of iterative recoding and writing as required.

We refer to this set of software operations as a CONSTRUCTED-TOOL because it is a combination of separate uses of the software conducted together. We have described the process we chose to fulfill this ANALYTIC TASK at a high level to indicate what a CONSTRUCTED-TOOL is like—we do not expect you to be able to reproduce the process from this description. That is the purpose of the *Harnessing Components* videos on the companion website, which lend themselves to demonstration of the detailed steps to fulfill ANALYTIC TASKS similar to this one.

Figure 6.13 displays the ANALYTIC PLANNING WORKSHEET for this task. This shows that there is an additional chosen COMPONENT for the writing and visualizing purposes of the task as well as the COMPONENTS representing the UNITS of the task—Framework Matrix SOURCES to support the interpretation and writing purpose. Figure 6.13 displays a description of the sequence of planned actions that comprise the CONSTRUCTED-TOOL in the Level 4/5 column.

Using Constructed-Tools as a Customized Way to Harness the Program

Some ANALYTIC TASKS call for a customized way to harness the program, regardless of the number of UNITS and purposes. This means that the straightforward way to use the COMPONENTS does not seem to offer a solution to the requirements of a task. By *straightforward* we mean simple and obvious; by *customized* we mean creative or unusual. Once a customized way of using a COMPONENT has served you well, it will join the category of simple and obvious.

To illustrate a custom use of COMPONENTS, we continue with the last ANALYTIC TASK, *watch videos of math lessons to identify types of interaction between students and teachers.* The CONSTRUCTED-TOOL we designed for this task, described earlier in Figure 6.13, led to a great deal of iterative analytic activity. One finding of this ANALYTIC TASK is that there is a great deal of difference in styles of interaction between teachers who interact with all students in a consistent style (teacher group 1) and those who interact very differently with students with apparently higher and lower math abilities (teacher group 2). To follow up this observation we obtain math ability information from the school, and we rename each student CASE with a prefix that indicates either higher or lower math ability.

As a result of all this analytic activity, a new ANALYTIC TASK emerged: *synthesize a general style of interaction typical of group 1 and group 2 teachers.* The purpose is *to characterize typical styles of student–teacher interaction among teachers with a consistent style toward all students and teachers whose style varies with students of different math ability.* We decide that typical styles in each teacher group are indicated by the most prevalent styles adopted by those teachers. Fulfilling this task involves three steps. First we would determine the prevalence of each style of interaction adopted by *group 1* and *group 2* teachers. Next we would view the video CODED-REFERENCES and read the interpretations in the

Level 2: ANALYTIC TASKS	Level 3: TRANSLATION	Level 4: SELECTED TOOL or Level 5: CONSTRUCTED TOOL
Watch videos of math lessons to identify types of interaction between students and teachers	_UNITS_ Videos of math lessons (unit of data) Types of interaction (unit of meaning) Students (unit of analysis) Teachers (unit of analysis) _PURPOSE_ To identify how students and teachers interact during math lessons _POSSIBLE COMPONENTS_ _(Not included for this illustration)_ _CHOSEN COMPONENTS_ Videos of math lessons = SOURCE Types of interaction = NODE (resulting in CODED-REFERENCES) Teachers = CASE _Additional components from writing/visualizing purpose of task_ Interpretation of interactions = Framework Matrix SOURCE _EXPLANATION (Full explanation in the chapter text)._	Constructed tool: • View video SOURCES and code to new or existing _style of interaction_ NODE • Create a Framework Matrix source of all teacher cases and _style of interaction_ NODES, in which interpretations are written at each intersection

FIGURE 6.13   First example of a CONSTRUCTED–TOOL

Framework Matrix SOURCES for the most prevalent of these styles for each teacher group. Finally, we would synthesize this information into a general style of interaction for each teacher group.

It is beyond the scope of this chapter to illustrate the full range of possible ways to TRANSLATE this ANALYTIC TASK into CONSTRUCTED-TOOLS—that is the purpose of the *Harnessing Components* videos on the companion website. The purpose of this example is only to illustrate what a customized CONSTRUCTED-TOOL is like. Here we describe one way to fulfill the current task using CASES, SETS, and the Matrix Coding Query in a customized manner.

We could put all our teacher CASES as columns and all the styles of interaction NODES as rows in a Matrix Coding Query. But we don't want columns for all the teachers—there may be dozens. We want just two columns in the table, one for the *group 1* teachers and one for the *group 2* teachers. We can do this one of two ways—either by applying ATTRIBUTE-VALUES to the teacher CASES or with a customized use of SETS & SEARCH-FOLDERS. Here we describe the use of SETS & SEARCH-FOLDERS for this purpose. We can create a SET for each teacher group and add CASES in which *group 1* teachers are present to the *group 1* SET and CASES in which *group 2* teachers are present to the *group 2* SET. We can then select these two SETS as the columns of the Matrix Coding Query, leaving the rows as before for each *style of interaction* NODE. We now have the number of CODED-REFERENCES in each cell that we want in order to determine their prevalence for each group of teachers, and we can easily navigate to and watch each individual video REFERENCE to begin our synthesis of a general style of interaction for each teacher group. As we watch more videos and accumulate insights about each group of teachers, we add notes to a MEMO for that teacher group. We have already created these MEMOS, one for each teacher group, because the purpose of this task—*to characterize the typical styles of student–teacher interaction*—called for MEMOS as an additional COMPONENT in which to write the synthesis.

Figure 6.14 displays the ANALYTIC PLANNING WORKSHEET for this task, indicating the new purpose, the new chosen COMPONENTS, and a description of the actions planned for this constructed-tool in the Level 4/5 column.

Constructed-Tools for the Sample Analytic Task

Our discussions about the sample ANALYTIC TASK—*compare teachers' reactions to different kinds of bullying*—have all assumed that in the prior task we thought of *reactions* and *kinds of bullying* as two separate units of meaning. What if the TRANSLATION of the previous task had not been sufficiently guided by what was anticipated to come next, and we had decided to stick to the rule of thumb of two UNITS? The purpose of that previous task might have been well served by a single UNIT of meaning—*teachers' reactions to different kinds of bullying*—along with *teachers* as UNIT of analysis. We would have created NODES that specified in the name both the nature of the reaction and the kind of bullying, such as *disapproval of verbal abuse, censure of physical abuse, sympathy to cyber bullying,* and so on. This may have been efficient for the prior task, but not for the current task of investigating teacher reactions stimulated by different kinds of bullying, because the NODES do not distinguish *reactions* from *kinds of bullying*.

This sort of situation is common. No matter how much thought you give to the context of an ANALYTIC TASK and the actions that can be taken on its COMPONENTS in Step 4, unexpected new purposes emerge, and in hindsight the prior decisions are not always the most appropriate. We could go back and recode every REFERENCE to separate NODES for each reaction and kind of bullying, but this would be time consuming and perhaps demoralizing. In our experience an inability to work out a better solution leads researchers to stop using the software. Yet NVivo is flexible enough to easily fulfill our ANALYTIC TASK by CONSTRUCTING a TOOL. In this example we would do this by combining software operations, rather than by using the software in a customized way.

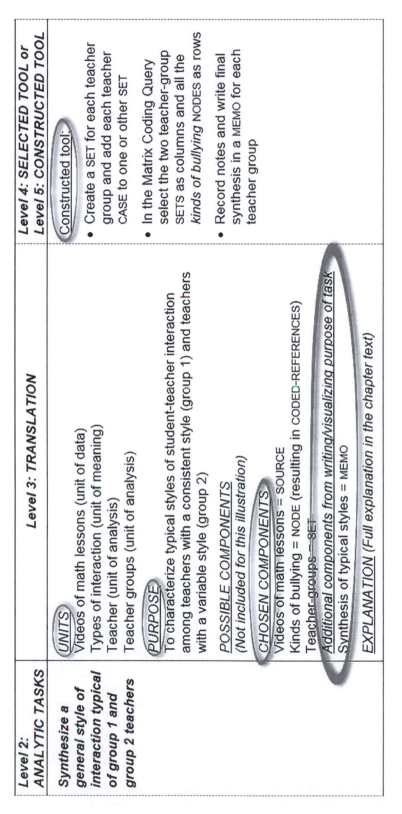

Level 2: ANALYTIC TASKS	Level 3: TRANSLATION	Level 4: SELECTED TOOL or Level 5: CONSTRUCTED TOOL
Synthesize a general style of interaction typical of group 1 and group 2 teachers	*UNITS* Videos of math lessons (unit of data) Types of interaction (unit of meaning) Teacher (unit of analysis) Teacher groups (unit of analysis) *PURPOSE* To characterize typical styles of student-teacher interaction among teachers with a consistent style (group 1) and teachers with a variable style (group 2) *POSSIBLE COMPONENTS* *(Not included for this illustration)* *CHOSEN COMPONENTS* Videos of math lessons = SOURCE Kinds of bullying = NODE (resulting in CODED-REFERENCES) Teacher-groups = SET *Additional components from writing/visualizing purpose of task* Synthesis of typical styles = MEMO *EXPLANATION (Full explanation in the chapter text)*	Constructed tool: • Create a SET for each teacher group and add each teacher CASE to one or other SET • In the Matrix Coding Query select the two teacher-group SETS as columns and all the *kinds of bullying* NODES as rows • Record notes and write final synthesis in a MEMO for each teacher group

FIGURE 6.14 Second example of a CONSTRUCTED-TOOL

Level 2: ANALYTIC TASKS	Level 3: TRANSLATION	Level 4: SELECTED TOOL or Level 5: CONSTRUCTED TOOL
	NEXT ANTICIPATED Determine whether patterns of most problematic or most productive reactions of teachers may inform mitigation of bullying behaviors	
Compare teachers' reactions to different kinds of bullying	UNITS Teachers (unit of analysis) Reactions to kinds of bullying (unit of meaning) PURPOSE To investigate whether individual teachers display similar or different reactions to different types of bullying POSSIBLE COMPONENTS (Not included for this illustration) CHOSEN COMPONENTS Teachers = SOURCE Reactions = QUERY-RESULT (resulting in CODED-REFERENCES) Kinds of bullying = QUERY-RESULT (resulting in CODED-REFERENCES) EXPLANATION (Full explanation in the chapter text)	Constructed tool: • Using a Coding Query, create QUERY-RESULTS for each group of NODES with the same reaction, and for each group of NODES with the same kind of bullying • Matrix Query: Select the reaction QUERY-RESULTS as rows, and the kinds of bullying QUERY-RESULTS, as columns

FIGURE 6.15 ANALYTIC PLANNING WORKSHEET for sample analytic task: CONSTRUCTED-TOOL

If our coding scheme has combined *reactions* and *kinds of bullying* into single NODES, we somehow need to separate them for our new purpose of investigating all the possible combinations of *reactions* and *types of bullying*. In this case the Coding Query—which did not suit our purpose in the earlier example (page 143)—will be just right, because it allows us to create new NODES based on combinations of other NODES connected by *operators*. For example, we can create a new NODE called *disapproval* that combines all the NODES for the disapproval reaction—*disapproval of verbal abuse*, *disapproval of physical abuse*, etc., by using the operator *OR*. We can repeat the process to create new NODES for each *reaction* and each *type of bullying*. Then we can use the Matrix Coding Query as before, but this time choosing the *reaction* NODES for the rows, and the *types of bullying* NODES for the columns.

We refer to this as a CONSTRUCTED-TOOL, rather than a pair of SELECTED-TOOLS performed one after the other, only because the two operations had to be thought out together in order to solve the problem. Once you are performing operations in the software, the distinction between SELECTED- and CONSTRUCTED-TOOLS is irrelevant. The distinction is only an aid to making better choices for harnessing NVivo. Figure 6.15 displays the sixth and final iteration of the ANALYTIC PLANNING WORKSHEET for the sample ANALYTIC TASK—using a CONSTRUCTED-TOOL. As we have described the thinking process in detail, the worksheet in Table 6.15 does not include a summary explanation in the TRANSLATION column.

This completes our instruction in the five steps of TRANSLATION. It also completes Part II, the application of the principles of the *Five-Level QDA* method that were introduced and described in Part I. In Part III and the accompanying video demonstrations on the companion website, we illustrate these principles in a variety of real-world research projects. Chapter 7 begins by suggesting how you can best take advantage of these illustrations.

References

di Gregorio, S., & Davidson, J. (2008). *Qualitative research design for software users.* Maidenhead, UK: McGraw Hill/Open University Press.

Lincoln, Y. S., & Guba, E. G. (1985). *Naturalistic inquiry.* Thousand Oaks, CA: Sage.

Naylor, P., Cowie, H., Cossin, F., Bettencourt, R., & Lemme, F. (2006). Teachers' and pupils' definitions of bullying. *British Journal of Educational Psychology*, 76(3), 553–576.

Rigby, K. (2014). How teachers address cases of bullying in schools: A comparison of five reactive approaches. *Educational Psychology in Practice*, 30(4), 409–419.

Silver, C., & Lewins, A. (2014). *Using software in qualitative research: A step-by-step guide* (2nd ed.). Thousand Oaks, CA: Sage.

Tracy, S. J. (2010). Qualitative quality: Eight 'big-tent' criteria for excellent qualitative research. *Qualitative Inquiry*, 16(10), 837–851.

PART III

Case Illustrations

Part III illustrates the *Five-Level QDA* method in a variety of real-world qualitative research projects. These projects are unlikely to be exactly the same as your own projects in terms of methodology or content. Chapter 7 explains how to learn by analogy from these case illustrations in order to transfer the underlying process to your own work. Chapter 7 also describes the content of the three sets of video demonstrations on the companion website that accompany the case illustrations. Chapters 8 and 9 contain the complete documentation of two full-case illustrations that are referred to in the video demonstrations. The documentation of many additional mini-cases is available with their videos on the companion website.

7

ORIENTATION TO CASE ILLUSTRATIONS

Case illustrations bring the *Five-Level QDA* method to life by illustrating the process in real-world research projects with accompanying video demonstrations that can be used as a guide in your own work. In this chapter we describe how these resources are organized and how they can be accessed. We first describe the characteristics of the case illustrations and how best to learn from them. Second, we describe the three series of video demonstrations available on the companion website and our format for presenting the full-case illustrations in Chapters 8 and 9.

Learning From Case Illustrations

A case illustration is not the same as a case study. A case study describes a real-world problem in order to reflect on the content of the case and learn to think like an expert in that field (Ertmer, Quinn, & Glazewski, 2014). The case study method is an established method of learning—the Harvard MBA program famously organizes its entire curriculum around a series of case studies. But in this book we are not studying the content of research methods or the strategy levels of research projects. We are instead studying the process of TRANSLATING from strategy to tactics. Successful TRANSLATION of an ANALYTIC TASK requires knowing its context—what has come before and what you plan to do next. We therefore need to know the full subject matter of these real-world research projects to provide the context for TRANSLATION. But we are not primarily focused on studying the projects themselves; we are only using them to teach the TRANSLATION of individual ANALYTIC TASKS, and in doing so, to demonstrate how NVivo can be harnessed powerfully throughout a whole project. We therefore call the projects *case illustrations*, and we draw on the content of the case as context for the instruction. In other words, we are interested here in process rather than content, but we need to be aware of the content to understand the process.

There is no comprehensive generic list of ANALYTIC TASKS that can be picked from and copied. ANALYTIC TASKS are the most specific level of detail in an analytic plan, specific to the context of a particular research project. This creates a quandary for illustrating the process of TRANSLATION. We cannot provide sufficient illustrations so that there will always be an ANALYTIC TASK within a project from the same discipline, guided by the same methodology, seeking to answer the same kind of research question with the same style of analysis that can then be directly copied to your project. Instead we provide a range of illustrations that will likely be different from your project in many ways but can be used as analogies. But they must be "productive analogies"—those that shed new light on what they are being compared with (Vosniadou & Ortony, 1989, p. 14). We must therefore consider how best to learn by analogy.

Learning by Analogy

Reasoning by analogy is a much studied psychological process (Gentner, Holyoak, & Kokinov, 2001). Analogies are based on the similarity between two things, which allows inferences to be drawn from one to the other. If a friend tells you that she felt like a fish out of water at a formal opera gala, you infer she was not comfortable in the alien surroundings. Thinking in this way is not a special skill but is at the core of our mental processes, as the "spotting of analogies pervades every moment of our thought" (Hofstadter & Sander, 2013, p. 18). This does not mean that all analogies are appropriate, correct, or helpful (Sunstein, 1993). If a student is told that the solar system is like an atom that has electrons circling around its nucleus, he may wrongly infer that planets jump out of their orbits when he is taught in another class that electrons jump from orbit to orbit around the nucleus.

We cannot know the context of the ANALYTIC TASKS in your own project and how you are drawing analogies from the ANALYTIC TASKS in our case illustrations. But we can draw attention to some aspects of learning by analogy. The most important issue is whether the similarity you see between a case illustration and your own project is based on *structural characteristics* of the case illustration or on its *surface features* (Gentner, 1989). Surface features refer to the individual details of a situation. The surface features of the fish out of water example are the fish and the wet and dry environments. The structural characteristic refers to the *relationships* among the surface features—the fish is not comfortable because it is out of water, or more generally, an alien environment produces discomfort. Drawing a productive analogy is based on noticing the similarity of the structural characteristics, that your friend felt discomfort because she was in unfamiliar surroundings. But drawing an analogy based on the surface features would lead you astray. If you concluded that your friend felt like a fish out of water because she is usually wet, perhaps spending most of her time swimming or walking in the rain, but is now feeling uncomfortable because she is dry, that would not have been the intention of her analogy and clearly makes no sense.

We have belabored the issue of needing to seek structural similarities rather than surface similarities, because psychologists report that in real situations people do not always spontaneously draw relevant, productive analogies from situations that are very different from their own (Holyoak & Koh, 1987, p. 334). The surface features of our case illustrations are the specifics of the projects— the discipline, methodology, type of research question, style of analysis, etc.—and are likely to be very different from your own. If you focus on these surface features, you may not find many ANALYTIC TASKS with the exact same combination of these surface features as in your own project. Conversely, shared surface features between projects do not imply that there are ANALYTIC TASKS with the same structural characteristics as your own. We know from Chapter 6 that the structural features of an ANALYTIC TASK are its units and purposes. If these features of an ANALYTIC TASK in a case illustration seem similar to a task in your own project, we suggest that you not be concerned whether the surface features—the discipline, methodology, type of project, or research question—are similar to or different from your own project.

The conclusion we can draw from the psychological research on analogies is that intentionally seeking analogies in case illustrations that are structurally similar to your own, regardless of whether there are any surface features in common, will make the analogy productive. It is beyond the scope of this chapter to go further into learning by analogy. For a fuller description of how to identify the structural characteristics of situations analogous to your own, see Mayer (1992).

Authentic Learning

The *Five-Level QDA* method is concerned with managing the contradiction between the emergent nature of qualitative analysis and the cut-and-dried nature of software. A similar contrast holds between learning the skill of TRANSLATION and learning to operate the software effectively. Donald Schön (1990) identified the problems of applying cut-and-dried technical knowledge to practice areas that are emergent in nature. Schön (1990) proposed that educational methods in these areas required the kind of practical knowledge only gained by engagement with real-world problems. In our field, learning to operate NVivo effectively requires technical knowledge of how the program works. But learning the process of TRANSLATION between strategies and tactics is based on the practical knowledge that only comes from engaging with real-world research projects. We therefore do not invent projects or fragments of projects to illustrate an idealized example of qualitative analysis or TRANSLATION. Instead we present projects that have been undertaken by experienced qualitative researchers who use NVivo. These contributing researchers have kindly described the entire progress of their qualitative analysis in the sequence that it occurred. Their project descriptions have two characteristics—they are *messy* and *unsanitized*.

In this context *messy* means *does not proceed in a straight line*. A qualitative project is a journey from a research question to a finding or a conclusion. This journey is not a predetermined series of steps, but to some degree iterative and emergent: the outcome of one analytic activity leading to reconsideration of what has gone before as part of the determination of what to do next. This sometimes proceeds smoothly, sometimes in fits and starts, and sometimes requires retracing of steps and adopting course corrections—all are part of a systematic yet emergent qualitative analysis process. We include this full messiness in our case illustrations so that the authentic structural characteristics of the ANALYTIC TASKS that we demonstrate are available for you to draw analogies to your own, inevitably messy, projects. The case illustrations are not intended as model or exemplar research projects, but simply real-world examples of a process.

We also present the case illustrations unsanitized. Our students consistently report that they do not learn much transferable knowledge from reading concise, highly ordered descriptions of a qualitative analysis in the methods sections of journal articles. In the interests of space these methods sections are boiled down to the main steps of analysis, missing out the detours that did not contribute to the findings in a direct way. They serve a different purpose from our case illustrations. For learning purposes we describe how a qualitative analysis actually progressed, including the detours that are not mistakes but an intimate part of the process, in the order in which they occurred. This is particularly important regarding NVivo, as the inevitable detours involve harnessing the software in ways that may have an impact on what comes next and how the exit from the detour is accomplished.

Most of the case illustrations are completed projects with published articles. Some are still in progress at the time of writing, and others reached a certain point and will never be completed, either because the funding ran out or for some other reason. Whatever the current status of the project, the progress that was made and reported was authentically done.

Learning From Multiple Illustrations

In the video demonstrations of TRANSLATION we always include a pair of contrasting examples. There are two reasons for this. One purpose of the *Five-Level QDA* method is to counteract the wrong impression that there is a "correct" way to use NVivo. This may be due to what we call the default software mind-set: that there is always a correct way to use software that must be discovered. Our demonstrations of TRANSLATING an ANALYTIC TASK inevitably lead to harnessing particular

COMPONENTS, which contributes to an inappropriate assumption that this is how those COMPONENTS should always be used, or this is the only way this ANALYTIC TASK could be accomplished. We therefore always include a contrasting demonstration of a different way to use the COMPONENTS or a different way to fulfill the ANALYTIC TASK, to show that this is not the case.

A second reason for including multiple ANALYTIC TASKS in each video demonstration is based on the recommendations of educational psychologists. Qualitative analysis is an example of an "ill-structured activity." "Ill" does not mean that there is anything wrong with it, but that there is uncertainty or incomplete information about how a conclusion can be reached, and there is no single correct outcome that can be considered "correct"—almost a definition of qualitative analysis (see Box 1.1, page 15). Gaining skill in such ill-structured activities requires learning multiple perspectives using multiple contrasting examples, which Spiro, Coulson, Feltovich, and Anderson (1988) refer to as "criss-crossing the conceptual landscape" (p. 6). For both reasons we therefore ensure that each demonstration of the TRANSLATION of an ANALYTIC TASK is accompanied by a contrasting example.

Video Demonstrations of Case Illustrations

This book has three sets of video demonstrations. The first set—the *Component Orientation* videos—provide a short orientation to how each COMPONENT works. These videos are described in Chapter 5. The second set—*Case Illustration* videos—demonstrate the two full cases documented in Chapters 8 and 9. The third set—the *Harnessing Components* videos—demonstrate both the two full cases and a series of mini-cases documented on the companion website. Here we describe the second and third sets of videos and the full cases and mini-cases. Figure 7.1 provides an overview of the different sets of videos.

Case Illustration Videos

The *Case Illustration* videos demonstrate the two full cases described in Chapters 8 and 9. Both are real-world projects conducted using NVivo. The first, described in Chapter 8, is a more straightforward project contributed by Elizabeth Pope, a PhD candidate at the University of Georgia. The second, described in Chapter 9, is a more sophisticated project contributed by Dr. Kristi Jackson, President of Queri, an independent research consultancy, based in Denver, Colorado. The purpose of the chapters and the *Case Illustration* videos is to demonstrate the progress of these real-world projects in the sequence in which the analytic activities occurred. Your current project may not be like either of these studies, but as we discussed earlier, the surface features do not have to be similar in order for productive analogies to be drawn.

Accompanying the *Case Illustration* videos are *Translating an Analytic Task* videos that demonstrate in detail the TRANSLATION process for a selection of the ANALYTIC TASKS in the project. The associated ANALYTIC PLANNING WORKSHEETS that are demonstrated in the videos are also downloadable as PDF documents.

There is often more than one way to fulfill an ANALYTIC TASK. It is likely that harnessing one COMPONENT to fulfill an ANALYTIC TASK will be more effective than harnessing another, based on the context—what has been accomplished previously, the purpose of the ANALYTIC TASK, and what is anticipated to come next. But there will also be alternative ways. In the *Translating an Analytic Task* videos for the more sophisticated project in Chapter 9 we therefore demonstrate contrasting ways to TRANSLATE the same ANALYTIC TASK, and we discuss the pros and cons of each with the case contributor, Dr. Kristi Jackson. This ensures that there is no misunderstanding that there is a single "correct" way to accomplish an ANALYTIC TASK.

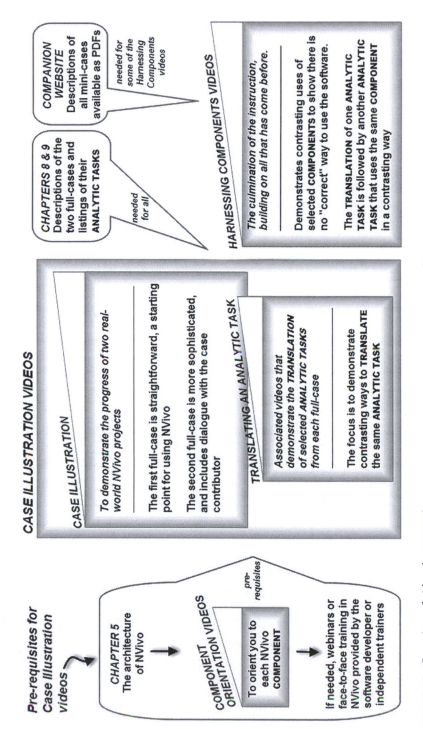

FIGURE 7.1 Overview of video demonstrations

Harnessing Components Videos

The *Harnessing Components* videos are the culmination of the book—they build on everything that has come before to demonstrate different ways to harness NVivo powerfully. These videos are organized by COMPONENT. Each video demonstrates how a COMPONENT can be harnessed by TRANS-LATING an ANALYTIC TASK into SELECTED- or CONSTRUCTED-TOOLS that use that COMPONENT.

There is no one correct way to harness a COMPONENT. Each COMPONENT can be harnessed in different ways based on the units and the purpose of an ANALYTIC TASK. In the *Harnessing Components* video we therefore demonstrate contrasting examples of the use of a selection of COMPONENTS to illustrate that there is no single "correct" way to harness that COMPONENT. This emphasizes that the use of the software is driven by the needs of the analysis, not by the "correct" use of the software. To accomplish this in the *Harnessing Components* videos we begin by choosing one ANALYTIC TASK of interest from a case illustration. We then select a second ANALYTIC TASK that harnesses the same COMPONENT in a different way or for a different purpose. We then demonstrate the TRANSLA-TION of both ANALYTIC TASKS, going through the ANALYTIC PLANNING WORKSHEETS, which are also downloadable as PDF documents.

The two full-case illustrations in Chapters 8 and 9 do not provide sufficient variety for all the necessary contrasting examples for all COMPONENTS. We therefore illustrate ANALYTIC TASKS from additional mini-cases that are not described in the book. We provide descriptions of these mini-cases in PDFs on the companion website in the same format as Chapters 8 and 9, but in abbreviated form, with a short summary of the project's purpose, methodology, and ANALYTIC STRATEGIES. These mini-case descriptions are two-page overviews that provide the necessary context for the *Harnessing Components* videos.

Accessing Video Demonstrations

All video demonstrations and associated PDF documents are available at the companion website. To register and log in go to www.routledgetextbooks.com/textbooks/5LQDA. You will be directed to choose among the available videos. Within each category you will then be directed to choose the videos for either a COMPONENT or a particular stage of one of the full cases, as appropriate.

The Two Full-Case Illustrations

Chapters 8 and 9 describe the full cases in a standard format. Each chapter begins with a narrative overview of the entire project in straightforward language without any terms or jargon words that would not be understood outside that field. The purpose is to facilitate productive analogies without any required knowledge of the surface features of the research topic, discipline, or methodology. The narrative overview includes the background of the project, the objectives and methodology, and any unexpected and unplanned detours that occurred. This is the same format that is used in abbreviated form for the mini-cases which are available on the companion website.

Following the narrative overview we list all the project's ANALYTIC TASKS in a standard format. In collaboration with the contributors we have grouped all the ANALYTIC TASKS for a project into a number of analytic phases, or simply *phases*, in which each phase reflects a coherent set of tasks. For more convenient demonstration in the videos, all the phases of the project have been further grouped into a small number of *stages* of the project, so that each stage can be demonstrated in a separate video. The videos refer to the written descriptions of the stages, phases, and ANALYTIC TASKS in Chapters 8 and 9. Figure 7.2 displays a schematic of these stages, phases, and ANALYTIC TASKS, and Figure 7.3 explains their presentation in Chapters 8 and 9.

Chapters 8 and 9 are a collaboration between the case contributors and the authors of this book. The text of each chapter is a synthesis of the contributors' initial descriptions of their projects, the authors' questions and comments, and the contributor's responses. The contributors have approved the final text as an accurate representation of what occurred. The video demonstrations rely on the text of these chapters, as they provide the context for the videos as well as the detailed listing of ANALYTIC TASKS in each stage of the project. Neither the chapters nor the accompanying videos are intended to be independent standalone instruction; they are intended to be read and viewed together in order to be meaningful.

Case Illustration 1: A Literature Review

The first full case in Chapter 8 is a more straightforward project, a literature review conducted as part of a PhD dissertation. This project provides a starting point for those with little or no experience in qualitative research or for those with no prior experience in using NVivo. The *Case Illustration* and *Translating an Analytic Task* videos demonstrate on screen the progress of the project described in the chapter, and we assume that you have read the chapter prior to watching the videos. Although this case illustration is intended for those with no prior experience of NVivo, we hope that those with more experience will also find the videos helpful in becoming enculturated into *Five-Level QDA* thinking.

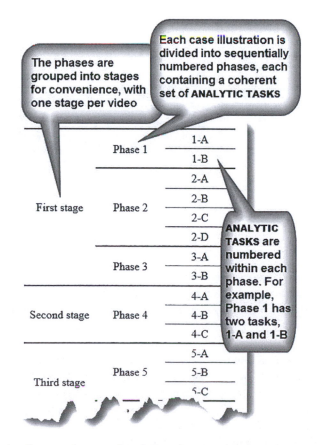

FIGURE 7.2 Schematic of stages, phases, and analytic tasks

Phase 6: Plan the write-up of the [This figure displays Phases 6 from Chapter 9. This phase has two **ANALYTIC TASKS**: 6-A, 6-B, 6-C, and 6-D]

6-A	*Generate and prioritize ide*
	• *Team members reviewed* ... *ed ideas for the themes that should be included in the report in a Microsoft Word file.*
6-B	*Collate socio-demographic characteri* [ANALYTIC TASKS in *italics* do not involve the use of NVivo]
	• *We created a Microsoft Excel fi* *information about the roun* *the int* *e* *in the project, the type of violence prevention initiative they contributed to, their gender, and a few Likert S* [ANALYTIC TASKS in *regular type* are **TRANSLATED** into software operations using NVivo] *developing an evaluation plan" plan to project success").*
6-C	Plan interrogations to inform writing of report sections
	• The whole team met to discuss the coding of the first round interviews and the potential themes for inclusion in the report generated in 6-A.
	• We imported the interviewee characteristics collated in 6-B into the master NVIVO-PROJECT as ATTRIBUTE-VALUES linked to the interview SOURCES.
	• We discussed ways in which potential th [The *names* of the **ANALYTIC TASKS** in Chapters 8 & 9 are the same as on the **ANALYTIC PLANNING WORKSHEETS** on the Companion Website...] interrogated and identified how we cou
6-D	Investigate co-occurrences between sets report
	• We ran a series of Matrix Coding querie coding, based around the potential themes identified in 6-C.
	• We retrieved the CODED-REFEREN intersection in each Matrix Coding QUERY-RESULT and review
	• While reviewing the ... but the *summary descriptions* of the tasks in Chapters 8 & 9 are replaced by the details of the **TRANSLATION** process in the **ANALYTIC PLANNING WORKSHEETS** on the Companion Website identifying five repo Recommendations, and Implications).
	• Each Primary Coder was allocated a section to write up

FIGURE 7.3 Presentation of stages, phases, and analytic tasks in Chapters 8 and 9

Case Illustration 2: A Program Evaluation

The second full case in Chapter 9 is a more sophisticated project, a program evaluation. This is intended for those with some experience in both qualitative research and NVivo. This also serves as a second step of learning for those who have watched the videos of Case Illustration 1.

In addition to demonstrating the progress of the project on screen, the *Translating an Analytic Task* videos include a dialogue with the case contributor, Dr. Kristi Jackson, an experienced qualitative research consultant and NVivo trainer. The dialogue focuses primarily on the extent and manner to which NVivo was harnessed powerfully, rather than on the project's strategy—the objectives, research questions, and development of the analytic plan. Discussions include the pros and cons of the choices made in this project's research context compared with other contexts and the pros and cons of possible alternative choices for fulfilling the analytic plan. The purpose is to explore the implications and consequences of alternative ways to harness the program.

References

Ertmer, P. A., Quinn, J. A., & Glazewski, K. D. (Eds.). (2014). *The ID casebook: Case studies in instructional design* (4th ed.). Boston: Pearson.

Gentner, D. (1989). The mechanisms of analogical learning. In S. Vosniadou & A. Ortony (Eds.), *Similarity and analogical reasoning* (pp. 199–241). New York: Cambridge University Press.

Gentner, D., Holyoak, K. J., & Kokinov, B. N. (2001). *The analogical mind: Perspectives from cognitive science.* Cambridge, MA: MIT press.

Hofstadter, D., & Sander, E. (2013). *Surfaces and essences: Analogy as the fuel and fire of thinking.* New York: Basic Books.

Holyoak, K. J., & Koh, K. (1987). Surface and structural similarity in analogical transfer. *Memory & Cognition, 15*(4), 332–340.

Mayer, R. E. (1992). Chapter 14: Analogical reasoning. *Thinking, problem solving, cognition* (2nd. ed., pp. 415–454). New York: W. H. Freeman and Company.

Schön, D. A. (1990). *Educating the reflective practitioner: Toward a new design and teaching and learning in the professions.* San Francisco: Jossey-Bass.

Spiro, R. J., Coulson, R. L., Feltovich, P. J., & Anderson, D. (1988). *Cognitive flexibility theory: Advanced knowledge acquisition in ill-structured domains.* Paper presented at the Proceedings of the 10th Annual Conference of the Cognitive Science Society. Montreal, Quebec, Canada.

Sunstein, C. R. (1993). On analogical reasoning. *Harvard Law Review, 106*(3), 741–791.

Vosniadou, S., & Ortony, A. (1989). Similarity and analogical reasoning: A synthesis. In S. Vosniadou & A. Ortony (Eds.), *Similarity and analogical reasoning* (pp. 1–17). New York: Cambridge University Press.

8

CASE ILLUSTRATION — AN EXPLORATORY LITERATURE REVIEW

Exploring the Literature on Interfaith Dialogue

Elizabeth M. Pope

This chapter and the accompanying videos illustrate what a straightforward real-world qualitative analysis executed in NVivo is like. The contributor, Elizabeth Pope, is a PhD candidate in Adult Education at a major U.S. research university. We asked Elizabeth to contribute this case from her dissertation because PhD students take their dissertation projects very seriously—it is their first piece of original research and they want to make sure it is an example of good scholarship. Elizabeth's project is therefore documented in detail, and it is easy to follow how she moved the project forward. Her dissertation is a qualitative case study examining an interfaith dialogue group between Jewish, Christian, and Muslim adults. This chapter illustrates only the literature review part of her dissertation. However, a literature review is a qualitative research project in itself, as it takes a large body of unstructured materials—articles, books, etc.—in order to make sense of them and provide a framework for the research project.

The purpose of the chapter is to provide the context for the ANALYTIC TASKS that are referred to in the video demonstrations. The first section of the chapter—*Analytic Strategies*—contains the objectives and guiding methodology of the project, that is, Level 1 of the *Five-Level QDA* method. The second section—*Stages of the Analysis*—is Level 2, the analytic plan, which unfolds in six stages, including the generation of ANALYTIC TASKS at each stage. This is the point at which Level 3 begins, that is, TRANSLATING the ANALYTIC TASKS into software operations. Each stage is demonstrated in a separate video, including commentary on the choices made and on possible alternative choices for fulfilling the analytic plan using NVivo. To view a video after reading a stage please go to www.routledgetextbooks.com/textbooks/5LQDA and follow the on-screen instructions.

This case illustration demonstrates the *Five-Level QDA* method, which is independent of the CAQDAS package used. Elizabeth originally conducted the study using ATLAS.ti, but the identification of ANALYTIC TASKS in an analytic plan and their TRANSLATION into software operations can be illustrated using any package. This chapter and the accompanying videos illustrate the TRANSLATION and fulfillment of her ANALYTIC TASKS using NVivo.

Now we turn over the chapter to Elizabeth.

Analytic Strategies

I have presented the context for the case illustration in three sections: "Background," describing my dissertation as a whole; "Focus of This Case Illustration," describing the conceptual framework for my dissertation, which determined the scope for the literature review; and "Guiding Methodology" for the literature review.

Background

This literature review is for my dissertation, a qualitative case study titled *This Is a Head, Hearts, and Hands Enterprise: Interfaith Dialogue and Perspective Transformation*. The study was conducted in the southeastern United States and explored a community-based interfaith dialogue program between Jewish, Christian, and Muslim adults.

The context for the study is the continuing problem of religious conflict. The history of violence, fear, prejudice and bigotry, misunderstandings, misinformation, and a general lack of knowledge about different faith traditions has led to negative perceptions of the "religious other." Many scholars of religion believe that interfaith dialogue could be an invaluable method for resolving religious discord. But although interfaith dialogue can be successful, it can just as often fail. One explanation is the many idealized and varied goals of interfaith dialogue. Unanticipated challenges in practice and implementation can also be a detriment. And Jewish–Christian–Muslim dialogue has its own particular difficulties, including the expectation that each group is speaking on behalf of an entire faith tradition, a lack of trust between participants, historical disagreements, etc.

Most academic literature on interfaith dialogue is conceptual, aiming to understand the impact of interfaith experiences. There is little empirical research that examines the effects and process of interfaith dialogue, the nature of learning in such an interfaith experience, or how perceptions of the "religious other" can be transformed through interfaith dialogue. The need for research into these issues is the rationale for my dissertation.

Focus of This Case Illustration

The purpose of my dissertation is twofold. First, it is to examine the nature of learning in interfaith dialogue. Second, to understand if, and how, "perspective transformation" in people of different faiths occurs through interfaith dialogue. The research questions guiding the study are as follows:

1. What happens when Jewish, Christian, and Muslim adults engage in interfaith dialogue?
2. How do facilitators of interfaith dialogue prepare for and guide group meetings?
3. In what ways, if any, does interfaith dialogue foster perspective transformation in regard to the religious other?

Before beginning the research I needed to review the existing literature about interfaith dialogue across academic fields. In this chapter I use the term *literature* interchangeably with *resources* to mean all items I gathered, whether journal articles, books, or other electronic resources. This literature review gave me an extensive overview of interfaith studies and allowed me to understand how interfaith dialogue has and has not been researched in a wide variety of disciplines.

Prior to conducting the literature review I created a conceptual framework for the whole dissertation to serve as the "analytic lens" through which I would view and interpret my data and conduct my analysis. This determined what literature I would need to review, and so I begin by describing how I created this conceptual framework. I began with two main elements: the concept of "dialogue" and the concept of "transformational learning." I based my understanding of dialogue on Martin Buber's (1923) seminal work *I and Thou*. Buber (1923) distinguishes two types of dialogic relationships, the "I-It" and "I-Thou" relationships. In the "I-It" relationship, the "It" is a person seen as an object to be used to achieve a certain goal. In the "I-Thou" relationship, in contrast, there

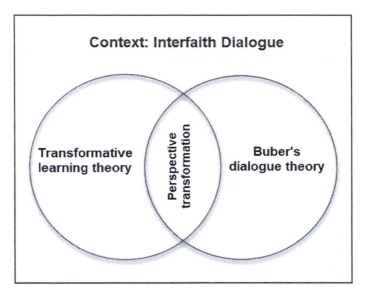

FIGURE 8.1 Theoretical framework for dissertation

is a "mutual and holistic existence of two entities" (Morgan & Guilherme, 2012, p. 982) between people. I based my understanding of transformational learning on Mezirow's (2012) "transformative learning theory," which defines transformational learning as a process that "transforms our taken-for-granted frames of reference to make them more inclusive, discriminating, open, emotionally capable of change, and reflective" (p. 76). Within transformative learning theory one concept plays a crucial role, that of "transforming perspectives of the world." For my conceptual framework I proposed that the transformation of perspectives toward the "religious other" during interfaith dialogue can be understood through the intersection of Buber's (1923) and Mezirow's (2012) theoretical standpoints. Combined, these theories provide a way to conceptualize "perspective transformation" in interfaith dialogue groups in terms of both the individual experience of transformation and the relational experience of dialogue. Figure 8.1 illustrates a big-picture view of this framework.

Guiding Methodology

The guiding methodology described here concerns just the conduct of the literature review, not the entire dissertation. First I thought through the purpose of the review. The conceptual framework for the dissertation indicated that I needed to review the academic literature that used transformative learning and/or Buber's dialogue theory to examine intercultural or interfaith interactions. I also needed to identify any gaps in the literature regarding adult learning through interfaith dialogue in order to find areas in which further study was necessary. This search introduced me to resources in a wide variety of academic fields. I paid particular attention to the theoretical frameworks, data collection methods, analytical methodologies, and findings of these empirical articles in order to learn from and build on the existing research in this field.

I primarily searched for resources electronically, but I noticed that when I went to the library with a list of books to find, I often ended up finding other relevant resources through physical proximity to the books I was looking for. Visiting the library led to a serendipitous literature review that did not happen with electronic searching, and this became part of my personal guiding methodology.

My literature review was exploratory because my conceptual framework consisted of the inter-section of two separate theories, and I was not aware of any existing framework that combined these theories which could be used to analyze the disparate items of literature. I therefore sought an inductive approach to the analysis, as inductive approaches do not start with a predetermined ana-lytic frame but rather start with specific observations or statements in the data and move logically to a more general explanation. I chose the inductive thematic analysis approach described by Braun and Clarke (2006), which is based on the work of Boyatzis (1998), as my guiding methodology because in the absence of an existing framework that combined transformative learning theory and dialogue theory I needed to generate data-driven themes. This approach is a "bottom-up" coding of the data to identify themes and patterns that are strongly linked to the data, which in this case are the various literature resources. This allowed me to note key themes and moments of importance as they became clear through my reading of the literature rather than relying on a predetermined coding frame to interpret them.

I implemented Braun and Clarke (2006)'s methods in practice by first immersing myself in the literature with wide reading and marking segments of text that struck me as interesting. I then cre-ated descriptive NODES to capture the concepts I was seeing in the literature and applied them to the segments I had identified as interesting. During this phase I generated 141 descriptive codes. I then grouped these NODES into higher-level categories to indicate similarities and differences among the descriptive NODES and to organize the relationships I was identifying between them. During this phase I reduced the number of descriptive NODES to 139 by merging those that essentially repre-sented the same concept and grouped them into 12 categories. Finally, I identified themes for rep-resenting a holistic picture of the broad literature on interfaith dialogue. The result was the creation of eight higher-level themes that grouped the categorized codes.

My process was informed by my general understanding of grounded theory methodology. In writing up my literature review methodology I felt I needed to name the stages of my process using established terms. I therefore borrowed two grounded theory terms to describe my process. I referred to the descriptive coding phase as "open coding," which I took to mean the creation of tentative labels for the concepts identified that summarize what is discussed. However, I only coded segments within the literature that related to the focus of my review, rather than coding all of each resource, as is typically how "open coding" is described in grounded theory texts. In the next step, I created the categories in an intuitive way, but referred to this as "axial coding" (Grbich, 2013) as this process of relating NODES to one another is the second stage of grounded theory (Strauss & Corbin, 1998) and well describes what I did. My use of grounded theory terms ended there, because my intention in developing themes did not have the purpose of generating a core theory that reflects all the data in the analysis, as a grounded theory analysis does. Rather, I developed several themes that reflected how interfaith dialogue is discussed and has been researched across academic disciplines.

Stages of the Analysis

The analytic plan for reviewing the literature evolved as the work progressed. There were six stages of analysis, with each stage planned in light of the outcome of the previous stage and my current thinking about the literature. The six stages reflect turning points in the progress of the literature review, and I named the stages after the fact when reflecting on the process for this chapter. The six stages are listed in Table 8.1.

The first stage was like a mini-review in order to produce a first draft of my literature review during a course on how to conduct a literature review offered in my program. This initially involved lots of paper, and I soon realized I needed to use some kind of software to manage all the resources. After consulting Professor Paulus, one of my teachers at the University of Georgia, I

TABLE 8.1 The six stages of analysis

Stages of the project (one video on the companion website for each stage)	
Stage 1: Preliminary partial literature review	Analysis of initial resources gathered in order to complete first draft for literature review class.
Stage 2: Review and rationalize the first stage	Reconsideration of the analysis produced in the first stage and refinement and reorganization of the process for continued analysis to be included in dissertation prospectus.
Stage 3: Expand the scope of the literature review	Addition of more literature into the review and integration of them into the analysis.
Stage 4: Identify themes in the literature	Development of themes that came to frame the rewriting of the literature review.
Stage 5: Rewrite the literature review	Integration of the new analysis to the initial literature review to complete dissertation prospectus.
Stage 6: Ongoing expansion of the literature review	Continued adding of literature as identified.

chose ATLAS.ti and continued the project in that software package. However, for the purposes of this chapter I am recounting what I would have done had I decided to use NVivo.

When I came back to the project several months after the class had ended I discovered that I couldn't get back into my original thinking due to the lack of organization in my analytic process. This led to rationalizing the analysis, meaning that I reconsidered the first approach and reorganized the process; otherwise, I would be continuing to add to the disorganization. This was time consuming but turned out to be beneficial. The subsequent stages are similar to the first stage, but are more refined and systematic, and always included defining NODES and making notes continuously about insights and the process. The result of these later stages was the development of themes that are now framing the dissertation data analysis. The literature review has been ongoing throughout my dissertation, and my refined and more precise process now allows me to easily add new resources into the framework whenever additional literature is published in the various academic fields.

First Stage: Preliminary Partial Literature Review

I submitted my dissertation prospectus for approval, including a first major draft of the literature review, during the spring semester of 2016. I began collecting literature in the spring semester of 2015 during a graduate course called "Critique of the Literature in Adult Education." The first stage of the project involved reviewing these resources for the purpose of this course. In retrospect this was the first iteration of the literature review.

The course taught doctoral students the steps of completing a literature review for their dissertations and how to examine and critique research questions and conceptual frameworks. During the class I collected 56 articles using the "Multi-Search" capability of the university library's website, which searched all available databases that the university subscribed to. I used the key terms *interfaith, interreligious, transform**, and *dialog** to identify resources. At this early stage I needed to get "the lay of the land" and sought a broad range of conceptual, experiential, and empirical literature. I understand conceptual literature to mean theoretical articles about the process or effects of interfaith and intercultural experiences. Experiential literature describes the author's experience within an interfaith or intercultural context. Empirical literature means research on human subjects to examine interfaith or intercultural interactions and contexts. As the purpose of my dissertation is to add to the scholarly understanding of interfaith dialogue through empirical research, I was particularly interested in finding empirical studies involving interfaith or intercultural interactions using transformative learning or dialogue theory in their conceptual frameworks. The search identified both electronic and print resources. All electronic resources identified by the university's Multi-Search capability are automatically available as full-text PDF downloads, and all the print resources identified were available for checking out in the library or were obtained by the library for me through interlibrary loan.

I read the downloaded PDF files of articles in Adobe Acrobat Reader, highlighting interesting sections of text and bibliographical information, and sometimes annotating sections using the comment tool. As I read and marked the resources, I wrote an appraisal of each one in a separate Microsoft Word file. At this stage, this appraisal writing was not very systematic, sometimes it was a summary of the resource, and sometimes an abstract, a synopsis, or just notes about my initial reflections.

After reading, marking up, and appraising the resources, I imported all the PDF files into NVivo as individual SOURCES and organized them into FOLDERS that represented topical areas such as *Adult Learning Theory*, *Dialogue Theory*, and *Transformative Learning Theory*. The highlighting carried over into NVivo, but the annotations I had written using the comments tool in Adobe did not. I had highlighted sections to help familiarize myself with the literature but this also served as a precoding process, because once inside NVivo, the highlighted portions served as triggers for sections that would probably require coding, and this acted as a roadmap of pertinent information later in the review process.

In the Description area for each SOURCE within NVivo I recorded the full citation and pasted in the article abstract and notes I had written about my initial impressions of the article. This was very time consuming, but I felt it was an important task because it would later help me to reference the resources and access my initial thoughts about each article.

I began coding this first set of articles in NVivo by creating 141 descriptive NODES based on the text. By "descriptive code" I mean a single word or very brief phrase that identifies the topic of a particular portion of the resource. As a major purpose of my literature review was to understand and catalogue what literature existed on interfaith dialogue, using descriptive coding was my natural, research instinct. Initially I did not organize or define the NODES in any way, as I thought they were self-explanatory and that I would remember their meaning from the short NODE name. I later realized the NODES were of different types and needed to be organized to reflect this and that it was necessary to define new NODES at the time of creating them to avoid reviewing this coding work in detail later in order to make sense of what I had done and be able to build on it in later stages, which occurred months later.

After all the articles were coded I reviewed all the CODED-REFERENCES and organized the NODES into higher-level categories by adding prefixes to the NODE names to indicate category names. I organized most of the NODES into categories in this way, but a few remained uncategorized, because I thought of them as categories in their own right. Examples of uncategorized NODES were, "Empathy," "Effects of Globalization and Modernity," and "Pluralism."

When I had finished categorizing the NODES I exported all the CODED-REFERENCES associated with each NODE as a text file. I used this to write the first draft of my literature review, which was organized by the categories I had created using my prefix system. However, I also had the hard-copy resources I had gathered with accompanying Word files of appraisals, separate from NVivo. While writing my first draft based on the outputs of coded PDFs from NVivo I also flipped through the separate hard-copy resource looking at the areas I had marked in order to fit the relevant topics into the draft of the literature review. This was extremely unsystematic and inefficient, which is why in later phases of the project I extended the color coding system from NVivo to the hard-copy resources.

This stage of the project contained eight ANALYTIC TASKS. For ease of presentation in Table 8.2 and in the video demonstrations, I have grouped these ANALYTIC TASKS into three analysis phases. Figures 7.2 and 7.3, pages 161–162, review the format and numbering system for stages, phases, and ANALYTIC TASKS. Note that bullet points in italics do not involve the use of NVivo.

TABLE 8.2 First Stage (Phases 1–3): Preliminary partial literature review

Phase 1: Identify and become familiar with resources	
1-A	*Collect literature to review* • *I used the UGA Library's Multi-Search capability to identify literature that relates to the dimensions of the conceptual framework (see Figure 8.1) using the following key terms: interfaith, interreligious, transform*★, and dialog*★.* • *This process identified 56 relevant electronic resources, which I saved as PDF files on my computer hard drive.* • *I renamed each file using a consistent naming protocol (Author, Date, Title) and saved them in folders representing three types of resources: Conceptual, Experiential, and Empirical.* • *In addition I identified relevant hard-copy resources (either books or book chapters). I purchased my own copies of most of these and took the others out of the UGA Library.*
1-B	*Become familiar with literature and mark interesting sections* • *I read each resource and marked interesting sections of text and bibliographic information that related to the dimensions of my conceptual framework.* • *For the electronic resources I did this in Adobe Acrobat Reader, using the text highlighting feature. Sometimes I made notes about the highlighted sections using the Adobe commenting feature.* • *For the hard-copy resources that I owned, I used highlighter pens and made notes in the margins. For the hard-copy resources I took out of the library, I made notes in a hard-copy notebook.* • *I created a Microsoft Word file for each resource in which I wrote an appraisal about each one. Sometimes this was a summary of the content, and sometimes I also wrote a synopsis and reflection.*

Phase 2: Organize and initially categorize resources	
2-A	Create an analytic workspace to store literature and notes • I created and saved an NVIVO-PROJECT and imported all the marked-up electronic resources into it as individual SOURCES. Because of the way I had named the SOURCES they listed alphabetically by author in the Internals FOLDER. • I recorded the full citation and abstract for each electronic resource and pasted the appraisal I had written about each one in 1-B into a MEMO linked to each SOURCE.
2-B	Organize literature resources into subject areas • I created nine FOLDERS in the Internals area to represent the broad subject areas covered by the resources (e.g. "Adult Learning Theory," "Dialogue Theory," "Transformative Learning Theory," "Muslim & Christian interfaith dialogue," etc.), and moved each SOURCE into the relevant FOLDER. These FOLDERS were mutually exclusive (i.e., each electronic resource belonged to only one FOLDER).
2-C	Apply descriptive nodes to the relevant segments of literature and take notes • I opened each SOURCE and coded the sections I had highlighted in 1-B to new descriptive NODES. This resulted in 141 descriptive NODES. Most reflected relevant concepts I identified (for example, "Intercultural Communication," "Learning and Faith," and "Value of Interfaith Dialogue"). However, some were more practical (for example, "Design," "Hole in Literature," and "Future Research"). • The vast majority of REFERENCES were coded to only one descriptive NODE. • I created MEMOS to record my thoughts as I was coding, for example, "Challenge of method and design," "Community Organization," and "Challenge of language and culture." One MEMO called "Problem of sameness" summarized my thinking about the literature so far as this was a common challenge I had noticed in the conceptual literature. An additional set of notes about "What is faith?" that I had written in a Microsoft Word file was pasted into a MEMO.
2-D	Organize descriptive codes into initial categories • I retrieved the CODED-REFERENCES linked to each NODE and reviewed them for equivalence, changing any coding where necessary. • I organized the descriptive NODES into categories by adding prefixes to their names, so that they were listed alphabetically in the List View according to their category. Examples of categories are "Aims," "Definitions," "Categories," and "Outcomes."

Phase 3: Write first draft of literature review	
3-A	Extract coded literature by category • Every NODE created in Analysis Phase 2 was outputted with all their CODED-REFERENCES into a file.
3-B	*Write a first draft literature review* • *Using this output I wrote the first draft of my literature review. I displayed the NVivo Output on one side of my computer screen and opened a Microsoft Word file on the other side. Referring to the CODED-REFERENCES in the Output and the content of the MEMOS I had written I wrote my review, which I organized according to the categories created in 2-C.*

Second Stage: Review and Rationalize the First Stage

I came back to the project several months after writing the first draft of the literature review to continue adding new resources and also to use the project to help prepare for my comprehensive exams. However, I discovered that I couldn't get back into my original thinking by simply reviewing the NVIVO-PROJECT as it was not well organized and I hadn't defined the NODES or made notes of my analytic process. It became clear that my previous assumption that the NODES were self-evident was not correct, and I had to review all my previous work in detail before planning how to continue and build on what I had previously done.

The review and rationalization process involved retrieving all the CODED-REFERENCES at each NODE, merging any NODES that represented the same concept, and then defining each NODE in the Description area. I dated the definitions so that if I later redefined them I would be able to track the development of my thinking. Reviewing each NODE involved reconsidering the categories I had created in the first stage to ensure they adequately grouped the descriptive NODES, but I only made one change to the categories.

I also reviewed the FOLDERS I had created to store the literature SOURCES and combined some of them so that they more meaningfully represented the way I was now thinking about collections of resources. While reviewing the work I had previously done and making changes to the NVIVO-PROJECT I was fully re-engaging with the literature. I began making analytical notes to keep track of my insights and in particular the relationships I was seeing among the resources. For example, I wrote about individual articles, themes I was noticing across articles, and areas of disconnect or discord in the literature.

This Second Stage was time consuming yet immensely beneficial because it both reimmersed me in the literature and forced me to reflect upon the analytical decisions I had made at the outset of the project. I recognized that if during the First Stage I had written about the analytical decisions I was making, I may not have struggled as I did when returning to the project months later. As a result of this stage, the next stages of my review were much more focused because the reconsideration of my earlier approach meant that I refined and reorganized the process. This ensured that I did not continue to add to the disorganization that I had created in the First Stage.

Table 8.3 displays this stage of the project, which contains three ANALYTIC TASKS in a single analytic phase. These three ANALYTIC TASKS actually happened simultaneously, but they are presented as separate tasks to illustrate the process clearly.

TABLE 8.3 Second Stage (Phase 4): Review and rationalize the First Stage

Phase 4: Review and reorganize the analytic workspace	
4-A	Review and refine coding and the coding scheme • I retrieved all the CODED-REFERENCES linked to each NODE in the First Stage and based on these defined each NODE in the Description field, adding dates to the definitions. • Any NODES that I identified as repetitive or that were linked to CODED-REFERENCES that represented the same concept were merged. • Most of the NODE name prefixes that I had created in 2-B remained the same, other than renaming the "Aims' prefix as "Purpose." This resulted in a rationalized list of 139 NODES.
4-B	Review and refine broad subject-areas covered by literature resources • I reviewed the FOLDERS created in 2-A to store SOURCES and combined some of them to reduce the number from nine to five: "Adult Learning," "Buber & Dialogue Theory," "Empirical Studies on Interfaith Dialogue," "Interfaith Dialogue & Interactions," and "Transformative Learning."
4-C	Reflect on the literature and coding achieved so far • While undertaking 4-A, I appended the MEMOS created in 2-A with additional insights about each electronic resource. • I also added commentary to the analytical MEMOS I had created in 2-C, concerning areas of disconnect or discord I was seeing. This led to two additional analytic MEMOS to capture insights relating to "Tolerance" and "Communicative Learning."

Third Stage: Expand the Scope of the Literature Review

From the summer of 2015 to the early spring of 2016 I added more articles to the project in a piecemeal fashion. I used the same search criteria to identify additional resources as I had used in the first stage and followed the same process of downloading the article, reading it in Adobe, highlighting as necessary, adding the resource to the NVIVO-PROJECT, and coding the highlighted portions. I no longer made annotations using the comment feature in Adobe as I now knew they would not transfer into NVivo, so I wrote all my notes about the articles as I read them in a Microsoft Word file. I also decided to add the new resources to the NVIVO-PROJECT in smaller batches, around 10 at a time, and coded those articles before bringing in the next batch. This was a practical decision, to avoid the tedium of adding the citation, abstracts and notes to the MEMOS for several dozen resources at a time, and because I found it overwhelming to code more than 10 SOURCES at a time.

Each batch of resources was coded to the existing categorized NODES that had been rationalized in the Second Stage. Because I had just completed the review and rationalization of the project, I was very familiar with the categorized NODES and therefore this process was straightforward. Where I identified text in a resource for which I did not yet have a NODE, I immediately categorized the new NODE into one of the existing categories when I created it. The review and rationalization that I had undergone in the Second Stage meant I was now able to think at a higher level of abstraction when reading new literature. I no longer needed to first create a descriptive label for a new NODE and then think about which category this NODE belonged to, but could conceptualize segments of text into my scheme immediately. This meant the process of coding the new literature was both quicker and more analytically focused than had been the case in the First Stage.

Table 8.4 displays this stage of the project, which contains four ANALYTIC TASKS grouped into two analytic phases. Because I was adding new resources to the NVIVO-PROJECT in small batches I repeated these tasks several times, so this stage comprises several iterative cycles of identifying resources, becoming familiar with resources, integrating resources, and categorizing resources.

Fourth Stage: Identify Major Themes in the Literature

This stage focused on identifying the major themes in the literature, and was based on the categorization process undertaken in the Second Stage. In order to generate themes I reflected on my previous work, and in doing so I began identifying relationships between the categorized codes. To capture these relationships I linked NODES to one another using Relationship NODES and created SETS.

Representing relationships within and between categories involved using relations such as "is associated with," "is part of," "is an outcome of," "is a cause of," and "contradicts" to link NODES. I created a total of 23 pairs of linked NODES in this way. Most of the relationships I created were between NODES within the same category, for example:

- "DEF: Dialogue *is part of* DEF: Discourse" (where DEF is the prefix for the category "Definitions")
- "CHAL: Culture and context *is associated with* CHAL: Language and translation" (where CHAL is the prefix for the category "Challenge of Dialogue")
- "ALT: Ambivalence *contradicts* ALT: Ambiguity" (where ALT is the prefix for the category "Adult Learning Theory")

Linking NODES in this way helped me to think about how the categorized NODES related to one another, and this informed the development of the themes. To represent the themes I created and named SETS and added categorized NODES into them. I created eight themes. Each theme was mutually exclusive rather than overlapping, meaning that no NODE belonged to more than one theme. This

TABLE 8.4 Third Stage (Phases 5–6): Expand the scope of the literature review

Phase 5: Add resources to the analytic workspace

5-A	*Overview:* The same process as outlined in 1-A was used to identify additional relevant resources, except that now I scanned hard-copy resources and added them to the NVIVO–PROJECT along with electronic articles. Eight additional books were included in the review at this stage.
	Collect literature to review (ANALYTIC TASK 1-A repeated)
	• I used the UGA Library's multi-search capability to identify literature that relates to the dimensions of the conceptual framework (see Figure 8.1) using the following key terms: interfaith, interreligious, transform*, and dialog*.
	• This process identified additional relevant electronic resources, which I saved as PDF files on my computer hard drive.
	• I renamed each file using a consistent naming protocol (Author, Date, Title) and saved them in folders representing three types of resource: Conceptual, Experiential, and Empirical.
	• In addition I identified relevant hard-copy resources (either books or book chapters). I purchased my own copies of most of these and took the others out of the UGA Library.
5-B	*Overview:* The same process as outlined in 1-B was used to become familiar with identified new resources.
	Become familiar with resources (ANALYTIC TASK 1-B repeated)
	• I read each resource and marked interesting sections of text and bibliographic information that related to the dimensions of my conceptual framework.
	• For the electronic resources I did this in Adobe Acrobat Reader, using the text highlighting feature.
	• For the hard-copy resources that I owned, I used highlighter pens and made notes in the margins. For the hard-copy resources I took out of the library, I made notes in a hard-copy notebook.
5-C	Integrate additional resources into the analytic workspace
	• I added newly identified electronic resources to the NVIVO–PROJECT as SOURCES.
	• I assigned each resource to the relevant FOLDERS and recorded the full citation and abstract for each electronic resource in its linked MEMO in the same way as I had done in 2-A.

Phase 6: Categorize new resources and adjust existing coding scheme

6-A	Apply categorized codes to the relevant segments of literature and take notes
	• After each new electronic resource had been added to the NVIVO–PROJECT the sections highlighted in 5-B were coded to the existing NODES rationalized in 4-A.
	• Where new concepts were identified in highlighted sections, NODES to represent them were created and defined in the Description field. These new NODES were immediately organized into categories by using the prefixes rationalized in 4-A.

was because the themes served to represent the core aspects of interfaith dialogue in terms of how it has been discussed in the literature and previously researched. I developed the themes to identify the gaps and clusters in the focus of research on interfaith dialogue, and to reach an understanding of the current status of scientific knowledge in this area. My thematic analysis was inductive in that the NODES, categories, and themes I developed were grounded in the data. However, it was not about generating a theory from the data, but to map out and analyze patterns in previous work on interfaith dialogue. For this reason mutually exclusive themes represented by SETS were most appropriate. Although no one NODE belonged to more than one theme, some of my themes did contain NODES from different prefixed categories. For example, the theme "The Practice of Interfaith Dialogue" included the NODES belonging to the following categories: "challenges of interfaith dialogue," "impact factors on dialogue," "outcomes of dialogue," "purposes of dialogue," and "types of interfaith dialogue."

As I organized my categorized NODES into themes I also color-coded them. These colors served two purposes. First, they were a signal of the theme to which each NODE belonged, which appeared in the margin area where they were applied to REFERENCES, and this was helpful when reviewing SOURCES. Second, and more importantly, they corresponded to the colors of highlighting and tabs I used in the hard copy books. Although my literature review is 95 percent paperless, I used several print books. Coloring the themes meant that I was able to directly relate work done within NVivo to my paper-based work.

Because I had organized my NODES categorically using prefixes, I continued to work with a long list of NODES throughout the project. I did not reduce the number of NODES as I moved from the descriptive "open coding" phase, through the categorization "axial coding" phase, into the phase of developing the themes. At this stage I was working with 168 NODES, because during the Third Stage when I expanded the literature review I generated almost 30 new NODES. Some of the NODES were repeated within the categories, because the categorical system determined the situation within which the NODE was used. For example, the NODE "mutual learning" appears in the both the category of "outcomes of interfaith dialogue" and the category of "purposes of interfaith dialogue." But the definition of "mutual learning" is different in each category and applied to different types of text segments.

- *OUTCOME: Mutual Learning*—An outcome of interfaith dialogue is that individuals learn about other traditions while the members of other traditions learn about them.
- *PURPOSE: Mutual Learning*—A purpose of interfaith dialogue is to promote mutual learning, which means that while you are learning about and from another religious tradition, you are also learning about your own and the other participants of interfaith dialogue are doing the same.

These two "mutual learning" codes reflect different concepts in how interfaith dialogue is discussed in the literature. This way of working with codes provided me with a way to represent the nuances of the literature in my codebook. The way I organized NODES into categories and themes meant that

TABLE 8.5 Fourth Stage (Phase 7): Identify major themes in the literature

Phase 7: Recategorization	
7-A	Reflect on coding and analysis • I revisited hard–copy resources, retrieved CODED–REFERENCES, and reviewed definitions I has written on the categorized NODES. • I added to MEMOS in relation to potential higher-level themes.
7-B	Create and explain relationships between codes within categories • I linked NODES to one another using Relationship NODES to express relationships between the codes within the categories and creating Relationship Types such as "is part of," "is associated with," and "is an outcome of." • I wrote about the relationships I was seeing and the links I was making in MEMOS.
7-C	Generate and explain themes • I created SETS to represent potential themes; at this stage I had four themes: "Adult Learning & Theory in Interfaith Dialogue," "Empirical Research on Interfaith Dialogue," "The Practice of Interfaith Dialogue," and "Transformative Learning." • I assigned categorized NODES to the relevant SETS and assigned color to NODES based on the SET they were assigned to. • All the NODES belonging to each SET were assigned the same color so that the themes were reflected in the list of NODES. • In MEMOS I wrote about the themes and reflected on the links between NODES and categories. The tasks undertaken in 7-A, 7-B, and 7-C were repeated until I had identified eight themes that accurately reflected the conceptual, experiential, and empirical emphasis of the literature. Themes were mutually exclusive, meaning each NODE only belongs to one SET, but NODES with different category prefixes belong to different SETS.
7-D	Integrate hard-copy resources into themes • I reorganized the hard-copy resources so sections relevant to each of the themes identified in 7-C were easily retrievable, using tabs in the same colors.

the number of NODES never became overwhelming for me. I included a high level of detail within my coding scheme, which now that I was defining my concepts, I was able to easily keep track of my thinking, and the high level of detail contained within the coding scheme became be very useful when writing up my findings in the next stage.

Table 8.5 displays this stage of the project, which contains four ANALYTIC TASKS in a single analytic phase.

Fifth Stage: Rewrite the Literature Review

To write up my findings from my literature review, I exported my themes by generating outputs based on my SETS. I outputted by NODES because they represented the nuances of my themes. Because I was writing a thematic literature review, organizing the output in this way was most conducive to writing up my findings. I also outputted my MEMOS, so I had each step in my analysis process outputted and could use the output files as the basis for my literature review. Because I had used the same colors for themes within NVivo and for tagging the print books, the organization and structure of my NVivo project actually organized the physical books I used in my literature review. This was invaluable when writing up my findings as I could follow a system of colors to be sure each resource was considered in the write-up at the appropriate time. It also allowed me to keep the same organization system across my in-print books and my electronic articles, which led to a harmonious relationship between my two types of resources.

In rewriting the review, the NODE definitions informed my explanation of the nuances within each theme and category, and the exported CODED-REFERENCES provided an easily accessible list of citations. As a result the writing-up process in this stage was streamlined I was able to complete a draft over the course of a few days.

Table 8.6 displays this stage of the project, which contains two ANALYTIC TASKS in a single analytic phase.

Sixth Stage: Ongoing Expansion of the Literature Review

At the time of writing this chapter, I am continuing to add to my literature review. I continue to add no more than 10 articles to the NVIVO-PROJECT at a time. I aim to read several articles each week, add them the NVIVO-PROJECT, and integrate them into my analytic structure as described earlier. Because of the detailed setup of the coding system, it is a seamless process to bring newly identified literature into the analytical framework. The extensive work I did in the early stages of the literature, particularly the first and second stages, with regard to organizing and interrogating my coding system, has made the longitudinal nature of my literature review extremely manageable. My use of NVivo is integral to this process, as I do not believe that I would be able to complete as comprehensive a literature review if I was not using such a program.

TABLE 8.6 Fifth Stage (Phase 8): Rewrite the literature review

Phase 8: Rewrite the literature review	
8-A	Extract coded data by categories and themes
	• I outputted all CODED-REFERENCES, with linked MEMOS, theme by theme into a file.
8-B	*Rewrite the literature review*
	• *Using this output I wrote the second draft of my literature review. I displayed the NVivo output on one side of my computer screen and opened a Microsoft Word file on the other side. Referring to the CODED-REFERENCES in the output and the MEMOS I rewrote my review, which I now organized according to the themes created in 7-C.*

TABLE 8.7 Sixth Stage (Phase 9): Ongoing expansion of the literature review

Phase 9: Integrate new resources cumulatively	
9-A	*Repeat analytic process as new relevant resources are identified*
	• *Every few months I searched the UGA Library catalog and when new relevant resources are identified I repeat Phases 5–7 and integrate new knowledge into my literature review.*

TABLE 8.8 Summary of the nine phases of analysis

Stages of the project (one video on the companion website for each stage)	*Phases within each stage (one ANALYTIC PLANNING WORKSHEET on the companion website for each phase, describing the TRANSLATION of each of its ANALYTIC TASKS)*
Stage 1: Preliminary partial literature review	Phase 1: Identify and become familiar with resources
	Phase 2: Organize and initially categorize resources
	Phase 3: Write first draft of literature review
Stage 2: Review and rationalize the First Stage	Phase 4: Review and reorganize the analytic workspace
Stage 3: Expand the scope of the literature review	Phase 5: Add resources to the analytic workspace
	Phase 6: Categorize new resources and adjust existing coding scheme
Stage 4: Identify themes in the literature	Phase 7: Recategorization
Stage 5: Rewrite the literature review	Phase 8: Rewrite the literature review
Stage 6: Ongoing expansion of the literature review	Phase 9: Integrate new resources cumulatively

I am currently analyzing the data I generated for my dissertation through observations, interviews, focus groups, and gathering SOURCES, and I currently have a separate NVIVO-PROJECT for the literature review and the data analysis portions of my dissertation. Upon completion of the data analysis I will be able to compare and contrast my analysis with what exists in the current literature. I do not plan to combine my literature review and dissertation data NVIVO-PROJECTS because the volume of materials in each may become unmanageable. Additionally, each NVIVO-PROJECT has its own analysis plan, and I do not anticipate these merging successfully. I intend this examination to enhance the discussion chapter of my dissertation, providing a clearer understanding of how my findings compare to, contrast with, and contribute to the existing body of scholarship on interfaith dialogue. Table 8.7 displays this stage of the project, which contains a single ANALYTIC TASK, and Table 8.8 provides a closing summary of all nine phases.

Acknowledgments

I would like to thank my committee members, Dr. Aliki Nicolaides, Dr. Kathryn Roulston, and Dr. Carolyn Jones-Medine, as well as Dr. Trena Paulus at the University of Georgia for their guidance and consideration throughout the course of my research.

References

Boyatzis, R. E. (1998). *Transforming qualitative information: Thematic analysis and code development.* Thousand Oaks, CA: Sage.

Braun, V., & Clarke, V. (2006). Using thematic analysis in psychology. *Qualitative Research in Psychology, 3*(2), 77–101.

Buber, M. (1958). *I and thou* (R. G. Smith, Trans.). New York: Scribner. (Original work published in 1923).

Grbich, C. (2013). *Qualitative data analysis: An introduction*. Thousand Oaks, CA: Sage.

Mezirow, J. (2012). Learning to think like an adult: Core concepts of transformation theory. In E. Taylor & P. Cranton (Eds.), *The handbook of transformative learning: Theory, research, and practice* (pp. 73–95). San Francisco, CA: Jossey-Bass.

Morgan, W. J., & Guilherme, A. (2012). I and thou: The educational lessons of Martin Buber's dialogue with the conflicts of his times. *Educational Philosophy and Theory, 44*(9), 979–996.

Strauss, A., & Corbin, J. (1998). *Basics of qualitative research: Procedures and techniques for developing grounded theory* (2nd ed.). Newbury Park, CA: Sage.

9

CASE ILLUSTRATION — A PROGRAM EVALUATION

Violence Prevention Initiative

Kristi Jackson

This chapter and the accompanying videos illustrate what a real-world program evaluation executed in NVivo is like. The contributor is Dr. Kristi Jackson, president of Queri, an independent research consultancy based in Denver, Colorado. We asked Kristi to contribute this case because of her long-standing role as a consultant in the use of NVivo and because of her research interests in the usability and impact of CAQDAS packages and practice of leveraging such software to teach qualitative methods.

The purpose of the chapter is to provide the context for the analytic tasks that are referred to in the video demonstrations. The first section of the chapter—"Analytic Strategies"—contains the objectives, guiding methodology, and overview of the analytic plan of the project, that is, Levels 1 and 2 of the *Five-Level QDA* method. The second section—"Stages of the Analysis"— unfolds the analytic plan in six stages, including the generation of analytic tasks at each stage. This is the point at which Level 3 begins, that is, TRANSLATING the ANALYTIC TASKS into software operations. Each stage is demonstrated in a separate video and includes dialogue with Kristi about the pros and cons of possible alternative choices for fulfilling the analytic plan using NVivo. To view a video after reading a stage, please go to www.routledgetextbooks.com/textbooks/5LQDA and follow the on-screen instructions.

The project was originally undertaken in NVivo Version 2. We have converted the project to NVivo Version 11, which led to no changes in process or procedure, except for changing the names of the COMPONENTS to their NVivo Version 11 names. We have used the Version 11 COMPONENT names even when discussing Version 2 operations to avoid confusion for readers who have not used Version 2 of NVivo.

Now we turn over the chapter to Kristi.

Project In Brief

The Violence Prevention Initiative was launched in 1995 and was funded by the Colorado Trust to prevent violence in twenty-six communities throughout the state of Colorado. Each community had a separate violence prevention program with its own objectives and activities, and the whole initiative was evaluated by OMNI Research and Training, Inc., an evaluation research firm in Denver, Colorado. I was employed by the evaluation team as an analyst as part of my full-time employment in the organization while working on approximately five other evaluation research projects. I was the only team member with prior experience using the software and conducting violence prevention research.

The Colorado Trust's approach was to engage the community-based directors of each violence prevention program in an ongoing process evaluation that was customized for each program. The overall philosophy was known among stakeholders as the Learning Lab. The Learning Lab was centered around the process evaluation, which examined the efficacy of the innovative efforts in all twenty-six communities. Based on the ongoing evaluation, program directors were encouraged to change their approach to violence prevention during the course of the initiative, assisted by a community development facilitator assigned to each program. The intention was for the Learning Lab approach to have a positive impact on the facilitators, which in turn would have a positive impact on the specific violence prevention program in each community.

This case illustration focuses on the qualitative part of the evaluation and describes the design and conduct of the evaluation of interview data collected during the first two years of the Initiative.

Analytic Strategies

I have presented the context for the case illustration in three sections: "Overall Project Objectives," where I outline the objectives of the whole project; "Focus of this Case Illustration," where I describe the qualitative part of the project, which is the focus of this chapter; and "Guiding Methodology," where I describe the approach to the qualitative analysis and the broad and more specific research questions that sensitized the analysis.

Overall Project Objectives

The overall objective of the initiative was to facilitate improvements to the local violence prevention programs, the services provided by the assigned facilitators, and to the overall structure of the initiative as managed by the Colorado Trust. Three forms of data were collected over the initiative's four-year period:

- *Social indicator data.* Rates of arrest, truancy, calls to emergency services, and other quantitative data that were directly or proximally related to violence in the community.
- *Program tracking.* A customized Microsoft Access database that was used to assess the quarterly reports from the individual programs for changes in their customized goals, objectives and activities, and the rationale for these changes.
- *Semi-structured interviews.* Over 200 individual interviews with program managers, front-line staff, service recipients, and the assigned facilitator in each community. The interviews explored their perceptions of the effectiveness of the community-based program and their opinions of the Learning Lab approach of the entire initiative.

This evaluation design included two types of research questions—*formative* questions focusing on process and *summative* questions focusing on outcomes—and at two levels—the overall initiative level and the site level, resulting in a quadrant of research questions. Table 9.1 provides examples of research questions in each quadrant.

TABLE 9.1 Examples of formative and summative research questions at the initiative level and the site level of the Violence Prevention Initiative

	Formative (regarding process)	Summative (regarding outcomes)
Site-level questions	1. How did you identify the initial focus of your violence prevention program (e.g., youth violence, elder abuse, hate crime)? 2. What events or understandings changed the goals, objectives, or activities of the program? How did they change? 3. What kinds of assistance have been provided by the facilitator/consultant (e.g., board training, meeting facilitation, evaluation design, conflict mediation)? 4. What is your understanding of the expectations of the Colorado Trust?	1. What impact has the program made in the community? 2. What impact has the initiative had on the hosting entity in the community? 3. What effect did the facilitator/consultant have on the design of the program? 4. How has (or hasn't) the group of community stakeholders been expanded and/or diversified as a result of the initiative?
Initiative-level questions	1. Where is there coherence or diversity regarding perceptions of the Learning Lab (between staff at the Colorado Trust, facilitators/consultants, and community members)? 2. What is gained and lost by inserting a facilitator/consultant in the relationship between funder and grantee? 3. How does the Learning Lab change "business as usual" for the Colorado Trust? 4. What lessons can be learned in order to effectively implement a Learning Lab model for other initiatives?	1. How do social indicator data change during the course of the initiative? 2. How do agencies change as a result of the initiative and the Learning Lab approach? 3. What impact does the initiative have on the way community development facilitators/consultants provide services to grantees? 4. How does the Learning Lab approach affect the way the evaluation of the entire initiative is implemented?

Focus of This Case Illustration

This case illustration focuses on the first four waves of interviews conducted during the first two years of the initiative in the twenty-six communities, a total of 200 interviews. Each round of interviews had the following focus:

- *First round.* These interviews addressed early expectations about the purpose and structure of the initiative.
- *Second round.* These interviews asked participants about their relationships with other members of the initiative during the planning process of the local program.
- *Third and fourth rounds.* These interviews asked about key events and lessons learned during program implementation that either reinforced the direction of the local program or suggested changes.

The evaluation team anticipated several topics to emerge from the four rounds of interviews, and these aspects informed the analysis:

- What was learned through the unfolding of the process
- The relationships developed between the facilitators and the members of the project and/or community
- The role of the local evaluation in guiding the project

Guiding Methodology

The methodology guiding the qualitative part of the project discussed in this chapter was a team-based longitudinal program evaluation. The evaluation team comprised five researchers: two lead analysts, one of whom was the Principal Investigator; myself, who acted as the "NVivo Project Czar"; and two additional analysts. The evaluation was undertaken collaboratively and was therefore structured around frequent team meetings. For example, the whole team met several times to plan each stage, and smaller subteams met more frequently in order to refine aspects of the analysis. These meetings were important in planning and managing the project, ensuring consistency in the analysis, and in enabling me to build the team's capacity with NVivo based on lessons learned along the way. We employed a consensus approach to decision making involving several rounds of review and refinement to resolve analytic dilemmas and to ensure the final analysis represented a collaborative approach.

We took a mixed-methods approach to the analysis. This involved different approaches to qualitative analysis for each round of interviews, including cross-referencing interview data with quantitative community-level social indicator information—for example, location (whether the community was urban or rural) and type of violence (whether elder abuse, youth violence, sexual assault, etc.)

We developed the following broad evaluation plan in conjunction with the Colorado Trust before collecting any interview data;

- **Descriptive coding of the first two rounds of interviews.** Descriptive coding focused on perceived attitudes within the partnership, understandings of local program design and logic, perceptions about the content and purpose of the local program evaluation and the entire initiative, and the characteristics of the Learning Lab.
- **Concept sensitization analysis of the third and fourth rounds of interviews.** This analysis focused on experiences of and changes to program implementation.
- **Identification and interrogation of patterns across all interview rounds.** The goal of this analytic activity was to investigate the co-occurrence of concepts identified in the interviews and comparisons by program characteristics (geography, type of violence, etc.)
- **Initiative- and site-level memoing throughout.** The purpose of this ongoing writing was to ensure effective feedback to all stakeholders at key points during the analysis.

We anticipated that this plan would be subject to change as the project unfolded, and this was the case in practice, as described in the next section.

Stages of the Analysis

We started the multiyear study in 1995, and the initial analytic plan was refined as the work progressed. In terms of the *Five-Level QDA* method there were six stages of analysis, with each stage planned in light of the previous stage. The six stages reflect turning points in the progress of the project, and we named the stages retrospectively by reflecting on the process for this chapter.

We refocused the project in the Fourth Stage in response to feedback from the Colorado Trust on the findings thus far. This resulted in refocusing the latter stages of the project on community-level issues. The six stages are listed in Table 9.2. The stages and the phases of analysis within each stage are illustrated in Figure 9.1.

TABLE 9.2 The six stages of analysis

Stages of the project (one video on the companion website for each stage)	Description of analytic activities
First Stage: Planning the analysis of first-round interviews	Planning the analysis of three rounds and piloting descriptive thematic coding for the first-round interviews
Second Stage: Descriptive thematic analysis of first-round interviews and first report	Analysis of first-round interviews using *a priori* and emerging descriptive themes, focusing on perceptions and expectations and write-up of first report
Third Stage: Concept sensitizing and descriptive thematic analysis of second-round interviews and second report	Planning, piloting, and analysis of second-round interviews using *a priori* descriptive and concept-sensitizing themes, focusing on "what counts" as learning, and write-up of second report
Fourth Stage: Critical incident analysis of third-round interviews and third report	Planning the remaining analysis and critical incident analysis of third round of interviews, with a focus on community-level issues and realities, and write-up of third report
Fifth Stage: Discourse analysis of fourth round of interviews and integration of all stages	Planning, piloting, and analysis of fourth round of interviews, with a focus on discursive practices, and integration of all stages of analysis
Sixth Stage: Synthesis of all stages and final report	Interrogation of all rounds of analysis to identify patterns and planning and write-up of the final report

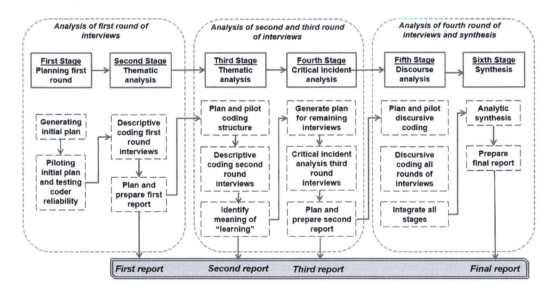

FIGURE 9.1 Stages and phases of analysis

First Stage: Planning the Analysis of First-Round Interviews

The first stage involved planning and piloting the analysis of the first round of interviews. The evaluation team met several times during this stage, including two whole-day team retreats as well as shorter meetings, during which we planned collectively. All of the first-round interviews had been conducted by the same team prior to the first team meeting, for which we had each prepared by reviewing the evaluation specifications and deliverables, research questions, two interview transcripts, and list of potential codes generated by the interviewers. During this meeting we identified three broad topic areas to guide the analysis: *learning*, *relationships*, and *evaluation*. Together we sketched out a draft coding scheme, which was subsequently written up and circulated for review. We then met again to finalize the coding scheme and plan the specifics of how the descriptive coding of the first-round interviews would be undertaken within NVivo. During this meeting I led the creation of the NVIVO-PROJECT, which we referred to as the *analytic shell*, and in which the structure for the analysis was created and the interview transcripts were imported (see Table 9.3, Task 1–E).

We undertook three rounds of pilot coding (Phases 2 and 3 in Table 9.3), during which the *a priori* coding scheme was piloted. First, pairs of analysts coded together; then we each worked independently. (We refer to team members as either *analysts* or *coders* depending on the task they were performing.) After each round, I combined the separate NVIVO-PROJECTS, and we met to discuss the coding and make any necessary changes to the NVIVO-PROJECTS. The final part of this process was to formally test the level of coding agreement. Because we were using NVivo Version 2, which did not have a tool designed specifically for this purpose, we used a Matrix Coding Query (see Table 9.3, Phase 3). Once agreement had been achieved we again refined the NVIVO-PROJECTS in preparation for the descriptive analysis of all the first-round interviews, the focus of the Second Stage.

The pilot coding was important in ensuring the interviews would be consistently coded, but also because we were all fairly new to NVivo and therefore this iterative process enabled us to build capacity around our use of NVivo. In addition, because of the complexity of the project, it was important that procedures were put in place to enable everyone to contribute. Therefore, we implemented a protocol for consistent use of NVivo MEMOS, involving the use of heading levels to denote different sections within MEMOS—for example, all writing about "coding questions," "issues for next team meeting," "interpretations, hypotheses, and theories," etc. In the iterative cycles of merging, two things were thus made possible:

- All analysts' old MEMOS (merged in from another analyst's project) could be deleted after the merge (so only the newest MEMOS for each analyst remained)
- We could auto-code by content area to efficiently access MEMO sections

This stage of the project contained sixteen ANALYTIC TASKS. For ease of presentation in Table 9.3 and in the video demonstrations, we have grouped these ANALYTIC TASKS into three analysis phases. *Figures 7.2 and 7.3, pages 161–162, review the format and numbering system for stages, phases, and analytic tasks. Note that bullet points in italics do not involve the use of NVivo.*

Second Stage: Descriptive Thematic Analysis of First-Round Interviews and First Report

The Second Stage involved putting into practice the plan generated in the First Stage and undertaking the descriptive thematic analysis of the all the first-round interviews. The descriptive code names we had created served as summaries or distillations of the speech to which they were linked during the coding. We had a high degree of confidence that the participants would agree with these descriptive codes, which attempt to capture the conscious perceptions of the speaker, not hypotheses by or inferences from the analyst.

I first duplicated the NVIVO-PROJECT, and each analyst received their own copy. Each analyst was allocated the transcripts of the interviews they had conducted themselves and used the *a priori*

TABLE 9.3 First Stage (Phases 1–3): Planning the analysis of the first round of interviews

Phase 1: Generate an initial plan	
1-A	*Identify topics likely to emerge from interviews in relation to research questions* • *We discussed the project objectives and brainstormed topic areas anticipated to emerge from the interviews.*
1-B	*Create an a priori descriptive coding scheme* • *We mapped out an initial a priori coding scheme on a whiteboard, after which the two lead investigators created a Microsoft Excel file containing code names, definitions, and examples, which was distributed to all team members.*
1-C	*Review the proposed a priori descriptive coding scheme* • *We each reviewed four interview transcripts (two that we had conducted ourselves and two that we had not) and made suggestions for clarifications and additions to the a priori coding scheme.* • *The two lead investigators amalgamated our suggestions into the Microsoft Excel file and distributed this for review.*
1-D	*Plan the descriptive coding strategy* • *We discussed the initial coding scheme, the suggestions generated in 1-D, and the planned stages of coding and how they would be implemented. We updated the Microsoft Excel file to reflect our decisions.*
1-E	Create an analytic "shell" to store interviews and codes • We created, named, and saved a master NVIVO-PROJECT, in which we created and defined a structure of NODES to store our initial descriptive coding scheme. • We named each interview transcript using a consistent structure that identified the interviewee's community, his or her role, the interview round, and the interviewer. • We imported all the interview transcripts into the NVIVO-PROJECT as SOURCES. • We duplicated the NVIVO-PROJECT twice and renamed each version.
Phase 2: Piloting the initial descriptive coding structure	
2-A	Trial application of *a priori* codes on two interview transcripts (in pairs) • We selected two transcripts to pilot the coding, and four of the team members split into two pairs. Each pair coded these SOURCES in a separate NVIVO-PROJECT, using the NODES created in 1-F. • While coding, each pair recorded their discussions in a Microsoft Excel file and suggestions for refining NODE definitions, examples (i.e., exemplary quotes), and counterexamples (i.e., quotes that may initially appear to fit, but belong in another NODE).
2-B	Combine code applications undertaken in the two separate analytic "shells" • The Project Czar merged the two NVIVO-PROJECTS used in 2-A.
2-C	Review trial application of codes and adjust the coding • We together reviewed the work undertaken in 2-A within the merged NVIVO-PROJECT created in 2-B and discussed differences.
2-D	Adjust the analytic "shell" to reflect additions to the coding scheme and store the analyst's notes • We added NODES to the NVIVO-PROJECT to capture the additional themes identified in 2-A. • We created a NODE for each analyst, under which they could create any new NODES they wished to generate inductively from this point on. • We created a MEMO containing the same section headings for each analyst to keep analytic notes.
2-E	Trial application of revised *a priori* codes on one interview transcript (as a team) • Together we coded another SOURCE and discussed the process.
2-F	Duplicate revised analytic "shell" for further piloting • We duplicated the NVIVO-PROJECT four times and renamed each version with the date and name of the analyst.
2-G	Trial application of revised *a priori* codes (as individual coders) • We independently coded the same three SOURCES in our version of the NVIVO-PROJECT. • We noted issues for discussion with the wider team in our personal MEMO created in 2-D. • When necessary, we created new NODES under our own NODE created in 2-D.

Phase 3: Test the level of coder agreement in the pilot coding

3-A	<u>Combine code applications undertaken in the two separate analytic "shells"</u> • We sent our separate NVIVO-PROJECTS to the Project Czar, who renamed the three coded SOURCES in each NVIVO-PROJECT to indicate who had done the coding. • The four NVIVO-PROJECTS were merged. The coding merged as the NODE names had not been changed, but the SOURCES did not merge because they had been renamed. The result was one NVIVO-PROJECT containing four versions of each of the three coded SOURCES (twelve total).
3-B	<u>Compare the application of codes to sample interview transcripts by different coders</u> • We ran a separate Matrix Coding Query for each of the three interview transcripts. Each QUERY-RESULT contained four columns representing the same SOURCE that had been coded by a different coder. Each row was occupied by one of the NODES in the coding structure. • We inspected each QUERY-RESULT row, one cell at a time, to identify areas of coding disagreement and discussed how coding inconsistency and disagreement could be avoided in the future.
3-C	<u>Adjust the coding scheme to reflect pilot coding</u> • We altered the coding scheme in the NODE structure by moving, merging, and renaming nodes as required.

coding scheme created during the First Stage to code the transcripts. Each analyst coded independently, adding any emerging concepts in their area of the coding scheme as required, and keeping detailed notes in the MEMOS as they progressed (see Table 9.4, Task 4-B).

Each analyst's coding was then reviewed by a secondary coder, who had no prior contact with anyone in the program. The secondary coder reviewed the primary coder's NVIVO-PROJECT, marking and explaining where and why they may have coded differently. The two analysts then met to discuss any discrepancies and where they could be resolved adjustments were made. This was not a "blind" or independent review process aimed at achieving coder reliability in a quantitative sense, but was focused on enabling us to learn from each other, to develop skills in coding and thereby reach a richer qualitative understanding of the data. The intention of using secondary coders who had not been directly involved in the programs or data collection was to help leverage the insights of "outsiders" (see Table 9.4, Tasks 4-C and 4-D).

I then combined the four NVIVO-PROJECTS so the NODES and SOURCES merged (unlike the process described earlier to compare coders in a Matrix Coding Query) and the Principal Investigator reviewed and refined all the coding. The refined NVIVO-PROJECT was then shared among the team, along with all analysts' reflections, in order to facilitate ongoing training and review, as well as to contribute to ensuing subsequent coding would be as consistent as possible (see Table 9.4, Tasks 5-A and 5-B).

We then met to review our work and plan the write-up of the first report for the Colorado Trust. During this meeting I imported demographic information about interview respondents into the NVIVO-PROJECT and showed the team how NVivo could be used to interrogate patterns in coding in relation to these aspects (see Table 9.4, Tasks 6-C and 6-D). Based on these queries we planned the sections of the report, and each section was allocated to a different team member to write up. The draft sections were passed to the two most experienced members of the team, who reviewed the QUERY-RESULTS generated for each section in the NVIVO-PROJECTS to ensure the interpretation was sound, edited the sections, and collated them into one draft report. This was shared with the whole team who provided feedback, and once suggestions had been incorporated the report was passed to the Colorado Trust (see Table 9.4, Phase 7).

This stage of the project contained fourteen ANALYTIC TASKS, grouped into four analysis phases, as illustrated in Table 9.4.

TABLE 9.4 Second Stage (Phases 4–7): Descriptive thematic analysis of first-round interviews and first report

Phase 4: Descriptive coding of round one interviews

4-A	Create a master analytic workspace for analyzing first-round interview transcripts • In the refined NVIVO-PROJECT created in 3-C we created two MEMOS for each analyst to recommend for changes and to keep track of emerging ideas: "Nodes and Descriptions" allowed individual analysts to provide recommended adjustments in names and definitions. "Ideas" contained heading levels for topics such as "coding questions," "issues for next team meeting," and "interpretations, hypotheses and theories." • We duplicated the NVIVO-PROJECT four times and renamed each version to indicate which coder was working on it.
4-B	Primary coders apply *a priori* and emerging codes to first-round interviews • Each coder was assigned eight to ten interview transcripts, which were imported into their NVIVO-PROJECT as SOURCES. • We each coded our SOURCES using the NODES created in 3-B, adding any new NODES we felt were needed under our named NODE created in 2-B, defining them in the Description field. • We kept notes as we coded in the MEMOS created in 4-A. • When relevant REFERENCES within MEMOS were linked to the specific CODED-REFERENCES to which they referred in the interview SOURCES, using See Also Links.
4-C	Independently review coding undertaken by primary coders • A second coder retrieved the CODED-REFERENCES applied to NODES by the primary coders in 4-B and reviewed for potential disagreement. • Where potential disagreement was identified, the second coder changed the font color of the CODED-REFERENCE and commented on it using an ANNOTATION to record their explanation. • Any new NODES they felt were relevant to the research questions were created under their named NODE and defined in the Description field.
4-D	Review coding of primary and secondary coders • The CODED-REFERENCES where potential disagreement had been identified in 4-C were retrieved and discussed between the primary and secondary coders. • When resolved, the font color of CODED-REFERENCES was returned to black and the ANNOTATION was removed. • Any CODED-REFERENCES where consensus could not be reached between the primary and secondary coder were linked to a MEMO in which their differences in opinion were explained. This included questions for the principal investigator (PI) that might help resolve the differences.

Phase 5: Refine coding of first-round interviews

5-A	Combine code applications undertaken in the four separate analytic "shells" • The four separate NVIVO-PROJECTS were merged by the Project Czar.
5-B	Review and refine coding • The PI reviewed the MEMOS created in 4-D that contained unresolved differences in coding and retrieved and reviewed the CODED-REFERENCES and ANNOTATION remaining after 4-D. • The PI made necessary changes to the NODES, CODED-REFERENCES, and NODE Descriptions, clarifying the reasons for his decisions in the MEMO.
5-C	Share coding and reflections • The MEMO containing the PI's explanations for the decisions made in 5-B was exported from the NVIVO-PROJECT and shared with primary and secondary coders. • All the other MEMOS were also exported together with the See Also Links generated in 4-B and shared with all team members.

Phase 6: Plan the write-up of the first report

6-A	*Generate and prioritize ideas for themes to include in the report* • *Team members reviewed all the MEMOS exported in 5-C and prioritized ideas for the themes that should be included in the report in a Microsoft Word file.*
6-B	*Collate sociodemographic characteristics about interviewees* • *We created a Microsoft Excel file containing sociodemographic information about the round one interviewees (for example, their role in the project, the type of violence prevention initiative they contributed to, their gender, and a few Likert scale ratings including "Experience developing an evaluation plan" and "Relevance of a local evaluation plan to project success").*

6-C	Plan interrogations to inform writing of report sections
	• The whole team met to discuss the coding of the first-round interviews and the potential themes for inclusion in the report generated in 6-A.
	• We imported the interviewee characteristics collated in 6-B into the master NVIVO-PROJECT as ATTRIBUTE-VALUES linked to the interview SOURCES.
	• We discussed ways in which potential themes needed to be further interrogated and identified how we could use NVivo queries to do so.
6-D	Investigate co-occurrences between sets of codes and identify data for the report
	• We ran a series of Matrix Coding queries to identify co-occurrences in coding, based around the potential themes identified in 6-C.
	• We retrieved the CODED-REFERENCES at each intersection in each Matrix Coding QUERY-RESULT and reviewed them.
	• While reviewing the QUERY-RESULTS, we planned the report structure, identifying five report sections (Node Summary, Strengths and Recommendations, Agreement and Difference, Intersections, Lessons and Implications).
	• Each analyst was allocated a section to write up.

Phase 7: Preparing the report

7-A	Draft report sections
	• Based on the queries and report planning undertaken in 6-C and 6-D, each analyst wrote up a first draft of their report section in a Microsoft Word file.
7-B	Collate draft report sections, review interrogations, and revise report
	• The two most experienced evaluators collated the individual report sections, compiled them, and edited them for consistency.
	• They reviewed all the QUERY-RESULTS to ensure the write-ups were accurate and revised the report.
7-C	*Review report*
	• *Each team member reviewed the draft report and made suggestions for edits.*
	• *Suggestions were incorporated and the report submitted to the Colorado Trust.*

Third Stage: Concept Sensitizing and Descriptive Thematic Analysis of Second-Round Interviews and Second Report

The Third Stage involved analyzing the second round of interview transcripts. The evaluation team met again and planned and trialed the coding approach, which integrated the descriptive thematic coding undertaken on the first-round interviews with concept sensitizing coding (see Table 9.5, Phase 8).

Our approach to concept sensitization was a two-pronged strategy for capturing community-level reflections and initiative-level reflections. First, at the community level, we wanted to do more than simply code descriptively and hoped to develop a framework for understanding and representing the world-views of the community members, particularly in terms of the issues in their communities that they were most aware of, concerned about, or "tuned in to" relative to their violence prevention programs (e.g., the overrepresentation of people of color in the criminal justice system, the changing demographics in the community, substance use). We also wanted to know, although it was more difficult to ascertain, what issues the community members were less aware of, but were evident in the social indicator data for their community. Therefore, in alignment with basic understandings of *sensitization* in psychology, this first community-oriented prong attended to the things participants were sensitized to observe and the things they were perhaps sensitized to ignore (see Table 9.5, Phase 9).

The second prong of concept sensitization had a far more reflexive role for the researcher. Because the Learning Lab was such an experimental model at the initiative level, there were many meetings, retreats, and discussions among the staff at the Colorado Trust, the community

TABLE 9.5 Third Stage (Phases 8–11): Concept sensitizing and descriptive thematic analysis of second-round interviews and second report

Phase 8: Plan and pilot the coding structure	
8-A	Add second-round interview transcripts to the analytic workspace • We imported the second-round interviews into the NVIVO-PROJECT as SOURCES.
8-B	Identify concepts likely to capture community- and initiative-level issues • The whole team met and discussed the objectives for analyzing the second-round interviews. We identified concepts that would potentially allow us to capture community-level aspects that participants were sensitized to observe and ignore. • These concepts were added to the coding scheme as NODES and defined in the Descriptions.
8-C	Trial application of a priori codes on two interview transcripts as a team • Together we coded two SOURCES using the NODES created in 8-B and discussed the process.

Phase 9: Concept sensitizing and descriptive coding of second-round interviews	
9-A	Duplicate master analytic "shell" • We duplicated the NVIVO-PROJECT four times and renamed each version with the name of the coder and the date.
9-B	Apply a priori and emerging codes to second round interview transcripts • Each analyst was assigned 8–10 interview transcripts, which were imported into their NVIVO-PROJECT as SOURCES. • We each coded our SOURCES using the NODES created in 8-B and those used in the Second Stage, adding any new NODES we felt were needed under our named NODE created in 2-B, defining them in the Description field. • We kept notes as we coded in the MEMOS created in 4-A. • When relevant REFERENCES within MEMOS were linked to the specific CODED-REFERENCES to which they referred in the interview SOURCES, using See Also Links.

Phase 10: Identify what "counts" as learning from different perspectives	
10-A	Combine code applications undertaken in the four separate analytic "shells" • The four separate NVIVO-PROJECTS were merged by the Project Czar.
10-B	Review and refine coding • During a team meeting we together reviewed the work undertaken in 9-B within the merged NVIVO-PROJECT created in 10-A by retrieving CODED-REFERENCES and identifying differences in how the NODES had been applied. • We refined the coding by adjusting the REFERENCES to which NODES had been applied where inconsistencies were identified.
10-C	Identify instances of learning and different perspectives on learning • We created NODES to capture examples of where learning was (and was not) evident in the second-round interview SOURCES and for the different perspectives that were evident such as characteristics of learning (flexibility/adaptability, mutuality, distributed), definitions of learning (internalized, can be communicated, usable in the future) sources of learning (feedback, failure, local knowledge), and outcomes of learning (sustainability, pride, social networks). • We created a MEMO in which we described the rationale for focusing on instances of learning from different perspectives. • We reviewed all CODED-REFERENCES created in 9-B and recoded them to the learning and perspectives NODES.

Phase 11: Plan and write up the second report	
11-A	Generate and prioritize ideas for themes to include in the report • We exported the MEMOS created in 10-C and reviewed them during a team meeting. • We prioritized ideas for the themes that should be included in the report in a Microsoft Word file and assigned report sections for each analyst to draft.
11-B	*Draft report sections* • *Analysts wrote up a first draft of their report section in a Microsoft Word file.*
11-C	*Collate draft report sections, review interrogations, and revise report* • *The two most experienced evaluators collated the individual report sections, compiled them, and edited them for consistency.*
11-D	*Review report* • *Each team member reviewed the draft report and made suggestions for edits.* • *Suggestions were incorporated and the report submitted to the Colorado Trust.*

consultants/facilitators, and the evaluators. We did not want to burden the grantees with all of these discussions and reflections on the meaning of "learning," so the community members were less focused on the role and structure of the Learning Lab at an initiative level. Instead, they were focused on what the Learning Lab meant in their communities. At the juncture between the initiative at large and the individuals in the communities, we evaluators needed to make sense of the ways the Learning Lab from the initiative perspective and the Learning Lab from the community perspective were (or were not) mutually informing. We therefore developed NODES and reflective MEMOS to dig more deeply into what did or did not "count" as learning from particular perspectives and why. Based on this work we prepared the second report (see Table 9.5, Phase 10 and 11).

We followed a similar process as in the Second Stage, planning, trialing, coding, combining, and reviewing. However, by this stage the analysts were more confident in the use of NVivo and the level of shared agreement with regard to the meaning of the concepts we were using to code the transcripts was greater. Therefore we did not use secondary coders to review the primary coders' work as we had done in the Second Stage.

This stage of the project contained twelve ANALYTIC TASKS, grouped into four analysis phases, as illustrated in Table 9.5.

Fourth Stage: Critical Incident Analysis of Third-Round Interviews and Third Report

The Third Stage of the evaluation was tremendously helpful to the Colorado Trust, but they questioned whether continued explorations with this emphasis would be helpful for the grant-ees. Therefore, to ensure a focus on community-level issues and realities, the Fourth Stage adopted the critical incident technique to help ensure that the researchers were focusing on the community realities rather than the model of the initiative. This resulted in the adoption of a critical incident technique to the third round of interview transcripts during this Fourth Stage of the evaluation.

The critical incident technique is a data collection and analytic strategy that attends to participant-identified events that contribute (either positively or negatively) to a larger process or phenomenon (e.g., if/how a free pizza night brought youth in the community together to discuss bullying). Critical incidents can be gathered in various ways, but typically respondents are asked to tell a story about an experience they had. The analyst subsequently attends to the details of the incident, issues that are proximally related to the incident (e.g., historical events or longstand-ing loyalties), responses to the incident, and reflections on how/why the responses did or didn't adequately leverage the usefulness of the incident. Although this technique tends to focus on incidents that are perceived as negative, in this study we asked participants to identify both nega-tive and positive incidents.

During a team meeting we first summarized the evaluation findings so far and identified the types of incidents that were likely to be present in the interview transcripts, added these to our "analytic shell" in the NVIVO-PROJECT, and together trialed the coding on two transcripts (see Table 9.6, Phase 12). We then duplicated the NVIVO-PROJECT for each analyst, who then coded their set of third-round interview transcripts using the *a priori* critical incident codes. I then combined their work by merging the NVIVO-PROJECTS, and during another team meeting we together reviewed and refined the coding (see Table 9.6, Phase 13). This stage culminated with writing up a third report for the Colorado Trust, which was planned, written, and revised in a similar way as the first and second reports during the Second and Third Stages (see Table 9.6, Phase 14).

TABLE 9.6 Fourth Stage (Phases 12–14): Critical incident analysis of third-round interviews and second report

Phase 12: Generate an analytic plan for remaining rounds of interviews

12-A	<u>Summarize findings so far and review analysis of previous phases</u> • *During a team meeting we discussed the analysis of the second wave of interviews, reviewed the coding scheme, and summarized our findings so far in a Microsoft Word file.* • *We discussed the project objectives and decided that to ensure a focus on community-level issues and realities we needed to adopt the critical incident technique to help ensure the next wave of analysis focused on community realities rather than the model of the initiative.*
12-B	<u>Identify types if incident likely to be present in the interviews</u> • We identified the characteristics of incidents that were identified by participants, such as conflicts, awards, surprises, large scale (e.g., social indicator data, textile plant closures, news items), and small scale (e.g., personal differences, sarcastic comments, kind gestures). • We added NODES to the NVIVO-PROJECT and defined them in Descriptions.
12-C	<u>Add third-round interview transcripts to the analytic workspace</u> • We imported the third-round interviews into the NVIVO-PROJECT as SOURCES.
12-D	<u>Trial application of a priori codes on two interview transcripts as a team</u> • Together we coded two SOURCES using the NODES created in 11-D and discussed the process.

Phase 13: Critical incident coding of third-round interviews

13-A	<u>Duplicate master analytic "shell"</u> • We duplicated the NVIVO-PROJECT four times and renamed each version with the name of the coder and the date.
13-B	<u>Analysts apply a priori and emerging critical incident codes to third round interviews</u> • Each analyst was assigned eight to ten interview transcripts, which were imported into their NVIVO-PROJECT as SOURCES. • We each coded our SOURCES using the NODES created in 11-B, adding any new NODES we felt were needed under our named NODE created in 2-B, defining them in the Description field. • We kept notes in the MEMOS created in 4-A as we coded. • When relevant, reflections within MEMOS were linked to the specific CODED-REFERENCES to which they referred in the interview SOURCES, using See Also Links.
13-C	<u>Combine code applications undertaken in the four separate analytic "shells"</u> • The four separate NVIVO-PROJECTS were merged by the Project Czar.
13-D	<u>Review and refine coding</u> • During a team meeting we together reviewed the work undertaken in 12-B within the merged NVIVO-PROJECT created in 12-C by retrieving CODED-REFERENCES and identifying differences in how the NODES had been applied. • Where inconsistencies were identified, we refined the coding by adjusting the REFERENCES to which NODES had been applied.

Phase 14: Plan and write up the third report

14-A	<u>Generate and prioritize ideas for themes to include in the report</u> • We exported the MEMOS created in 12-B and reviewed them during a team meeting. • We prioritized ideas for the themes that should be included in the report in a Microsoft Word file and assigned report sections for each analyst to draft.
14-B	<u>*Draft report sections*</u> • *Analysts wrote up a first draft of their report section in a Microsoft Word file.*
14-C	<u>*Collate draft report sections, review interrogations, and revise report*</u> • *The two most experienced evaluators collated the individual report sections, compiled them, and edited them for consistency.*
14-D	<u>*Review report*</u> • *Each team member reviewed the draft report and made suggestions for edits.* • *Suggestions were incorporated and the report submitted to the Colorado Trust.*

This stage of the project contained twelve ANALYTIC TASKS, grouped into three analysis phases, as illustrated in Table 9.6.

Fifth Stage: Discourse Analysis on Fourth-Round Interviews and Integration of All Stages

The Fifth Stage involved analyzing the fourth and final round of interviews, integrating the analysis of all rounds, and writing up the final report for the Colorado Trust. We took a discourse analysis approach to the analysis of the fourth-round interviews. Our approach paid attention to discursive practices that systematically reflect and shape the world to which they refer. These practices place boundaries around phenomena and categorize them to direct the attention of both speaker and listener. An example in this study was the use of pronouns "us, we, ours" versus "them, they, theirs" as well as the use of metaphors such as "uplifting" and "roadblock."

We began as in the previous stages, meeting to plan and pilot together the way we would identify and code for discursive practices. I then duplicated the master NVIVO-PROJECT and the coders applied *a priori* and emerging discursive practices NODES to all rounds of interview transcripts. As in previous stages, I then combined their work by merging the NVIVO-PROJECTS, and we met again to review and refine the coding and to share the analysis and our reflections (see Table 9.7, Phases 15 and 16).

The next task was to integrate the different kinds of analysis across all four rounds of interview transcripts. This involved the application of the critical incident codes used in the Fourth Stage to the first- and second-round interviews and applying the descriptive thematic codes to the third- and fourth-round interviews. I then combined their work and we met again to review, refine, share, and reflect (see Table 9.7, Phase 17).

This stage of the project contained twelve ANALYTIC TASKS, grouped into three analysis phases, as illustrated in Table 9.7.

Sixth Stage: Synthesis of All Stages and Final Report

The sixth and final stage of the project synthesized all rounds of analysis in order to prepare for and deliver the final report to the Colorado Trust. We first collated the sociodemographic information about the interview respondents, which I imported into the master NVIVO-PROJECT that contained all the rounds of qualitative analysis. The evaluation team met to discuss the whole analysis and to generate and prioritize themes to include in the final report. We discussed how the themes needed to be further interrogated, and I demonstrated how this accomplished with NVivo queries (see Table 9.8, Tasks 18-A and 18-B).

We had a planning meeting with the project funder, The Colorado Trust, during which we outlined our main findings and discussed their priorities for inclusion in the final report. We then met again and together ran a series of Matrix Coding queries and retrieved and reviewed the results. While doing so we planned the final report structure, identifying four key areas:

1. Program Implementation Lessons
2. Initiative Management Lessons
3. Evaluation Lessons
4. The Role of Learning in the Development of Sustainable Grantee Programs

Each analyst was allocated one report section to write up (see Table 9.8, Task 18-C). These were collated, the QUERY-RESULTS upon which the analysis was based were reviewed, and the whole report

TABLE 9.7 Fifth Stage (Phases 15–17): Discourse, critical incident, and thematic descriptive analysis on all rounds of interviews

Phase 15: Plan and pilot discursive practices coding	
15-A	Add fourth-round interviews transcripts to the analytic "shell" • We imported the fourth-round interviews into the NVIVO-PROJECT as SOURCES.
15-B	Identify discursive practices • During a team meeting we identified discursive practices that may be used to reflect and shape the worlds that interviewees refer to, for example, the use of pronouns and metaphors. • We created NODES in the coding scheme to capture these discursive practices.
15-C	Trial application of discursive practice codes on two interview transcripts as a team • Together we coded two SOURCES using the NODES created in 14-B and discussed the process.
Phase 16: Discursive practice coding of all rounds of interviews	
16-A	Duplicate the analytic "shell" • We duplicated the NVIVO-PROJECT four times and renamed each version with the name of the coder and the date.
16-B	Analysts apply a priori and emerging discursive practice codes to all rounds of interviews • Each analyst was assigned eight to ten interview transcripts, which were imported into their NVIVO-PROJECT as SOURCES. • We each coded all of our SOURCES, from all rounds of the project, using the NODES created in 14-B, adding any new NODES we felt were needed under our named NODE created in 2-B, defining them in the Description field. • We kept notes as we coded in the MEMOS created in 4-A. • When relevant reflections within MEMOS were linked to the specific CODED-REFERENCES to which they referred in the interview SOURCES, using See Also Links.
16-C	Combine code applications undertaken in the four separate analytic "shells" • The four separate NVIVO-PROJECTS were merged by the Project Czar.
16-D	Review and refine coding • During a team meeting we together reviewed the work undertaken in 14-B within the merged NVIVO-PROJECT created in 14-C by retrieving CODED-REFERENCES and identifying differences in how the NODES had been applied. • We refined the coding by adjusting the REFERENCES to which NODES had been applied where inconsistencies were identified.
Phase 17: Integration of all stages of analysis	
17-A	Duplicate the analytic "shell" • We duplicated the NVIVO-PROJECT four times and renamed each version with the name of the coder and the date.
17-B	Analysts apply critical incident codes to first- and second-round interviews • Each analyst recoded their first- and second-round interview SOURCES using the NODES created in 12-B and kept notes as we coded in the MEMOS created in 4-A.
17-C	Analysts apply thematic codes to third- and fourth-round interviews • Each analyst recoded their third- and fourth-round interview SOURCES using the NODES finalized in 5-B and kept notes as we coded in the MEMOS created in 4-A.
17-D	Combine code applications undertaken in the four separate analytic "shells" • The four separate NVIVO-PROJECTS were merged by the Project Czar.
17-E	Review and refine coding • During a team meeting we together reviewed the work undertaken in 15-A and 15-B within the merged NVIVO-PROJECT created in 15-C by retrieving CODED-REFERENCES and identifying differences in how the NODES had been applied. • We refined the coding by adjusting the REFERENCES to which NODES had been applied where inconsistencies were identified.

TABLE 9.8 Sixth Stage (Phases 18–19): Synthesis of all rounds of analysis and preparation of the final report

Phase 18: Analytic synthesis	
18-A	*Collate sociodemographic characteristics about interviewees*
	• *We created a Microsoft Excel file containing sociodemographic information about the round two, three, and four interviewees (for example, their role in the project, the type of violence prevention initiative they contributed to, their gender, and a few Likert scale ratings, including "Experience developing an evaluation plan" and "Relevance of a local evaluation plan to project success").*
18-B	Plan interrogations to inform writing of report sections
	• The whole team met to discuss the analysis and the potential themes for inclusion in the final report.
	• We imported the interviewee characteristics collated in 17-A into the master NVIVO-PROJECT as ATTRIBUTE-VALUES linked to the interview SOURCES.
	• We discussed ways in which potential themes needed to be further interrogated and identified how we could use NVivo queries to do so.
18-C	Investigate co-occurrences between sets of codes and identify data for the report
	• We ran a series of Matrix Coding Queries to identify co-occurrences in coding, based around the project objectives.
	• We retrieved the CODED-REFERENCES at each intersection in each Matrix Coding QUERY-RESULT and reviewed them.
	• While reviewing the QUERY-RESULTS, we planned the report structure and analysts were each allocated a section to work on and write up.
Phase 19: Write the final report	
19-A	Draft report sections
	• Based on the queries and report planning undertaken in 17-B and 17-C, each analyst wrote up a first draft of their report section in a Microsoft Word file.
19-B	Collate draft report sections, review interrogations, and revise report
	• The two most experienced evaluators collated the individual report sections, compiled them, and edited them for consistency.
	• They reviewed all the QUERY-RESULTS to ensure the write-ups were accurate and revised the report.
19-C	*Review report*
	• *All the team members reviewed the draft report and made suggestions for edits.*
	• *Suggestions were incorporated and the report submitted to the Colorado Trust.*

revised (see Table 9.8, Tasks 19-A and 19-B). The report was then circulated to all members of the evaluation team for review. Their suggestions for edits were incorporated by the Principal Investigator and the final report was submitted to the Colorado Trust.

This stage of the project contained thirteen ANALYTIC TASKS, grouped into two analysis phases, as illustrated in Table 9.8.

Stakeholders, Published Works, and Funders

The Executive Summary of the final report for the Violence Prevention Initiative, titled "Building Capacity for Violence Prevention," is available on the Colorado Trust website: www.coloradotrust.org/find?search_api_views_fulltext=violence%20prevention

In addition, several publications reference the lessons learned from the initiative:

Easterling, D. (2016). How grantmaking can create adaptive organizations. *Stanford Social Innovation Review*, Fall, 45–53.

Easterling, D., & Main, D. (2016). Reconciling community-based versus evidence-based philanthropy: A case study of the Colorado Trust's early initiatives. *The Foundation Review, 8*(4), 80–107.

Appendices

APPENDIX 1

Three Levels of Detail of Analytic Tasks

Common overly general ways for describing analytic activities	Appropriate level of detail for translation	Overly specific tasks requiring a sequence of similarly overspecific tasks
INTEGRATING Bring all our work together *or* Show differences in coding	Compare each team member's separate coding of each focus group transcript	Print out all data segments coded by each team member
	Review together the thematic and discursive coding of media representations of local politicians to identify overlaps and connections	Retrieve all the data coded to themes
ORGANIZING Revisit the analytic framework *or* Reflect on emerging codes in relation to theory	Review and refine codes and the coding scheme	Read names of codes
	Compare theoretical and emerging concepts and explain their similarities and differences	Prepare separate lists of theoretical and emerging concepts
	Refine the initial conceptual framework in light of the themes generated from the data	Prepare a representation of the initial conceptual framework
EXPLORING Find out what's going on in the data *or* Explore the data with regard to content and meaning	Read interview transcripts to identify potential concepts for coding	Read the first interview
	Search for evocative terms in newspaper articles	Prepare notes on meaning of evocative
	Watch videos of math lessons to identify types of interaction between students and teachers	Sort videos by student–student and student–teacher interaction
	Review field notes to summarize athletes' body language with same- and opposite-gender coaches	Highlight sections of all field notes referring to same-gender coaches
REFLECTING Think about differences in types of interaction *or* Show connections between concepts	Summarize differences in verbal and nonverbal interaction between doctors and patients	Prepare separate lists of types of verbal and nonverbal interaction
	Create and explain relationships between concepts	List each possible type of relationship
INTERROGATING Show relationships between themes and participants *or* Find out differences in attitudes expressed	Compare teachers' reactions to different kinds of bullying	Extract data for first teacher's reactions to bullying
	Identify related concepts by investigating co-occurrences among concepts in the data	List all the concepts used in the study
	Interpret media representations of local politicians in relation to attitudes expressed by focus group respondents	Separate media representations of local and nonlocal politicians

APPENDIX 2

Five Analytic Activities

Silver and Lewins (2014) developed a framework of five analytic activities independent of methodology to assist in developing analytic plans that connect a project's objectives with the detailed tasks to be accomplished. It is not a method of analysis to be adopted, as it does not consist of specific action steps. Rather, analytic activities are a high-level guide to thinking through the purposes of each element of a developing analytic plan in relation to other elements. Each activity has two or three dimensions, and Figure A2.1 illustrates the web of connections among the

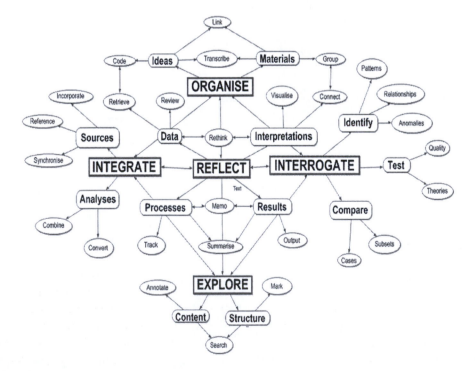

FIGURE A2.1 Silver and Lewins's (2014) five analytic activities

Silver, C., & Lewins, A. (2014). *Using software in qualitative research: A step-by-step guide* (2nd ed.). Thousand Oaks, CA: Sage, p. 45. Reproduced with permission.

various activities. The diagram is not a flow chart indicating a fixed sequence of activities, as projects engage in them in different ways, to different extents, and in different sequences. Once the purpose of a specific ANALYTIC TASK has been identified and the task written, it is no longer important which analytic activity it represents, and many ANALYTIC TASKS fulfill aspects of more than one activity. For example, the ANALYTIC TASK in Table 6.1 *Create and explain relationships between codes within categories identified in the literature* may have been the result of a *reflection* activity, but may also involve *organizing* activities. The purpose of the framework is only to stimulate thinking about the purpose and relationship of analytic activities. The following summaries introduce the five activities. For further details and their application to a number of case studies see Silver and Lewins (2014, p. 45).

Integration

The purpose of integration is to combine parts into a whole. This involves bringing together research materials, analytic methods, and the contributions of team members. Integrating materials may involve connecting data files related to the same respondent or setting, or to synchronize media data with corresponding transcripts. Integration of methods relates to mixed-methods analyses, which may involve analyzing one dataset using two or more approaches, analyzing different sets of data using different methods, linking qualitative and quantitative data, or representing qualitative analyses numerically. Integration in team projects may involve combining and comparing the analytic contributions of different team members or refining the definitions of concepts used to reflect team members' multiple perspectives to ensure shared understandings.

Organization

The purpose of organization is to arrange something in a systematic or orderly way. This involves sorting data according to similarities and differences based on what is meaningful in relation to the objectives. Organizing may involve ordering similar concepts with a prefixing protocol, organizing a coding scheme hierarchically, or linking concepts to represent their relationships. Notations in transcripts may represent nonverbal hesitations, pauses, etc., or transcripts may be formatted to represent repeated structures, such as topic areas discussed, or track contradictions by linking contradictory statements with a named relationship. Sociodemographic characteristics may be used to group respondents, and metadata such as when social media content was downloaded, who are the authors of journal articles, or when articles were published, may be used to organize materials.

Exploration

The purpose of exploration is to examine something in detail. This involves exploring both the content of data and its structure. Regarding the content, exploring may involve identifying surface features, such as counting how often particular words or phrases are used, or identifying nonverbal interactions in video recordings. Another purpose looks beyond the surface features to the implicit meaning, such as developing detailed accounts, or "thick descriptions." Exploring may involve familiarization with a large volume of data before commencing analysis, such as by generating a high-level overview of words and phrases in the text. Regarding the structure of data, exploration may involve capturing repeated content, such as discussions about the same topics or responses from the same respondents.

Reflection

The purpose of reflection is to think deeply or carefully. This core activity in qualitative analysis involves thinking deeply about the data, the analytic processes, the interpretations generated, and the results to be presented. Two key reflective activities are writing and generating visualizations. Reflection on data may involve summarizing or appraising its content by writing analytic notes or drawing diagrams. Regarding analytic processes, reflection may involve recording the progress of the analysis or visually representing the stages of the project or the contributions of different team members. Regarding interpretations, reflection may involve illustrating the validity of an explanation in terms of respondents' accounts. Regarding results, reflection may consider which data extracts are most illustrative or how best to represent an argument graphically.

Interrogation

The purpose of interrogation is to follow up what has already been done. This involves asking questions about, investigating, or visualizing in order to identify patterns, relationships, and anomalies in the data to test hypotheses or to generate theories. Patterns may identify similarities in how respondents discuss an issue or experience, relationships may establish connections within a concept or between respondents' accounts, and anomalies may find counterexamples of what appears to be a general trend or variances in how an event is experienced. Another purpose of interrogating may be to visually represent differences between established thought and what is emerging from a different context or setting.

APPENDIX 3

Examples of Units in Analytic Tasks

Types of units	Definition	Units (with examples of an instance of that unit)
Units of analysis	The entities that are the subject of the analysis A project commonly has one major unit of analysis and several additional units	Articles (e.g., a journal paper for a literature review) Artifacts (e.g., a historical document) Documents (e.g., a transcript of an interview) Individuals (e.g., a named respondent) Groups (e.g., a female participant) Organizations (e.g. a hospital) Regions (e.g., a county) Events (e.g., a political meeting) Settings (e.g., a church) Interventions (e.g., a health promotion effort) Programs (e.g., a science curriculum) Etc.
Units of data	The form of the materials or resources that comprise the data Smaller units of data may be embedded within a larger unit	Transcripts (e.g., a written record of a research encounter) Field note entry (e.g., a summary of an observed event) Journal articles (e.g., an academic paper on a specific topic) Survey responses (e.g., an answer to an open-ended question) Image (e.g., a participant-generated photograph) Video recording (e.g., a recording of a science class) Video clip (e.g., a segment of a film) Audio recording (e.g., a recording of a focus group discussion) Etc.
Units of meaning—concepts	A concept that is created because it is meaningful in the analysis Several units of meaning may be identified for different purposes	Concept (a general unit for all kinds of abstract entities) *Specific conceptual units defined by the methodology, for example:* Topics (e.g., a broad area of discussion) Codes (e.g., an evocative term used in a political speech) Categories (e.g., a group of related evocative terms) Themes (e.g., the persuasive effect of evocative terms across contexts)
Units of meaning—segments of data	Segments of data identified as being meaningful Several units of meaning may be identified within the same unit of data	Responses (e.g., an answer to a survey question) Speaker section (e.g., the comment of a respondent in a conversation) Interaction (e.g., a nonverbal communication in a video recording) Post (e.g., a response to a thread in an online discussion forum) Paragraph (e.g., an opening section in a news article) Phrase (e.g., a named theory discussed by scholars) Etc.

APPENDIX 4

Identifying the Units of Analytic Tasks

Analytic task	Units	Discussion of the rule of thumb
EXAMPLES OF INTEGRATING—COMBINING PARTS INTO A WHOLE		
Overall purpose is bringing together the elements that make up a research project and thinking about how they relate to one another		
Compare each team member's separate coding of each focus group transcript	• Team members • Codes • Focus group transcripts	This ANALYTIC TASK conforms to the rule of thumb from an analytic perspective, having one unit of analysis (*codes*) and one unit of data (*focus group transcripts*). However, the task requires three UNITS because *team members* must be an additional UNIT for TRANSLATION purposes in order to track each member's contribution in the software for comparing their work when the NVIVO-PROJECTS are merged. Put another way, *team members* are not units at the strategy levels of the analytic plan, but they are UNITS at the tactics levels of harnessing the software.
Review together the thematic and discursive coding of media representations of local politicians to identify overlaps and connections	• Thematic and discursive codes • Media representations	Two UNITS jump out of the ANALYTIC TASK and conform to the rule of thumb. The context of the study is the media representations of local politicians' attitudes to a contentious issue (Brexit) in relation to the attitudes of local residents whom they represent to the same issue, captured in the focus groups. *Thematic and discursive codes* are units of meaning and *media representations* are units of data. However, once UNITS have been identified, the types of unit are no longer relevant for continuing the TRANSLATION process.
EXAMPLES OF ORGANIZING—CREATING STRUCTURES RELATED TO OBJECTIVES		
Overall purpose is creating structures that reflect meaningful aspects of the data in relation to project objectives		
Review and refine codes and the coding scheme	• Codes • Coding scheme	Conforms to the rule of thumb, but we might prefer to think about *codes* and *coding scheme* as one UNIT if the purpose of the codes and the coding scheme are the same. We cannot know this without knowing the purpose of the ANALYTIC TASK.
Compare theoretical and emerging concepts and explain their similarities and differences	• Concept	Note that even though this ANALYTIC TASK has but a single UNIT for purposes of TRANSLATION, it is by no means a straightforward task. The number of UNITS affects the ease or complication of the TRANSLATION process—the tactics—but has no bearing on the sophistication of the analytic activity—the strategies.
Refine the initial conceptual framework in light of the themes generated from the data	• Theme	As in the earlier example this ANALYTIC TASK has a single UNIT for purposes of TRANSLATION, but it is by no means a straightforward task.

Analytic task	Units	Discussion of the rule of thumb
		EXAMPLES OF EXPLORING—EXAMINING THE CONTENT AND STRUCTURE OF THE DATA *Overall purpose is considering the inherent nature of data*
Read interview transcripts to identify potential concepts for coding	• Interview transcripts • Potential concepts	Two UNITS jump out of the ANALYTIC TASK and conform to the rule of thumb. *Interview transcripts* are units of data and *potential concepts* are units of meaning. Now that these have been identified as UNITS, the types of unit are no longer relevant for continuing the TRANSLATION process.
Search newspaper articles for the use of evocative terms	• Newspaper articles • Evocative terms	Two UNITS jump out of the ANALYTIC TASK and conform to the rule of thumb. *Newspaper articles* are units of data, and *evocative terms* are units of meaning. Now that these have been identified as UNITS, the types of unit are no longer relevant for continuing the TRANSLATION process.
Watch videos of math lessons to identify types of interaction between students and teachers	• Videos of math lessons • Types of interaction • Students • Teachers	This ANALYTIC TASK has four UNITS, twice as many as the rule of thumb suggests. We could split the ANALYTIC TASK into two separate tasks—*watch videos of math lessons to identify types of interaction*, which contains the first two UNITS, and *identify types of interaction between students and teachers*, which contains the last three. To bring this second task down to two UNITS we could think of students and teachers as instances of a single UNIT—*participants*. Judging the wisdom of doing this comes with experience, depending on what we anticipate may come later. If students and teachers are expected to be analyzed in similar ways in future ANALYTIC TASKS, considering them as instances of the single UNIT *participants* should be unproblematic. But if students and teachers are independent elements in other research questions or subquestions then TRANSLATING them as a single UNIT may not be the best way to go. Splitting the task may simplify TRANSLATION, but it comes at a cost. It means identifying *types of interaction* first without regard to *students* and *teachers* and then going back to identify each type in relation to *students* and *teachers*. This is both cumbersome and also implies easy separation of types of interaction from the people who are interacting. It may be best to think of these two dimensions at the same time as described in the original ANALYTIC TASK with four UNITS, and not worry about the slightly more involved TRANSLATION. Thinking in this way might give you another idea. If it is unproblematic to think of students and teachers as instances of one UNIT—*participants*—then the original ANALYTIC TASK has only three UNITS, not four. Maybe that is the best solution.
Review field notes to summarize athletes' body language with same- and opposite-gender coaches	• Field notes • Athletes • Body language	This ANALYTIC TASK has three UNITS. *Field notes* are a unit of data because as this is the form in which the data are stored, it needs to be a UNIT for TRANSLATION. The question is whether *athletes* and their *body language* are really two ways of expressing the same UNIT. This depends on the context—the objectives, methodology, and analytic plan. If the study is about self-identity in professional athletics, then *athletes* are the main entity of interest and would be a UNIT, a unit of analysis. *Body language* would be another UNIT, a unit of meaning. But if the study is about the meaning of different styles of body language in professional athletics, then the UNIT *body language* would be the main unit of analysis, and this ANALYTIC TASK might have only two UNITS—*field notes* and *body language*—and the ANALYTIC TASK might be better expressed *review field notes to summarize participants' body language*. Whether *athletes* would become a UNIT of a later ANALYTIC TASK is unknown at this point.

(Continued)

Analytic task	Units	Discussion of the rule of thumb
	EXAMPLES OF **REFLECTING**—CONSIDERING CAREFULLY AND DEEPLY *Overall purpose is recording analytic insights and what is going on in the project*	
Summarize differences in verbal and nonverbal interaction between doctors and patients	• Interaction • Respondents	At first sight this ANALYTIC TASK could be considered as having four UNITS—verbal interaction, nonverbal interaction, doctors, and patients. But the verbal/nonverbal distinction and the doctor/patient distinction refer to the action that will be taken, that is, summarizing differences. Unless the analytic plan suggests otherwise, verbal interactions and nonverbal interactions are instances of one UNIT that will be compared—interactions—and similarly for doctors and patients.
Create and explain relationships between concepts	• Relationships • Concepts	Two UNITS jump out of the ANALYTIC TASK and conform to the rule of thumb. *Relationships* and *concepts* are units of meaning. Now that these have been identified as UNITS, the types of unit are no longer relevant for continuing the TRANSLATION process.
	EXAMPLES OF **INTERROGATING**—FOLLOWING UP WHAT HAS BEEN DONE *Overall purpose is asking questions about data and the work we have done so far*	
Compare teachers' reactions to different kinds of bullying	• Teacher • Reactions • Kinds of bullying	This ANALYTIC TASK has three UNITS, but is clearly not amenable to being split into two separate tasks. Reducing to two UNITS requires thinking about whether any pair of these three UNITS is really a single UNIT for the purposes of TRANSLATION. As in the previous examples, this would depend on whether *teacher* is a unit of analysis in the study independent of the teachers' *reactions* to different types of bullying, or whether they are a single UNIT. A similar issue is whether *reactions* to bullying and concepts about *kinds of bullying* are best represented as a single unit of meaning or whether in subsequent ANALYTIC TASKS they will have different purposes and require two UNITS. How do we know all this from the ANALYTIC TASK as written? We don't. We know it from the analytic plan, which is conveniently displayed for reference in the ANALYTIC PLANNING WORKSHEET and that indicates the purpose of each ANALYTIC TASK.
Identify related concepts by investigating co-occurrences in the data	• Concepts • Data	This ANALYTIC TASK may seem to be at too broad a level of detail, because the types of concept and data are not specified. But an ANALYTIC TASK is at the most helpful level of detail for TRANSLATION purposes when the task naturally leads to the next task. In this example we know that the analytic plan requires finding out if there are related concepts, and if so which they are, in order to then generate a more specific ANALYTIC TASK. In practice (rather than out of context in this table) this would be known from the ANALYTIC PLANNING WORKSHEET, which indicates what has gone before and what is anticipated to come next.
Interpret media representations of local politicians in relation to attitudes expressed by focus group respondents	• Media representations • Attitudes • Focus group respondents	The final example further illustrates the role of purpose in identifying UNITS of ANALYTIC TASKS. This task has three UNITS, and the issue concerns *media representations*. The context of the study is the media representations of local politicians' attitudes to a contentious issue (Brexit) in relation to the attitudes of local residents whom they represent to the same issue, captured in the focus groups. Media representations are units of data, such as newspaper articles and online news clips, to be translated to COMPONENTS of the software. However, the purpose of the ANALYTIC TASK is to interpret these representations. These interpretations are concepts in the study to be TRANSLATED to software COMPONENTS, but the interpretations are not UNITS of the task. They are actions embodied in the purpose of the task. Therefore, although TRANSLATION is always based on the UNITS of the task, in some cases it is additionally based on the purpose of the task.

APPENDIX 5

Identifying the Purpose of Analytic Tasks

Analytic task	Purpose	Discussion of the rule of thumb
EXAMPLES OF INTEGRATING—COMBINING PARTS INTO A WHOLE *Overall purpose is bringing together the elements that make up a research project and thinking about how they relate to one another*		
Compare each team member's separate coding of each focus group transcript	One purpose: • To compare the coding undertaken separately by different team members	This ANALYTIC TASK conforms to the rule of thumb of containing one purpose. The action employed to fulfill the purpose is not evident in the way the task has been written, leaving us open to consider different ways of accomplishing the task.
Review together the thematic and discursive coding of media representations of local politicians to identify overlaps and connections	One purpose: • To identify overlaps and connections in the different types of coding	At first glance it may appear that this ANALYTIC TASK has two purposes: to review coding and to identify overlaps and connections between different types of coding. But the purpose of the task, *why* it is being undertaken, is to identify, and this is accomplished by reviewing the coding. Therefore this ANALYTIC TASK, although complex because it has several elements, conforms to the rule of thumb.
EXAMPLES OF ORGANIZING—CREATING STRUCTURES RELATED TO OBJECTIVES *Overall purpose is imposing structures that reflect meaningful aspects of the data in relation to project objectives*		
Review and refine codes and the coding scheme	Two purposes: • To look at the CODES that have already been created to check they are useful (review) • To make any necessary changes to the CODES or their position in the coding scheme (refine)	If we stuck to the rule of thumb of only one purpose we would have to split this ANALYTIC TASK into two: a) review the NODES and coding scheme, and b) refine the NODES and coding scheme. We could certainly do this, and we could translate each separate task with no problem. However, this would involve first reviewing the NODES to decide what all the required changes are and then going back to make those changes as a separate activity. In practice this is not how people work—when we see a needed change, we make it there and then. It therefore makes sense in this case to violate the rule of thumb and keep both purposes within one ANALYTIC TASK.

(Continued)

Analytic task	Purpose	Discussion of the rule of thumb
Compare theoretical and emerging concepts and explain their similarities and differences	Two purposes: • To compare concepts • To explain the similarities and differences that are found	If we stuck to the rule of thumb of only one purpose, we would have to split this ANALYTIC TASK in two: a) compare theoretical and emerging concepts to identify similarities and differences, and b) explain the similarities and differences identified between theoretical and emerging concepts. As in the previous example this would separate activities that naturally happen together. In comparing the concepts we would identify the similarities and differences and thus these insights would be at the forefront of our mind. To place them to one side would not only cost us time but also risk losing those valuable insights. This is therefore another example of when violating the rule of thumb is appropriate.
Refine the initial conceptual framework in light of the themes generated from the data	One purpose: • To refine the conceptual framework	This ANALYTIC TASK conforms to the rule of thumb of only one purpose. The action to fulfill the purpose is not evident in the way the task has been written, leaving us open to consider different ways of accomplishing the task.

EXAMPLES OF **EXPLORING**—EXAMINING THE CONTENT AND STRUCTURE OF THE DATA		
Overall purpose is considering the inherent nature of data		
Read interview transcripts to identify potential concepts for coding	One purpose: • To identify concepts that may be potential candidates for coding interview transcripts	This ANALYTIC TASK conforms to the rule of thumb of only one purpose. The way the task is written indicates that the purpose will be accomplished through the action of reading each interview transcript.
Search newspaper articles for the use of evocative terms	One purpose: • To find terms within newspaper articles that can be considered evocative.	This ANALYTIC TASK conforms to the rule of thumb of only one purpose. The way the task is written indicates that the purpose will be accomplished through the action of searching.
Watch videos of math lessons to identify types of interaction between students and teachers	One purpose: • To identify how students and teachers interact during math lessons	This ANALYTIC TASK conforms to the rule of thumb of only one purpose. The way the task is written indicates that the purpose will be accomplished through the action of watching.
Review field notes to summarize athletes' body language with same- and opposite-gender coaches	One purpose: • To summarize parts of field notes relating to body language	This ANALYTIC TASK conforms to the rule of thumb of containing one purpose. The way the task is written indicates that the purpose will be accomplished through the action of reviewing field notes and then writing summaries about body language.

EXAMPLES OF **REFLECTING**—CONSIDERING CAREFULLY AND DEEPLY		
Overall purpose is recording analytic insights what is going on in the project		
Summarize differences in verbal and nonverbal interaction between doctors and patients	One purpose: • To summarize identified differences	This ANALYTIC TASK conforms to the rule of thumb of only one purpose. The action to be employed to fulfill the purpose is not evident in the way the task has been written, leaving us open to consider different ways of accomplishing the task.

Analytic task	Purpose	Discussion of the rule of thumb
Create and explain relationships between concepts	Two purposes: • To create relationships between concepts • To explain why these relationships are meaningful	If we stuck to the rule of thumb of only one purpose, we would have to split this ANALYTIC TASK into two: a) create relationships between concepts, and b) explain relationships between concepts. We could certainly do this and TRANSLATE each separate task without difficulty, but in practice this would be cumbersome. While creating the relationships we would necessarily be thinking about the nature of the relationships, and postponing the explanation would be inefficient—the purpose of explanation is inseparable from the purpose of creation. It therefore makes sense in this case to violate the rule of thumb and keep both purposes within one ANALYTIC TASK.
EXAMPLES OF **INTERROGATING**—FOLLOWING UP WHAT HAS BEEN DONE *Purpose is asking questions about data and the work we have done so far*		
Compare teachers' reactions to different kinds of bullying	One purpose: • To investigate whether individual teachers display similar or different reactions to different types of bullying	This ANALYTIC TASK conforms to the rule of thumb of only one purpose. The action to be employed to fulfil the purpose is not evident in the way the task has been written, leaving us open to consider different ways of accomplishing the task.
Identify related concepts by investigating co-occurrences in the data	One purpose: • To identify concepts that are related	This ANALYTIC TASK conforms to the rule of thumb of only one purpose. The way the task is written indicates that the purpose will be accomplished through the action of investigating co-occurrences between concepts in the data.
Interpret media representations of local politicians in relation to attitudes expressed by focus-group respondents	One purpose: • To interpret the relationships identified	This ANALYTIC TASK conforms to the rule of thumb of only one purpose. The action to be employed to fulfil the purpose is not evident in the way the task has been written, leaving us open to consider different ways of accomplishing the task.

INDEX

Page references to figures are shown in italics. Tables and boxes are shown in bold.